IN CHEAP WE TRUST

The Story of a Misunderstood American Virtue

Lauren Weber

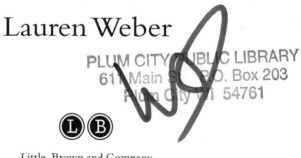

LB

Little, Brown and Company
New York Boston London

Little, Brown and Company
Hachette Book Group
237 Park Avenue, New York, NY 10017
Visit our website at www.HachetteBookGroup.com

First Edition: September 2009

Little, Brown and Company is a division of Hachette Book Group, Inc. The Little, Brown name and logo are trademarks of Hachette Book Group, Inc.

Library of Congress Cataloging-in-Publication Data
Weber, Lauren.
    In cheap we trust : the story of a misunderstood American virtue / Lauren Weber. — 1st ed.
        p. cm.
    ISBN 978-0-316-03028-1
    1. Thriftiness—United States.   2. Finance, Personal—Planning.
3. Finance, Personal—United States.   I. Title.
    HG179.W387 2009
    332.02400973—dc22   2009015516

10 9 8 7 6 5 4 3 2

RRD-IN

Printed in the United States of America

FOR MY FATHER,
A CHEAP AND GENEROUS MAN

CONTENTS

Contents

Cheap Thrills

C heap.

Cheap suit. Cheap date. Cheap shot. It's a dirty word, rife with negative associations. We hear the word *cheap* and we think, miser, whore, Wal-Mart, made in China, something that's going to fall apart. It's an insult, almost any way you look at it. An eighty-four-year-old man heard about my interest in cheapness and got so excited that he offered himself up for an interview about his frugal ways. At the end of our conversation, he said, sheepishly, "Please don't use my name....I don't want people to think I'm cheap."

My father has been called cheap for most of his life, by family members, friends, colleagues, and me. Dad is an economist in both senses of the word. He was an economics professor for thirty-three years at the U.S. Coast Guard Academy in New London, Connecticut. And he's also a master economizer, a legend in our extended family. I remember him dashing around the house turning lights off all the time, even if the room's occupant had just left to make a brief phone call. If I was in the shower for longer than a few minutes, I'd hear a knock on the bathroom door, followed by my father's voice saying, "Laur, you're using too much water." He refuses to use the dishwasher;

instead, he insists on washing all the plates and cutlery by hand. At some point, we discovered that he was using cold water and no soap; that explained why the knives and forks were often encrusted with the remnants of recent meals.

His latest conceit? He doesn't like to use the brakes on his car because he doesn't want to wear them out. So he coasts when he's approaching a red light, or employs a series of light taps and thrusts, a system he believes minimizes brake wear and tear. Dad also prefers to use hand signals out the window instead of the car's turning lights.

I recently learned that he uses his tea bags not three or four times, like most proud cheapskates, but *ten or twelve* times. ("I just dip it in for a few seconds, until the water gets a little color," he says.)

I spent my girlhood doing homework at the kitchen table, sock-clad feet nestling on the radiator, hands resting on the oven as it cooled down from dinner. This was the only way to stay warm during New England winters, when my father forbade us from turning the thermostat above fifty degrees. Cold? "Put on another sweater," he'd snap in his native Queens accent. Once he even tried to ration toilet paper, sitting the family down after dinner to tell us how much we could use for each bodily function. Proving too hard to enforce, however, these rules were eventually forgotten.

It's easy to mock these extremes of thrift, to marvel at the amount of time, thought, and emotional energy that some people will expend just to save a few dollars, even a few pennies. We call them eccentrics. We call them irrational. If we're related to them, and even if we're not, we complain bitterly about how *cheap* they are.

Then we turn into them—at least, I did. And maybe we realize they were onto something.

★　　★　　★

THIS BOOK IS a reconsideration of cheapness. It asks why we malign and make fun of people who save money. After all, when we as a nation and as individuals are so dangerously overleveraged, when we've watched our global financial system teeter and then tumble because of greed and ill-considered spending, when all of us could use a little more parsimony in our daily lives, why is it an insult to be called *cheap?*

The word *cheap* actually started out with a positive spin. It derives from the Latin word *caupo,* or tradesman; evolved into the noun *ceap* (a trade) in Old English; and came to be used in Middle English mostly in the phrase "good chepe," meaning "good bargain" or "good price." The opposite phrase was not "bad chepe" but "dear chepe," which referred to high prices. By the sixteenth century, *cheap* was employed, without judgment, as a synonym for "inexpensive."

But soon the word began assuming more malignant meanings. When the Earl of Clarendon wrote in 1674 of "the cheap laughter of all illiterate men," he referred to laughter too inexpensive, too easily obtained, and thus worthless. Cheapness came to indicate not just a low price but low quality as well. In 1820s America, a "cheap John" or "cheap Jack" was a man who peddled flimsy pots, ill-fitting suits, and inferior merchandise of all types, asking unreasonably high prices to begin with and gradually letting his customers haggle him down. And in 1880, a story in *Harper's Magazine* mentioned a character named Isaacson, "a traveling cheap-John who had opened a stock of secondhand garments for ladies and gentlemen in a disused fish-house on the wharf." It was a contemptible profession, and through that usage, the word *cheap* entered our vocabulary as a term of derision, an adjective synonymous with *miserly* or *stingy.*

Every culture, it seems, sustains a deep discomfort with the figure of the miser. A Native American legend tells of a hunter who refused to bring his kills back to share with his hungry tribe; he was punished by the gods. Jamie and Edmund Tyrone, the two sons in Eugene O'Neill's play *Long Day's Journey into Night*, blame their father's penny-pinching for their mother's drug addiction and the other woes they've endured. And Mr. Burns, from *The Simpsons,* lives by himself in his vast mansion, hatching schemes to multiply his fortune. He's a tragicomic figure of bewildered loneliness and pecuniary preoccupations, a modern version of Dickens's Scrooge.

The miser of legend offends the approved values of our religious and social traditions by favoring the base satisfactions of his pile of money over the rewards of spiritual wealth. He chooses his own personal comforts over selfless love and charity. But even as we scorn the miser, we admire the kindred qualities of saving and prudence. Miserliness has always been the dishonorable cousin of thriftiness, the habit of playing it close with money. So when writers, ministers, and wealthy elites in the nineteenth century admonished the poor and middle classes to be thrifty, they nearly always included a complementary warning against miserliness. But where is the line between hoarding and prudence? That's never been clear. Instead we're told, Save your money, but don't hoard it. Be thrifty and prudent, but generous as well. There is a narrow and nebulous band of acceptable behavior: spend "too much" (relative to one's circumstances, or perhaps to one's peers) and be labeled irresponsible; spend "too little" and be labeled parsimonious and stinting.

As cheap as he is, my father is also one of the most generous people I know. All my life, he has given time and money to causes he cares about, from homelessness and hunger to AIDS and political campaigns. He rarely passes a panhandler on the street without giving him the coins in his pocket. He's scrupulously honest; if a restaurant undercharges him, he points out the error and pays the higher check. After my grandmother's savings ran out, he and my mother began bankrolling all of her expenses at the assisted-living facility where she resides, rather than see her move into a Medicaid-funded home. When it came time for my sister and brother and me to attend college, we were never told to limit our sights to a state school or other lower-cost option. Instead, our parents sent us to some of the best and priciest schools in the country. Neither our father nor our mother ever complained about the high tuition. That was not only generosity in the extreme, but also a sign of my parents' priorities. The house may be freezing, and my father may still wear the maroon polyester blazer that he's owned for thirty years, but he and my mother provided three kids with priceless educations, and they continue to set an example of decency, generosity, and openhearted engagement with the world around them.

So is my father cheap or thrifty when he turns off lights, or when he refuses to use the car for what he calls "dippy-shit trips," like a quick run to the grocery store for a single forgotten item? Is he cheap or thrifty when he notes which station sells gas for a penny or two less than the competition? He always seems to be branded with the former adjective, even by relatives and friends who don't have two nickels to rub together and who could learn a thing or two from my father about low-cost living. Money stirs up fierce and deeply uncomfortable emotions, emotions like resentment, envy, guilt, self-righteousness, anxiety. It is a source of conflict; we war with ourselves and with others about it. And we feel a peculiar pleasure in judging what other people do with their money—how they spend it, how they save it, how and what they consume.

Since the earliest civilizations, philosophers and friends, prophets and lovers, have carped and quibbled about other people's excesses or austerities. Confucius warned that "he who will not economize will have to agonize," but the Greeks countered indirectly with the proverb "A miser is ever in want." The censure we heap on others for their expenditures is so intense that it calls to mind Freud's theories about projection. Teasing or censuring my father for being cheap seems to neutralize some of the confusion or shame his critics feel about their own relationships with money, and perhaps helps them validate their own choices. I'd call that a cheap shot.

PART OF THE reason I embrace the word *cheap* is that it embodies some of the contradictions, ambivalence, and confusion we feel about money. Our culture bombards us with a schizophrenic range of messages about how we steward our cash. On the one hand, personal finance experts tell us we're wildly unprepared for retirement, that we have to practice restraint and save for the future. On the other hand, presidents George W. Bush and Barack Obama, along with the Democrat-led Congress, passed "fiscal stimulus" plans in the last two years, giving us all tax rebates and telling us to spend them in order to keep the economy afloat. Editorial writers like David Brooks lament the lost virtue of thrift, but their employers—newspapers and magazines—stay in business by advertising pricey diamond jewelry and peddling images of a glamorous life that's far out of reach to most of us. Is it any wonder we're confused? We hold in our minds and in our culture an unrelenting tension between the twin imperatives of spending (for personal gratification, for economic growth) and saving (for our future security, for moral uplift).

If it's any consolation, this confusion is not new. When the sociologists Robert and Helen Lynd set out to capture the personality of America in the 1920s, they traveled to Muncie, Indiana, and studied the dynamics of this "typical" American town. In their seminal 1929 book, *Middletown,* they wrote that the local newspaper printed editorials over the course of a single year that offered perfectly contradictory opinions on the importance of both saving and spending. One editorial opined that "the American citizen's first importance to his country is no longer that of citizen but that of consumer. Consumption is a new necessity." But another editorial soon after the first expressed the opposite message: "Better start saving late than never," it warned. "If you haven't opened your weekly savings account with some local bank, trust company, or building and loan, today's the day."

GIVEN THE TURGID economic straits of the last couple of years, many commentators have been calling for a "return to thrift."

This phrase—a *return* to thrift—leaves me cold.

For one thing, I'm not convinced that ordinary Americans ever truly valued thrift in the first place. When I started researching the history of frugality, I assumed, as most Americans probably do, that we were once a thrifty nation but that we had become lazy and spoiled over time, a condition abetted by a cabal of corporations and advertising firms. I began this book with a single question in my mind: What happened to thrift in America? But as I got deeper into the subject I came to realize that what we consider old-fashioned thrift—some combination of resourcefulness, prudence, simplicity, and aversion to debt—was more the result of circumstance than virtue. Thrift was determined by necessity in the early days of the republic. Goods were scarce and often prohibitively expensive for the average family, so stockings were darned, clothes were patched, fruits were preserved and stored. People made do with what they had until the stuff fell apart or was used up. Very little went to waste when each cord of firewood or linen nightshirt was the product of one's own hard labor.

But when industrialization and financial innovation

brought Americans opportunities to make their lives easier and more comfortable—through new technologies like railroads and refrigerators, and the emergence of installment plans, mail-order shopping, and credit cards—by and large, they took advantage of them. Indeed, the truest story of America is not, as we might like to believe, the story of political freedom—slavery and the Japanese internments of World War II, for instance, put the lie to that—but the story of an ever-rising standard of living. Benjamin Franklin and John Adams envisioned a nation of thrifty, industrious farmers and artisans. But after the Revolutionary War, even many of the patriots who fought for independence from England celebrated Americans' new opportunities to get rich and spend lavishly. By the beginning of the twentieth century, politicians and ordinary consumers alike crowed about how the United States boasted the world's highest living standard, as measured by the consumption of modern conveniences like canned vegetables, washing machines, and automobiles. Thrift was a "virtue" many Americans couldn't wait to relinquish.

The idea, too, that our ancestors shunned debt and lived within their means turns out to be false. In his wonderful 1999 study of consumer credit called *Financing the American Dream,* the historian Lendol Calder refers to this misconception as "the myth of lost economic virtue." In fact, as Calder writes, "A river of red ink runs through American history." Debt has vexed Americans since the first European ships landed on these shores. Hard currency was scarce in the colonies and the British forbade Americans from printing their own money, so almost all business was transacted on credit. This led to a steady stream of lawsuits against delinquent debtors, and thousands of Americans were thrown in jail—debtors' prison—for taking on obligations they couldn't repay. While many of these were business debts (a shopkeeper restocking his inventory or a farmer buying an expensive piece of equipment), consumer debt piled up too, as early as the late 1700s and the first decades of the 1800s. Upwardly mobile planters and townspeople purchased pianos and parlor furniture on credit, ever confident that their circumstances would eventually rise to match their consumption. Similarly, loan sharks and pawnbrokers operated lively and lucrative businesses in the early twentieth century, offering advances to cash-strapped workers as well as to people who simply wanted to own the markers of the emerging "American dream"—a radio, a car, a family vacation. In every era, Americans have indulged the temptation to live beyond their means.

This is not to say that our cultural values haven't changed at all. Our attitudes toward debt have certainly relaxed further over the last hundred years. To many Americans, into the middle of the twentieth century, the only debt a person might respectably hold was a home mortgage. But new forms of credit invented by retailers, manufacturers, and financial institutions—installment plans in the mid-1800s, credit cards after World War II—made borrowing easier and more convenient. By the 1920s, even once-conservative banks were giving out loans for luxury items like jewelry and new suites of furniture. And the refinancing boom of the early 2000s led millions of Americans to use their homes as ATMs. Today, mortgage holders owe, on average, a balance of $129,789 on their homes. Credit card debt averages $3,161 per American man, woman, and child. And our personal savings rate plunged from around 10 percent in the early 1980s to less than 1 percent for much of the past decade. Recent generations have grown up with expectations of abundance and ready access to the fruits of consumer capitalism, not the experience of scarcity that drove our ancestors to conserve and save.

The other reason I dislike the phrase "return to thrift" is that it looks backward with the gauzy imprecision of nostalgia. No one can argue with thrift itself, as a word or a concept. It's solid, unimpeachable, respectable, like a sturdy old rocking chair or a pair of good jeans. But a "return to thrift" sounds stale, sober, and even a bit dour. It speaks of New England Puritans and Ben Franklin's folksy maxims, of religious sermons and laments over lost virtues. Like most of the things for which we feel nostalgic, the old-fashioned thrift some pundits long for exists more in the realm of myth than reality.

I imagine cheapness as a new framework for low-cost living, a twenty-first-century version of thrift. I'm not talking about getting a lot of stuff at low prices, even though I love a bargain as much as anyone else. I'm talking about living cheaply, consuming less, scaling down our needs and wants to modest levels that are economically and ecologically sustainable. Cheapness requires practical knowledge — a set of skills and strategies, such as knowing how to fix a leaky faucet or how to tile your own kitchen floor, driving at the speed limit to conserve gas, eating by the seasons to take advantage of bumper harvests, replenishing your wardrobe at thrift stores, or cooking lentils thirty different ways. But cheapness is also a mind-set, a habit of asking yourself, "Do I need this?" and "Is this a good use of my hard-earned money?"

Cheapness doesn't necessarily require abstinence and austerity — simply a thoughtfulness and care about how we live, and a skepticism toward the messages peddled by the retail-industrial complex. It means seeing oneself as an outsider in a world that values instant gratification and promotes the idea that we can understand and express our identities through the products we consume. It means embracing and even cultivating an adversarial relationship with consumer culture. It means rejecting the belief that spending money is the route to feeling good about ourselves or feeling better than, or the same as, or different from other people, that it can help us fulfill our longings or soothe our hearts.

THIS BOOK IS also a history of thrift, frugality, and cheapness in America. As you'll see, though, it's not a linear tale moving from our thrifty past to our profligate present. Though I tell the story chronologically, the history of thrift is cyclical; this is a virtue we've abandoned and then circled back to over and over again in the last four hundred years. Americans' interest in frugality has waxed and waned, usually in response to economic events like financial panics or political calamities such as the two world wars of the last century. We Americans are an intemperate and mercurial people, but perhaps these qualities also help us adapt to unfavorable circumstances. History shows that in hard times, we hunker down and make do with less. It also shows that as soon as the danger passes, we cheerfully reset our appetites a notch or two higher than before.

I tell the story of cheapness and thrift as a subjective, lived experience and also as an idea, one that has meant different things to different people over the course of our history. At certain moments, it has been proposed as a panacea for sin, luxury, moral corruption, poverty, alcoholism, marital discord, war, and urban vice and depravity. At other times, like the present, it's been blamed for recessions and for choking off the consumption needed to keep the economy chugging along.

I also explore the ways that thrift has been used and, at times, deployed like a weapon to judge, praise, and condemn those who were or weren't conforming to shifting standards of patriotism, Protestant Christianity, bourgeois convention, or psychological self-control. The history of thrift in America is as much about social conflict, class anxiety, and hardscrabble conditions as it is about evolving cultural values.

Thrift has always been a morally charged category, used to define a vision of the good life and to separate out the upright and righteous from the prodigal and wayward. Advocacy in favor of thrift can be roughly divided into two types: traditional, religiously based appeals that classify consumption in terms of vice and virtue, and pragmatic appeals couched in the language of social mobility, budgeting, and financial management. The former type dominated in the Puritan days and remained potent in the nineteenth and early twentieth centuries. The latter type found an audience in the 1800s and through the early 1900s as the Industrial Revolution fueled interest in concepts like efficiency and scientific management. No matter what the wording, though, one fact is undeniable: thrift advocacy has always carried a whiff and often a stench of preachiness.

Wealthy reformers in the nineteenth century, for instance, urged sailors, milliners, and other laboring people to practice thrift and put their cash away in newly opened savings banks. Doing so, promised the well-meaning but out-of-touch upper crust, would not only provide workers a measure of financial security, but would also induce in them piety, sobriety, and high moral standards. Such preaching papered over the reality that working people lived exceedingly precarious lives, vulnerable to the convulsions and insecurities of an unregulated economy. If many of them lived on the knife-edge of poverty, it was as much a result of their low wages and unsteady employment as any "thriftless" habits of alcoholism or gambling.

There have also been those who celebrated simplicity—thrift, frugality, nonmaterialism, cheapness—without trying to impose a way of life onto anyone else. Henry David Thoreau helped build the Transcendentalist movement of the mid-1800s on the premise that plain living cleared time for truth-seeking and spiritual satisfaction (though like just about every other thrift advocate, Thoreau didn't always live up to his own ideals). In the post–World War II era, the philosopher Paul Goodman recommended "decent poverty" as the aim of an equitable society, one that would allow individuals the leisure and freedom to pursue their creative goals. As the essayist Richard Todd has written, "There has seldom been an era in America where someone hasn't argued that the simple life is the good life."

I'VE GRAPPLED WITH this history of moralizing and sanctimoniousness, in part because with this book I insert myself into the long lineage of writers who have complained that Americans place too much stock in the ability of material pleasures to bring happiness. I've tried to look skeptically both at my antecedents and at the current incarnations of thrift advocacy, whether at the compulsive aspects of my father's and my cheap personalities or at the politics of freegans, a band of anticapitalist activists that I profile.

I've also attempted to take some of the moralizing out of the topic of cheapness and thrift. When I analyze the consumer nation that America has become, I try not to suggest that whether one is a cheapskate or a spendthrift reflects on one's moral or spiritual fiber. Instead, I approach these issues from a practical standpoint, arguing that cheapness is a virtue in the sense that it creates financial security at a time when government is exiting the business of providing economic safety nets to individuals. That it's better for the planet. That, in unhinging us from a cycle of working and spending to provide for our basic needs and our more extravagant desires, it can provide us with the freedom to pursue our true passions. The virtues of cheapness are autonomy, independence, a deeper sense of fulfillment, financial security, and a lighter footprint on the world around us.

But I don't mean to hold myself up as the embodiment of frugal virtue. After all, our uses of money are personal, often eccentric, and deeply inconsistent, adhering to a unique calculus we each concoct. I'll walk thirty minutes out of my way to get to my own bank's ATM (and thus avoid fees), but I use a French face cream that costs $60 an ounce. Like most of the people I write about — including the most fervent nineteenth- and twentieth-century moralists — I'm prone to temptation and too easily seduced. Not long ago I was visiting my sister in Chicago and we stopped in at a chic atelier. I spied a beautiful pair of shoes by a designer whose products I'd coveted but had never been able to afford. They were high-heeled oxfords, tooled from soft brown leather and criss-crossed with thick laces. The shoes were marked down from $360 to $99. I tried them on and traversed the store, admiring my feet in every mirror. Should I buy them? I asked my sister. I was midway through writing this book, and nearing the bottom of my advance. I went back and forth, talking myself into and then out of buying the shoes. There was absolutely no reason to fork over 99 bucks for a pair of shoes I certainly didn't need.

Reader, I bought them.

I'm not suggesting that anyone should be a purist or live in ascetic isolation from worldly pleasures. I don't believe one has to disavow all attachment to money and the things it can buy. Even my father believes in the occasional splurge, unable to give up his country drives despite gas prices that at one point rose north of $4 a gallon. But I am talking about moderation, about living below one's means, about spending less money and buying less stuff, about casting a critical eye over the exigencies of our late-capitalist consumer economy.

WHEN I STARTED working on this book, my friend Darcy suggested I call it "Thrift: A Short History of a Dying Virtue." But thrift—or cheapness, or frugality—is not dying at all. In fact, it's alive and well. I heard about a doctor who uses surgical forceps to hang up his tea bags so he can reuse them two or three times; about a computer programmer who ate peanuts for lunch every day, shells and all (he didn't want the shells to go to waste); about millionaires who refuse to turn on the air-conditioning in their enormous homes; about fathers and husbands and grandmothers who wash and dry their tinfoil; about my accountant's brother, a lawyer, who will spend a half hour in New York City traffic looking for a free parking spot rather than give in to a pricey garage.

I wrote sections of this book while staying (cheaply!) in East Hampton, New York. Even in this gilded zip code, I saw signs of cheapness everywhere. It was there in the line of Mercedeses and BMWs following the same weekend yard sale circuit as I, and in the crowds of women who responded to a newspaper ad for a designer shoe sale. Everyone—even the rich, maybe especially the rich—loves a bargain.

The Internet has breathed new life into the long tradition of Americans sharing strategies for saving money. Decades ago, this information passed seamlessly from father to son and mother to daughter, and was traded at general stores and cattle auctions. It filled the pages of women's magazines and, later, mimeographed newsletters. In 1990, a Maine housewife named Amy Dacyczyn (pronounced "Decision") began penning a monthly bulletin called *The Tightwad Gazette,* which garnered more than 100,000 subscribers during its seven-year run. In it, she offered instructions for making jump ropes from old bread bags and volleyball nets from plastic six-pack rings. She suggested cutting out the serrated edges of wax-paper boxes and using them to make the saw-tooth hangers on the backs of picture frames. She gave recipes for making chalk. She calculated that you can cook up your own chocolate syrup for 3 cents per ounce, less than half the cost of Hershey's.

Though no one can take the place of the Frugal Zealot, as Dacyczyn called herself, there are now dozens of websites and blogs devoted to the same kind of thrifty living. Many fall into the "frugal mommy" category, they are written by stay-at-home moms who manage the family budget and swear by chest freezers as the number one secret to conserving cash. Others are penned by reformed debtors, environmentalists, and those who have embraced their "inner cheapskate." One of my favorites, www.Fallenfruit.org, maps out public fruit trees in Los Angeles and encourages readers to gather up the bounty. Another, www.Swaporamarama.org, lists clothing swaps nationwide for people who want a new wardrobe without spending a dime. All these sites offer some combination of ingenious new ideas and tried-and-true methods for living on less.

My own cheapness hit its apex during the writing of this book. I've long been an advocate of washing and reusing plastic bags, and I'll sometimes walk thirty blocks rather than spend $2 on the subway. I also had dial-up Internet service until November 2007, when I finally upgraded to DSL, and, too frequently, I save money by skipping lunch if I'm too busy to make a sandwich before leaving my apartment (I've been a little better about that since a friend looked at me as though I was out of my mind and asked, "Is it because you think you don't deserve to eat?").

But the moment when I realized I had truly veered into

the Cheap Dimension came not long ago, when I decided to cut my budget by using up some of the older items in my kitchen pantry. I knew there was a can of baby clams in there, which I'd had for five years (okay, maybe seven). On my way home from the library one day, I bought spaghetti, parsley, and a lemon. These were all simmering on the stovetop that evening, along with garlic, olive oil, and white wine from my pantry, when I opened the can of clams. Inside, the mollusks were greenish blue. I sniffed; they smelled like old pennies. I considered throwing them away, but I just couldn't, not after I'd already cooked up the other ingredients. Forging ahead, I tried to cover up the metallic taste of the clams with extra Parmesan and salt. A few minutes later, I was sitting at my kitchen table eating the pasta with my laptop open in front of me, looking up the symptoms of botulism, *just in case*. The thought occurred to me, I may have gone too far this time.

Indeed, cheapness can become compulsive, pathological even. An acquaintance of mine briefly dated a man who weaseled out of taking her to dinner by claiming to have an eating disorder. I still haven't totally forgiven my father for keeping the house so cold that I could sometimes see my breath, and neither has my mother. I asked her recently how she had managed to coexist with Dad's stinginess. "I should've divorced him a long time ago," she said bitterly (turned out they'd had an argument about something else that morning, which partly explains the acrimony). According to a possibly apocryphal story, Hetty Green, the early-twentieth-century millionaire who was named by the *Guinness Book of Records* as the world's "greatest miser," refused to take her son to the hospital when he had gangrene, a decision that eventually cost him his leg.

On a broader scale, too, cheapness can come with a high price. Congress passed a national minimum-wage law in 1938 because employers, in a slack labor market, will happily offer their workers sub-subsistence pay if they can get away with it.

One hundred and forty-six women died in the 1911 Triangle Shirtwaist Factory fire in New York City because of poor ventilation and a lack of fire exits. That tragedy and others like it forced a reckoning that manufacturers, in pursuit of high profits, often skimp on safety precautions. It inspired the state legislature to pass regulations mandating fire exits, fire drills, and sprinkler systems, but there are innumerable examples of corporations still cutting corners to swell profits at the expense of employees, customers, or the environment. According to labor groups and even former executives, Wal-Mart has long fought workers' attempts to unionize, which has the effect of depressing wages and benefits and thereby keeping prices low. An investigation conducted after an explosion killed fifteen workers at a Texas oil refinery found that the owner, the British company BP, had severely reduced its capital and maintenance spending in the years before the accident. And in 2007, parents removed Thomas & Friends train sets from their kids' shelves because the toys were coated in lead paint. Why? Lead paint costs about half as much as lead-free paint in China, where the toys were made.

In addition, we've damaged our planet through our addiction to cheap commodities such as oil, food, and water. Gasoline at $1.50 a gallon should seem like a cheapskate's dream. But that low price is an illusion; it doesn't factor in long-term costs related to pollution and climate change or the political violence and instability sparked by competition for energy supplies. And we're unlikely to steward our resources carefully when, like the plastic necklaces thrown out of floats at Mardi Gras, they're cheap and plentiful. Only when the various costs of these commodities shoot up for good will we start getting really serious about challenges like global warming and energy independence.

So what's a tightwad to do? I opt for something I call ethical cheapness: reconciling my goal to live cheaply with my desire to consume conscientiously, shopping in a way that supports my values. One has to know which corners can be cut safely, on an individual level and on a broader scale. Laws and regulations that require employers to conserve resources and provide all Americans — ideally, all workers around the world — with healthful working conditions and a living wage might drive up the cost of consumer goods, but they also prove the maxim that "what's most dear is most cheap": environmental and labor regulations are more economical in the long run than a laissez-faire approach that burdens us with the costs of global warming and a deeply unbalanced distribution of resources.

But I can't tell you how to live. In a 2007 article in the *New York Times,* Carl Pope, the executive director of the Sierra Club, talked about his group's brand of environmental activism, and said, "We'll encourage companies to make more efficient SUVs, and we'll encourage consumers to buy them, but we do not find lecturing people about personal consumption choices to be effective." Hundreds of years of history tell us the same thing. Americans famous and unfamous have been preaching on the evils of overconsumption since the days of the Puritan minister Cotton Mather, and where has it gotten us? Our national debt rings up at more than $11 trillion and we've accumulated another $14 trillion in mortgage and consumer debt.

Americans slash their spending en masse only in times of national crisis — wars, economic depressions, periods of high inflation. Hard experience teaches quick lessons. Unfortunately, that may be one of the few silver linings of our current recession. Perhaps we will find we can live without four hundred cable channels. Perhaps we'll decide that big houses are too costly to heat, and we'll demand denser developments of apartment buildings and small homes. Perhaps we'll turn our rooftops into gardens that insulate our houses and provide low-cost vegetables. Perhaps I'll finally take up quilting so I can put all the fabric scraps from my old clothes to good use.

Perhaps, perhaps. As we figure out the way forward through these hard times and through the next cycles of prosperity and pain, we'll be reminded that there's no simple formula for finding the right mix of frugality and comfort, self-denial and self-indulgence, lentils and high-heeled oxfords. We've each got to craft our own solutions. In the meantime, I hope this book can help generate a new respect for values like prudence, resourcefulness, and economy. A new respect, even, for the cheapskates among us.

Chapter 1

"The Crowd Approved the Doctrine, and Immediately Practiced the Contrary"

In New York on June 5, 1757, Benjamin Franklin boarded the *General Wall,* a mail ship bound for London. Franklin, age fifty-one, was already a well-respected public servant in his adopted city of Philadelphia. He'd retired a rich man from his printing business and devoted himself to local politics, winning a seat in the Pennsylvania Assembly and jumping headfirst into the fractious relations between the Assembly and the colony's leading political family, the Penns. Franklin—genial, brilliant, irrepressibly funny, and pragmatic above all—was frequently called into service as a mediator and diplomat.

By the beginning of 1757, the battles between the Assembly and the Penns had hit a wall. The Assembly desperately needed to raise taxes to finance its military operations in the French and Indian War. But Thomas Penn kept insisting that he wanted full control of the revenues, effectively blocking plans for new levies. Finally, in exasperation, the Assembly dispatched Franklin to London to lodge a formal protest with the king.

In those days, the Atlantic voyage took at least four weeks, and Franklin, restless genius that he was, found himself a bit bored on the ship. Unexpectedly, he'd been stuck in New York for more than two months while waiting to sail, and he'd gotten all kinds of correspondence and administrative work out of the way then. So he tried his best to stay busy on the *General Wall*. He chatted with the captain, Walter Lutwidge, about the most efficient methods for loading a ship. Ever the scientist, he jotted down notes about the effect of oil on water, based on his observations every time the cooks threw out the ship's greasy scullery water. He began to chart the Gulf Stream. And he also sat down and wrote the preface to the coming year's edition of his most famous publication, *Poor Richard's Almanack*.

Maybe it was because he was trapped at sea with little else to do, but that year Franklin wrote a longer preface than usual. It was, in fact, a story woven around dozens of aphorisms and proverbs that had appeared in previous editions of the almanac. The parable opens with a crowd of shoppers waiting for a vendue—a market—to open. An old man, Father Abraham, happens along, and after one would-be shopper asks his opinion of the present economic depression, the old man begins sermonizing on the secrets of prosperity. "Plough deep, while sluggards sleep, and you shall have corn to sell and to keep," he says. "At the working man's house, hunger looks in, but dares not enter."

Father Abraham extols the benefits of hard work, but he counsels his listeners that earning money alone is no guarantee of prosperity. The secret to wealth was paying as much attention to the "outgoes" as to the "incomes"—practicing frugality, living within one's means, and setting aside something for the future. "Beware of little expenses; a small leak will sink a great ship." "'Tis hard for an empty bag to stand upright." "For age and want, save while you may; No morning sun lasts a whole day."

Father Abraham's final bit of advice was to heed his advice: "If you will not hear reason, she'll surely rap your knuckles."

According to Franklin, the crowd listened eagerly, "approved the doctrine, and immediately practiced the contrary, just as if it had been a common sermon; for the vendue opened, and they began to buy extravagantly."

After Franklin's boat landed in Falmouth on July 17, he made his way to London and sent his essay on a packet ship back to Philadelphia, where his former partner David Hall printed it up in the 1758 almanac. The preface soon came to be known by two names, "Father Abraham's Sermon" and, more popularly, "The Way to Wealth." It was a hit as soon as it appeared, reprinted as a stand-alone pamphlet and eventually making its way into the annals of American literature.

The essay stood out at the time, with its encouragement of industriousness and thrift, as a piece of uncommonly good sense. But the truest words in the whole sermon might well be the ones at the end, poking fun at the simple fact that, even though people usually know what's good for them, they rarely act on that information. Franklin knew this well: you can tell people to work hard and save their money, but when the vendue opens, all that good advice drains away like so many shillings in a torn pocket.

THERE WAS NOTHING revelatory about this observation. The fact is, Americans have had a troubled, complicated relationship with frugality almost since the first boatloads of Puritans landed on these shores.

Those pilgrims were followers of John Calvin, one of the great theologians of the Protestant Reformation in the sixteenth century. Calvin had emphasized an austere, rigid version of Christianity. He argued that man must do good works to glorify God, and that diligence and industry were just as important as prayer. Idleness, according to Calvin, left a person vulnerable to the devil's tricks.

Discipline, though, gave rise to prosperity, and prosperity brought its own set of dilemmas. Jesus Christ himself had cautioned that wealth had an insidious way of weakening a believer's relationship to God. After a rich young man balked at Jesus's command to sell all of his belongings if he wanted to enter heaven, Jesus turned to his disciples and pointedly told them that "it is easier for a camel to enter the eye of a needle than for a rich man to enter the Kingdom of Heaven."

So what were Christians supposed to do with their wealth? Calvin warned his followers not to allow worldly success to interfere with their worship of God. "What will become of thanksgiving, if you overcharge yourself with dainties or wine so as to be stupefied or rendered unfit for the duties of piety and the business of your station?" he wrote. "Where is gratitude toward God, if on account of our sumptuous and ornamented apparel, we admire ourselves and despise others?" He urged self-control and abstinence in all physical pleasures. It was a vision of worldly asceticism so fierce and uncompromising that, many years later, the cultural observer H. L. Mencken would describe Puritanism as "the haunting fear that someone, somewhere may be happy."

From their first arrival in the New World, the Puritan settlers had a hard time reconciling themselves to a doctrine of ascetic self-denial. They had entered "a howling wilderness," a forbidding land that had to be tamed. But it was also, as they discovered, a land of abundance, where six-foot lobsters washed ashore after storms and two-hundred-pound sturgeons glided through rivers. Arable soil and virgin forests were readily available to anyone who could withstand the early challenges of establishing a settlement. The bounty of the New World presented Puritan leaders with a paradox they never fully resolved: their faith taught diligence, modesty, and frugality, yet, by following this advice, believers could accumulate wealth that put every earthly temptation within reach. As the colonists set down roots, harvested grains and timber for export, and became enmeshed in a thriving system of local and international trade, this "puzzle of prosperity and piety," as the historian David Shi calls it, vexed religious leaders like no other question of the era.

John Cotton, a minister who came to Massachusetts in 1633, cautioned his followers to guard against spiritual slippage. Christians must exercise "diligence in worldly businesses, and yet deadness to the world," he said. In gymnastic locutions, he tried to explain how settlers could live in the realms of both heaven and earth at the same time. When a man applies himself to business matters and finds success, Cotton said, he "does it heavenly and spiritually; He uses the world as if he used it not." Don't loosen the reins on your desires; ignore the fruits of your own success.

But as much as the John Cottons of the early years wanted to believe that Americans had been elected to provide the world with an example of what virtuous men and women could accomplish, they noticed fissures early on. The colonists, it seems, had an insatiable appetite for walnut dressing tables, velvet breeches, and silver bowls. And no amount of hellfire sermons against pride and excess scared giddy American consumers away from enjoying the benefits of their burgeoning wealth and their vital trade with the rest of the world.

Just a few years after their arrival in America, Puritan officials began passing a stream of "sumptuary laws" that outlawed what they considered to be the most vulgar forms of consumption. In 1634, the Massachusetts General Court forbade colonists from making or buying clothing of "great, superfluous and unnecessary expenses." In 1639, the court outlawed, among other things, "knots of ribbon" and "double ruffs and cuffs." Lace was banned for allowing "the nourishing of pride and exhausting of men's estates." The settlers resented these regulations and mostly ignored them.

And no wonder. Not only did the laws stifle colonists' powerful longings for beauty and comfort and status, but the orders themselves smacked of ambivalence and hypocrisy. The colony's elders couldn't stomach the thought of their own followers decked out in lace and silks, but they were happy to see Puritans profiting from the vanity of nonbelievers. "So they allowed lace makers to continue in their callings as long as they promised to sell their handiwork only to 'such persons as shall and will transport it out of this jurisdiction,'" says the historian Patricia O'Toole. "The court also ended the drinking of toasts, declaring that they served no purpose, often led to drunken brawling, and wasted wine and beer. Such sentiments did not prevent the Puritans of Massachusetts from entering—and prospering in—the rum trade."

Another black mark on the anticonsumption effort: some of the laws were aimed only at the lower classes, whose aspirational consumption was considered an affront to the social hierarchy decreed by God and, not coincidentally, exploited and enjoyed by the upper classes. The gentry were offended by the sight of lowly laborers strutting around in silk vests or ruffled shirts, leading the Massachusetts legislature to declare in 1651 "our utter detestation and dislike that men or women of mean condition, educations, and callings should take upon them the garb of gentlemen, by the wearing of gold or silver lace, or buttons, or...to walk in great boots." Only a person whose estate was valued at more than £200, the magistrates decided, could wear such clothing; all others were fined 10 shillings per violation.

It appeared to be a losing battle. By the mid-1700s, ministers portrayed the original settlers as models of true piety and lambasted their own parishioners for having fallen so far in such a short time. The preacher Cotton Mather used the fire and brimstone approach to frighten his followers into frugality. "The cursed hunger of riches will make men break through all the laws of God," he thundered. "If you make an idol of this world, God will throw your idol into the Fire!" But while preachers continued to bemoan the turn to materialism, the direction of the society seemed clear. Colonists were tired of the constant blandishments to deny themselves, to live humbly despite the assets accumulating in their account books and storerooms. Puritan asceticism remained an ideal, but it was one that fewer and fewer people aspired to.

THE QUAKERS, ONE of the other early religions to set down roots in colonial America, mainly in Pennsylvania, encountered the same struggles and conflicts as their brethren to the north. But they were better able than the Puritans to maintain a focus on frugality and simplicity even in the face of prosperity. The Quakers' "Society of Friends" was founded in the mid-1600s in England by a roving preacher named George Fox. It was a more gentle and forgiving doctrine than Puritanism. Fox spread an egalitarian theology rooted in a quest for peace and social justice. God's grace, the Quakers believed, was available to everyone, not merely the elect, as Calvin had taught.

To the Quakers, frugality was a virtue because it proved one's immunity to the temptations of the world, but also because it promoted a spirit of sharing and mutual assistance. William Penn, the idealist who led the Quakers to America, believed that the earth's resources provided "enough for all;

let some content themselves with less; a few things plain and decent serve a Christian life."

But like the colonists in New England, the Quaker flock chafed against the restrictions imposed by their spiritual leaders. Penn's methods were sometimes extreme; he authorized sumptuary laws, imposed fines on rule breakers, and mandated monthly meetings where believers were expected to answer for any indiscretions they'd indulged in, like "superfluous buttons" on their coats or "broad ribbons" on their hats. Some Friends also grumbled about Penn's hypocrisy. How did his Delaware River estate—staffed by servants and slaves, decorated with damask drapes and satin-covered chairs, and containing formal gardens and even a vineyard—reflect a commitment to austerity and simple living? Even one of Penn's closest allies compared the Quaker leader's lifestyle with that of England's royal court.

At the same time, political turbulence in the colonies was forcing Quakers to assess whether their ideals were compatible with their role at the head of Pennsylvania's government. Violence between Indians and settlers in the western part of the colony, along with growing tensions between England and France, tested the Friends' commitment to pacifism, especially as Benjamin Franklin and his supporters agitated for the creation of a local defense force. In 1755, several Quakers resigned from the Pennsylvania Assembly, effectively relinquishing the sect's longtime hold on the colony's political affairs.

This loss actually helped the Quakers sustain their ideals, which had begun to slide when their headmen navigated the compromises of political leadership. Quakers were no longer the influential majority they had been at the founding of Pennsylvania, but their more modest role allowed for a stronger commitment to the piety, pacifism, and simplicity on which the faith had been built, the same values that define their doctrine today.

In 1749, Joseph and Daniel Waldo advertised that visitors to their Boston shop could find, among other things, horn and ivory combs, quill pens, necklaces, earrings, pendants, snuff-boxes, finger rings, watch chains, jacket buttons, cutlery, cane heads, and knee buckles. However, these trinkets remained well beyond the budgets of typical colonists.

As many as one third of pre-Revolutionary colonists were flat broke or barely scratching out a living, and the middle (or "middling," as the term went) class lived in states ranging from precarious comfort to relative prosperity. Estate inventories from the eighteenth century show that most middling families owned a few teacups, pewter plates, knives and forks, some furniture, and a few books, perhaps a Bible and an almanac.

Almanacs were a household essential. They did more than predict weather (inaccurately, most of the time) and lunar cycles (also inaccurately, usually). They were compendia of both goofy and vital information—homeopathic cures, riddles, aphorisms, poems, jokes, scientific articles, agricultural advice, and more. And they offered ingenious ways of saving money or maximizing income, with tips on repurifying tainted butter (melt it and add a piece of well-toasted bread; the bread soaks up the rancid odors and tastes), getting hens to lay more eggs, healing a bruise (soak a piece of bread in vinegar and mash it into a poultice with a few drops of laudanum), preserving herbs and vegetables, destroying rats (equal parts oxgall and oil of amber, blended into a paste with oatmeal), and optimizing a paint job (paint a house in winter; in summer, the wood is too absorbent). Many almanacs came with "interleaved" pages—blank sheets sewn into the binding, on which families could keep their accounts or write their own diary entries. It was an economical alternative to buying a separate notebook.

Hundreds of almanacs were published every year, and Franklin's was one of the most popular, selling ten thousand copies per edition for a few cents each, mostly out of his printing shop on Philadelphia's Market Street. Poor Richard was a humble, slightly daft, but ever so thoughtful narrator. One year, he told his readers, "To oblige thee the more, I have omitted all the bad Weather, being thy Friend R.S."

Richard's creator, on the other hand, was shrewd and vain (but still absurdly likable). Franklin's story is well known. He was the last son of Josiah Franklin, a poor Bostonian who raised seventeen children working at the lowly trade of candlemaking. Even as a youngster, Franklin was curious, cheeky, and independent-minded. Josiah was a freethinker, but Franklin vexed him all the same by questioning the edicts of the Christian church. Perhaps this was just as well; a good education cost a small fortune even then, and Josiah had already abandoned his plan to send Franklin to Harvard to study for the seminary. Instead, the youngster was dispatched to apprentice with his brother James, a printer, at the age of twelve. Though the work was physically tedious, it allowed Franklin to read every book he could get his ink-stained hands on, and even to publish some of his own writings, under an assumed name, in his brother's newspaper before he'd turned seventeen. Bristling under James's authority and the tedium of the apprenticeship, Franklin ran away from the printing shop. He made his way to Philadelphia, where, according to his own telling, he immediately caught the locals' eyes by wandering down the street with a fluffy loaf of bread under each arm and another clamped in his mouth. After working a few years for a shiftless printer, he decided he could capture much of the local printing work simply by practicing his signature virtues, industry and thrift.

The extroverted Franklin was a terrific businessman, a natural at making friends and negotiating deals. He built up a successful printing firm, publishing his almanacs and a newspaper and eventually setting up some of his employees with shops in other colonies, from which he earned a portion of the profits. While establishing himself as an honest and reliable tradesman, he pursued some of the other interests that ultimately gave him his reputation as an innovator and renaissance man. His scientific inquiries (he investigated lead poisoning and the causes of the common cold, designed the first urinary catheter used in America, and, of course, created a buzz with his famous kite) attracted international attention. Franklin also became active in civic affairs, organizing a library, philosophical society, streetlights, and the nation's first fire department.

He retired at age forty-two and then, living comfortably on the income from his publishing and other investments, distinguished himself as a philosopher, statesman, and diplomat, in England before the Revolution and in France afterward.

Franklin has been called "the first American" because of his folksy confidence, his respect for common sense, and what came to be seen as a uniquely American combination of shrewdness and optimism. His philosophies bore little resemblance to the religious commitments of the earliest settlers. Where the Puritans believed that actions should be determined by piety and worship of God, Franklin was skeptical of organized religion and most forms of authority. He was a prankster and a *bon vivant*. More than anything, he was a pragmatist. He promoted a kind of practical morality in which good deeds and upright living were rewarded in *this* life, with everything from business opportunities and wealth to a sterling reputation and meaningful friendships.

The same goes for his approach to thrift. Franklin managed to save money as a young man—according to his memoir, he became a vegetarian while apprenticing for his brother in order to cut down the cost of his meals and save the difference in board money his brother gave him. But frugality was never an end in itself, or a means of proving one's devotion to God. To Franklin, thrift was only a means to independence and freedom. When he was twenty-five, he proposed forming an international "party of virtue" to be called the "Society of the Free and Easy": "Free, as being by the general Practice and Habit of the Virtues, free from the Dominion of Vice, and particularly by the Practice of Industry & Frugality, free from Debt, which exposes a Man to Confinement and a Species of Slavery to his Creditors." The ultimate aim was to gain the freedom to pursue what he considered the highest calling of all, public service. "I would rather have it said 'he lived usefully' than 'he died rich,' " he wrote to his mother in 1750.

We know today that Franklin was a deft image maker, a careful tender of his own reputation even when he failed miserably at living up to it. So his autobiography has to be read partly as an exercise in self-invention. Franklin admits to having had his share of what he called "errata"—including numerous "intrigues with low Women" before he married—but he generally paints himself as the archetype of republican virtue. Though he saved money from his printing business and could afford to live as well as other Philadelphia pashas, for instance, he points out that he disapproved of his wife replacing his simple pewter porridge spoon with a silver one. Later on, with characteristic ambition, he tells of his experiment with "the bold and arduous Project of arriving at moral Perfection." According to this story, Franklin wrote up a list of thirteen virtues and resolved to master them one by one. In his notebook he sketched a grid and placed the virtues—temperance, silence, order, resolution, frugality, industry, sincerity, justice, moderation, cleanliness, tranquility, chastity, and humility — on the vertical axis, with the days of the week on the horizontal axis. He then attempted to get through one week without committing any offenses against one of the virtues; offenses in any of the others earned him a black mark on the respective part of the chart. He completed the thirteen-week course — one week for each virtue — four times a year, for several years, before limiting himself to one course per year, and then one every few years. Franklin had the hardest time with humility, since he was quite fond of himself. But that was all right. Ever the pragmatist, he determined after a few rounds that some imperfection was actually preferable to complete and total virtuousness, since "a perfect Character might be attended with the Inconvenience of being envied and hated."

In later life, Franklin embraced his sybaritic side, though mainly in private. While living in London from 1763 to 1775, he shipped crates of luxury goods — silk blankets, fine china and crystal, special material for curtains, damask tablecloths — back to the house he and his wife, Deborah, were building in Philadelphia. "The middle-aged Franklin, as generous and expansive as the young Franklin had been tight and guarded, sent presents left and right, a fine edition of Virgil to Harvard, fancy objects to friends," write the historians Claude-Anne Lopez and Eugenia Herbert.

But he also protected his long-cultivated image, and still answered to notions of common sense when it came to getting and spending. In a letter to his daughter, Sally, written during his diplomatic stint in Paris, Franklin chastised her for requesting some frippery.

> [Y]our sending for long black pins, and lace, and
> *feathers!* disgusted me as much as if you had put salt
> in my strawberries.... The war indeed may in some

degree raise the prices of goods, and the high taxes which are necessary to support the war may make our frugality necessary; and, as I am always preaching that doctrine, I cannot in conscience or in decency encourage the contrary, by my example, in furnishing my children with foolish modes and luxuries. I therefore send all the articles you desire, that are useful and necessary, and omit the rest.... If you wear your cambric ruffles as I do, and take care not to mend the holes, they will come in time to be lace; and feathers, my dear girl, may be had in America from every cock's tail.

Publicly as well, Franklin was always agitated with Americans' evident tendency to spend beyond their means and thereby risk the real fruits of the Revolution, their hard-won liberty and independence. As he saw it, Britain had grown weak in part because of the poor underclass crowding into cities. England's relatively small size and its age—the fact that most arable land had already been distributed among sons for many generations, and there was no room left for new generations—had displaced huge numbers of young men. Many of them migrated from the hinterland and made their way to the cities looking for factory work. Thanks to a confluence of factors—nascent industrialization, the development of global trade, and a cheap and exploitable labor force—England relied on a consumer-goods export economy as early as 1690.

For America, Franklin had a different vision altogether. Americans, he hoped, would forswear the types of luxuries imported from Europe, directing their savings instead toward investment at home. Those investments—in land, labor, and equipment—would increase the productive capacity of domestic farmers and craftsmen. Households, in his view, should make as much of their clothing, furniture, and food as possible, and what they couldn't produce at home, they should purchase from trained artisans who themselves would earn enough to employ apprentices and journeymen at good wages. America would thus be populated by independent, middle-class households, not the extremes of wealth and poverty that had led to tyranny all over Europe.

But while colonists admired Franklin, not everyone wanted to emulate him. By the mid-eighteenth century, Americans were deeply integrated into the international trading economy. They exported staples like corn, tobacco, and wooden shingles, and imported cloth and tea from England, silks from France, sugar from the West Indies, and, despite louder and louder rumblings about liberty and the rights of mankind, slaves from Africa.

Between their abundant harvests and the availability of cheap land and necessities such as firewood, the colonists enjoyed one of the highest standards of living in the world at that time, and they used the dividends of robust economic growth to participate in the consumer revolution that was already under way in Europe. England had felt the first tremors of the Industrial Revolution only a few decades earlier when small factories started churning out cutlery, ceramics, textiles, and other consumer goods. Colonists clamored for the new mass-produced British products, which were high in quality and cheaper than what the Americans could make at home. Newspaper advertisements trumpeted the latest shipments from Europe and touted the durability and style of British furniture and glassware. Between 1750 and 1773, imports more than doubled.

Franklin and other commentators castigated the colonists for their indulgence in new conveniences and comforts. In a letter to the *Boston Gazette* in 1764, one observer, writing under the pseudonym Philo Publicus, told readers that "we have taken Wide Steps to Ruin, and as we have grown more

Luxurious every Year, so we run deeper and deeper in Debt to our Mother Country." He noted the china and silver stacked on Bostonians' sideboards and concluded, "I wonder not that my Country is so Poor, I wonder not when I hear of frequent Bankruptcies."

These laments were about as effective as Cotton Mather's had been a hundred years earlier. But in 1767, King George and the British Parliament passed the Townshend Duties, imposing taxes on cloth, ribbons, shoes, paper, glass, tea, and a range of other items. These had the effect of electrifying the budding independence movement. In public meetings, political pamphlets, and newspaper stories, civic leaders began calling for a boycott of all the goods in question.

The boycotts were more than a temporary protest against England's taxation without representation. To men like John Adams, Thomas Jefferson, and Ben Franklin, they represented an opportunity to revive the old Puritan ideals of frugality, industriousness, and self-denial—ideals that would be essential in the struggle for independence from Great Britain. The ethos of the boycotts was summed up by the *Providence Journal* on November 7, 1767, when it announced them with a rousing headline that read, "Save your MONEY and you will save your COUNTRY!"

With their consumption cast in moral and political terms, Americans en masse began to rethink their spending. Many years later, the economist Thorstein Veblen would coin the term "conspicuous consumption" to describe the Gilded Age in America. What happened in the colonies in 1767 was the exact opposite; it was a period of what can be described only as conspicuous frugality.

Local assemblies held raucous meetings at which they passed resolutions calling on the colonists to promote thrift and give up silks, velvets, gold and silver buttons, ready-made clothes, snuff, mustard, and tea. In some villages, hundreds of men and women took oaths in front of their neighbors, swearing that they wouldn't buy imports from England.

The most obvious sign of patriotic self-denial was to don "homespun"—clothing made out of rough, American-made textiles—and Americans ostentatiously did so. Women dusted off their spinning wheels and held parties and contests to see who could produce the most yards in a day. Town fathers bragged about how many skeins of wool their ladies had woven or how many pairs of shoes a local cobbler had made. A man in Newport, Rhode Island, declared that he would vote in a coming election only for candidates who campaigned wearing American-made clothes. In the interests of maximizing local wool production, fire departments in Philadelphia announced that they would give up eating mutton for dinner in order to spare the lives of the city's sheep.

Indian or Chinese tea imported from England was a definite no-no; editorials referred to it as "a pestilential herb" and even implied that the stuff was poisonous. So ladies proudly served "Hyperion" tea made out of the red-root bushes that grew along the swampy banks of New England's rivers. In Boston, three hundred women from well-known Yankee families signed a petition against imported tea, a decision noted approvingly in the press.

At Harvard, Yale, and the College of Rhode Island (now Brown University), graduates wore homespun to their commencements in 1767. The following year, Harvard students vowed to stop drinking tea.

Colonists even promised to give up the beloved but pricey rituals associated with funerals, like wearing special commemorative rings and jewelry to the gravesite, giving away fancy English gloves and scarves to guests, and serving hot wine at the party afterward. When the wife of a certain Captain Curtis, of Marblehead, was buried "in the New Mode i.e. without Mourning [attire]," attendees applauded to show they approved of the new austerity.

"LITTLE BY LITTLE," the historian Ann Fairfax Withington writes in her book *Toward a More Perfect Union: Virtue and the Formation of American Republics,* "frugality entered the public consciousness as a virtue in itself and not just as a means of putting pressure on England."

This development was part of the patriots' grand design. In fact, frugality was an essential component of their vision for what their new nation would be.

Jefferson, Franklin, Adams, and hundreds of other Revolutionaries were building one of the first republics the modern world had ever seen. It was a radical dream: a nation governed by its people through elected leaders. But that simple definition belies what the Revolutionaries viewed as the complex requirements of a republic. For men (and it was all men at the beginning, since the only people who held the franchise in the new nation were white male property owners) to rule themselves, Jefferson and the others believed, they must be rational, public-spirited, and, above all else, virtuous. Without virtues like honesty, temperance, thrift, independence, and self-control, men would easily succumb to the vices of greed, degeneracy, corruption, and, ultimately, tyranny, the very vices that were weakening nations like England and France. As Franklin himself remarked, "Only a virtuous people are capable of freedom. As nations become corrupt and vicious, they have more need of masters."

On a practical level, Franklin believed, frugal citizens would direct their resources toward everyday necessities instead of luxuries, ensuring that everyone could maintain a basic standard of living. Frugal citizens would avoid falling into debt, which was the first and most serious threat to freedom. Frugal citizens would eschew baubles and trinkets, instead saving their money to invest in the land, labor, and equipment necessary to grow the domestic economy.

On a moral level, thrift and ascetic self-denial would hold men's ambitions in check and keep them honest, self-sufficient, and independent, all qualities that patriots believed were essential to the success of the American experiment. They used terms like *frugal* and *economical* as code for the character of the model American citizen. As one Virginia patriot noted, "Virtue is the vital principle of a republic, and it cannot long exist, without frugality, probity and strictness of morals."

THE PATRIOTS' VISION of a frugal citizenry was short-lived. The boycotts of the Revolutionary years galvanized opposition to British control, gave colonists a tangible way to assist the independence efforts, and fostered a renewed interest in thrift, but these effects were temporary. Americans (and by no means all Americans, since newspapers were full of notices accusing merchants of violating the resolutions) may have been largely willing to forgo comforts and delights in the service of a political emergency, but they could hold out for only so long.

As soon as the war ended, Americans' pent-up demand exploded in a frenzy of consumption and self-gratification. Private clubs for dancing and gambling opened in major cities. Ornate silk-covered chairs and rococo furniture, the style then popular in Europe, found their way into wealthy homes. The *Empress of China,* the first American ship bound for the Orient, sailed out of New York Harbor in 1784 and returned with porcelain designed by some clever marketer: dishes embellished with eagles, American flags, and the national seal. Only a few years earlier, coarse homespun was the way to trumpet one's patriotism; after the war, patriotism became just another commodity, available for purchase.

Now that the British were no longer their enemies, Americans seemed more eager than ever to emulate them. Young, upper-class men went off to Europe on months-long grand tours and came home with extravagant wigs and pretentious new habits, like flirting (practiced as an *art*) and ballroom dancing. Before the Revolution, only rich families had parlor rooms for such activities. But as gentility—a kind of social refinement based on European manners—spread as an ideal, the consumer revolution was spurred on further. Social identities in the new America became more fluid, and the Revolution's promise of freedom gave citizens a certain permission to invent themselves anew. Craftsmen, farmers, and clerks couldn't be gentry, but they could be genteel. One needed only a parlor, a mantel clock, and a punch bowl to fancy oneself a gentleman or a lady.

Republican leaders like Adams, Jefferson, and Franklin were alarmed by the consumer orgy, for they saw in it harbingers of the decline of the republic they had worked so hard to create. They knew it was crucial to somehow reconcile their classical republican vision with the new order of expansion and growth, but they couldn't abandon their conviction that prodigal self-indulgence was incompatible with self-rule. Observing the colonists' appetite for imported luxuries and modern conveniences, they despaired that the Revolution had failed. "I consider the extravagance which has seized them as a more baneful evil than Toryism was during the war," Thomas Jefferson wrote to a friend in 1786. "Would a missionary appear, who would make frugality the basis of his religious system, and go through the land, preaching it up as the only road to salvation, I would join his school." Even Franklin, optimistic and forgiving by nature, sadly admitted that Americans might be "lazy and indolent" at heart.

While these Revolutionaries lamented the decline of economic virtue, other Americans sneered at their moralism and celebrated the liberties the Revolution had unleashed. Defending his compatriots' freedom to get rich and spend their money as they pleased, the Virginia merchant Carter Braxton told his state convention: "These are rights which freemen will never consent to relinquish; and after fighting for deliverance from one species of tyranny, it would be unreasonable to expect they should tamely acquiesce under another."

With that sentiment, Braxton articulated the attitude that would find increasing currency among Americans. The common good, the virtuous republic, these were beautiful ideals and would always find some place in Americans' rhapsodic images of themselves. But in practical terms, the individualistic ethic of getting and spending would ultimately become the reigning credo of the prosperous new nation.

And what of Ben Franklin? The extraordinary American—inventor of bifocals, esteemed diplomat, signer of the Declaration of Independence—died in 1790 at age eighty-four, better loved in revolutionary France than in his native United States. In Paris, where the French fetishized his habit of strolling through the streets in rustic clothing and an old fur cap, Franklin's death was observed with three days of public mourning decreed by the National Assembly. At home, he was honored with a large funeral in Philadelphia (twenty thousand people attended, according to newspaper accounts) and members of the House of Representatives wore mourning badges for a month. But the Senate, led by Franklin's rival John Adams, refused to do the same, and President George Washington declined to wear mourning clothes, concerned that he might then have to observe the custom for every dead patriot. Franklin didn't receive an official eulogy until nearly a year after his death, and the lukewarm one that he finally got was delivered by a political enemy, the Anglican priest William Smith. By the end of Franklin's life, some of his fellow patriots and even friends had cut their ties to him because of political disagreements over the Constitution and Franklin's support for the messy French Revolution. One critic called him "a whore-master, a hypocrite and an infidel."

But he was not to fade into obscurity. Soon after his death, Franklin rose up to occupy a unique place in the American psyche. He was a comforting symbol of old virtues and new opportunities. As economic and political turmoil succeeded the Revolution, Americans searched for new myths to help explain and articulate their uncertain universe.

The familiar axioms of Franklin's "Way to Wealth" and other writings represented a popular font of common sense and business advice. And Franklin's own story of modest beginnings and great achievements enjoyed the status of myth. To many in the early 1800s, Franklin embodied the nascent ideology of upward mobility, the idea that one could rise from humble origins to stand before kings. By 1850, "The Way to Wealth" had been reprinted more than 145 times and had established thrift as an essential habit for anyone wanting to "get on" in the world.

The gospel of social mobility became one of the most powerful and enduring myths America has ever produced, and Ben Franklin was its poster child. A politician in Boston inaugurated the Franklin Lectures in 1831 to inspire young men to succeed; dozens of savings banks were named after him around the country. When the philanthropist Robert C. Winthrop unveiled a statue of Franklin in the park near Boston's city hall in 1856, he exhorted his audience, "Behold him, Mechanics and Mechanics' Apprentices, holding out to you an example of diligence, economy and virtue, and personifying the triumphant success which may await those who follow it!" (Winthrop himself had been born with silver spoon firmly in place.) In 1828, a poor farm boy in Pennsylvania came across Franklin's autobiography. That boy grew up to be the financier Thomas Mellon. He later described his reading of Franklin's story as "the turning point of my life" and installed a likeness of Franklin at the front of his first Pittsburgh bank.

Because of his beatification as the secular saint of capitalism, Franklin came to represent some of the worst traits of American culture to his many later critics. Mark Twain satirized the old patriot's self-improvement schemes, writing in 1870 that "his simplest acts were contrived with a view to their being held up for the emulation of boys forever—boys who might otherwise have been happy." And in a literary evisceration of the *Autobiography,* D. H. Lawrence complained: "The Perfectability of Man! Ah heaven, what a dreary theme! The perfectability of the Ford Car!" When Henry David Thoreau graduated from Harvard in 1837, he found both of the expected career paths—religion and business—lacking. "Neither the New Testament nor Poor Richard speaks to our condition," he sighed.

But both his critics and his champions have distorted Franklin's legacy. He wasn't a consistent embodiment of virtuous self-denial, but nor was he a self-interested capitalist pushing a vision of unbridled moneymaking. Franklin advocated thrift and industry as means to achieving a comfortable life and the time to pursue useful vocations. For him, this always meant intellectual inquiry and public service. After inventing the Franklin stove, a more efficient heater than the ones then found in most houses, he went further than declining a patent; he published a pamphlet with detailed instructions on how to build and operate the stove. "As we enjoy great advantages from the inventions of others, we should be glad of an opportunity to serve others by any inventions of ours," he said. No avarice there. But Americans have always needed their heroes, and Franklin has served ably as the personification of folksy American thrift, even as American culture drifted further and further from the ascetic republican virtues he promoted. The more we move away from our founding ideals, it seems, the more lovingly we tend them.

Chapter 2

A Nation of Savers

If Franklin represents our favorite thrifty archetype, then the nineteenth-century millionaire Hetty Green is the grasping, coldhearted Scrooge of American history. She's immortalized in the *Guinness Book of Records* as the world's "greatest miser," in an account that claims "she was so mean that her son had to have his leg amputated because of her delays in finding a *free* medical clinic," and continues, "She herself lived off cold oatmeal because she was too mean to heat it, and died of apoplexy in an argument over the virtues of skimmed milk."

Hetty Green has mostly faded into the shadows of the past. But while she lived, she was an object of surreal, almost fanatic fascination — a moneybags who lived like a pauper! Born in 1832 into a wealthy Quaker whaling family in New Bedford, Massachusetts, she multiplied the fortune she inherited a hundred times over thanks to her steel-willed dealings in railroads, real estate, and finance. Yet she spent most of her nights sleeping in frigid tenements in Brooklyn and Hoboken, and so commuted by public ferry to her office on Wall Street. She cut a proud figure walking along lower Manhattan's cobblestone streets wearing a threadbare black dress and a simple black bonnet. Some observer, noting her costume, gave her the nickname the "Witch of Wall Street," and it stuck for years. As she later told an interviewer, she'd learned a life-long lesson from her father, Edward Robinson. He taught her "never to owe anyone anything. Not even a kindness."

Hetty showed an unusual interest in money from her early childhood, perhaps because she'd been given the task of reading the financial pages to her grandfather after he lost his eyesight. There's a story that when she was six or seven years old, Hetty's family sent her to the dentist to have her teeth checked. The little girl kicked and screamed, forcing the dentist to back off until a servant pulled a silver half-dollar from his pocket and promised it to Hetty if she behaved. According to one of her biographers, Charles Slack, Hetty eyed the coin, considered the deal, and then gave in.

At the age of eight, when other children might have spent their coins on candy or games, Hetty preferred to think about compound interest and the stock markets. She asked to be escorted from the family manse down to the New Bedford Institution for Savings, where she handed over a small stash of cash and opened her first bank account. Of the list of depositors on file at the New Bedford Institution that year, wrote another of her biographers, there was no name "that represented such a complete faith in the thrift creed of the bank as did that of Hetty Robinson."

BY THE TIME Hetty opened up that savings account, banks were indeed the frontline institutions in the battle to inculcate thrift as an American virtue. But she wasn't the customer Thomas Eddy and other philanthropists had in mind when they started the earliest savings banks in the United States. The first banks were supposed to serve real paupers, the masses of poor and struggling Americans who filled the country's cities and towns.

Thomas Eddy was a wealthy Quaker insurance broker in New York City. Like other reform-minded elites, he was captivated by the penny banks in Scotland that served the "lower and middling sorts," the term used at the time to describe working people. He was convinced that if America's sailors, laborers, and widows could only be taught to save their money (rather than wasting it on lottery tickets and rounds at the tavern), the poverty rate would quickly fall. Banks would offer security, a small bit of interest, and incentives to save to all those who lived in the precarious zone between self-sufficiency and want. Even better, reformers hoped, banks might inspire long-lasting moral improvement.

Eddy was the main force behind the opening of the Bank for Savings in the City of New York, one of the first savings banks in the country, which took its maiden deposits on Saturday, July 3, 1819. On that day, between eleven a.m. and two p.m., eighty New Yorkers—including two spinsters, one teacher of the deaf and dumb, one sash-maker, one boot-cleaner, and four domestic servants—visited an old building on Chambers Street and surrendered their hard-won coins in exchange for a passbook and the promise of 5 percent interest.

The depositors may not have known it, but they were bit players in a grand plan to eradicate urban poverty from America. "A pecuniary gain to the indigent is not the only advantage to be expected from this institution," wrote Eddy in the bank's first report. "Their moral feelings it is hoped will be greatly benefited. It must have a direct tendency to induce habits of frugality, forethought, of self-assistance and self-respect."

Many of his contemporaries agreed. A Boston economist

named Willard Phillips, buoyed by the moral urgency of his cause, wrote that "the establishment of savings banks ought to be celebrated as a great event in the world, no less than the introduction of the compass, or the invention of printing."

THE FIRST AMERICAN savings banks were philanthropic organizations, usually sprung from the minds of prosperous men like Eddy, who managed the institutions without accepting salaries or dividends. Benevolent as they were, though, the early banks were based on fundamentally conservative ideas. Reformers laid the blame for poverty at the feet of thriftless, shiftless individuals when in fact, the market economy churned in a constant state of creative destruction, chewing up and spitting out workers when business cycles demanded it. A haphazard welfare system helped the very poorest, but there were no social insurance programs of the kind we have today—unemployment benefits, Social Security, sick leave, or disability pay—to keep ordinary Americans afloat when disaster struck. By focusing on personal responsibility instead of the structural inequities of the economy, reformers missed the deeper roots of poverty, and savings banks were proposed as a panacea for a problem they could not cure.

America's political and social establishment was preoccupied in the first decades of the nineteenth century with pauperism and the growth of what threatened to be a permanent underclass. After the Revolution, thousands of ex-soldiers, poor farmers, and free blacks (slavery was outlawed in most of New England in the 1780s) had poured into the cities along the East Coast, causing crowding and competition for jobs. Immigration from abroad grew as well. Slums rose up, filled with rickety tenements to house all the newcomers. While the majority of the American population still lived on farms, the agrarian utopia recently extolled by Thomas Jefferson was being transformed by a painful cycle of booms and busts and by the commercial opportunities opened up by America's increasing integration into the world economy.

In the face of all these changes, poverty escalated. Jobs, even once obtained, were insecure—subject to disruptions brought on by anything from foreign wars to droughts and storms to the seizure of commercial ships by pirates.

Officials at the almshouse in Philadelphia wrote in the last quarter of the eighteenth century that most of the paupers arriving at their doors were "naked, helpless and emaciated with Poverty and Disease to such a degree that some have died in a few days after their Admission." Beggars trolled city streets, hoping merchants or dowagers might toss them a few coins. Grueling work, infectious illnesses, and poor diets left workers vulnerable to periodic unemployment. According to some studies, one third to one half of the residents in early cities were poor or on the edge of destitution, and between the drafting of the Constitution in 1787 and the financial depression that started in 1837, poverty was the most urgent social problem in the United States.

Government provided some benefits to the worst off. Inspired by Britain's Poor Laws, officials during this period experimented with all types of welfare assistance: direct cash payments to down-and-out families, food donations, sending the poor to live in almshouses or asylums. Indigents also relied on charity doled out by relatives, churches, or philanthropic associations.

Surely the most colorful and questionable method of poor relief were "pauper auctions." These events were similar to slave auctions. They were usually held at the village inn, where a town father would describe the subject's qualities ("Here is Mr.____; he is a strong, hearty, sound man, who can eat anything, and a good deal of it") and then let locals bid to house and board him. The "winner"—who got another mouth to feed but also an extra pair of hands to put to work—was the householder who offered the lowest bid, which was then paid by the town.

The high levels of poverty around the turn of the century were disastrous for city budgets. Salem, Massachusetts, spent almost half its annual budget of $23,330 on poor relief in 1816. But no matter how many paupers they farmed out or how many almshouses they built, towns found poverty to be an intractable problem.

For republicans still high on the idealism and rhetoric of the Revolution, just as thorny as the practical challenge of providing for the down-and-out was the symbolic significance of poverty. The presence of so many poor people exposed the contradictions of a society suspended between political theory and market reality. The founders associated urban wretchedness with the decline of Europe, so the slums in their own towns were deeply troubling. What had become of Jefferson's and Franklin's idyllic agrarian economy driven by modest but successful farmers and artisans? What of their hopes that America's vastness, its cheap and fertile land, would guarantee every family the opportunity to be self-sufficient, independent, and free?

There's no question that those who spoke about poverty or tried to alleviate it—politicians, religious leaders, and wealthy reformers, mainly—wanted to help the people they trained their efforts on, whether for potential gain, prestige, or actual goodwill. But their methods and their language were often filled with such moral opprobrium, such "condemnation, voyeurism and paranoia," as the historian Seth Rockman says, that what's striking is both the heavy symbolic meaning of the problem and also the self-serving agendas that many of them were pushing. By suggesting that poverty was a character problem, an adjunct of idleness and an illness of the spirit, elites argued that the individual, rather than market forces or the structure of a competitive commercial society, was responsible for his own economic fate. If a man was poor, he wasn't working hard enough, or he was weak-willed, or he had allowed himself to be seduced by easy thrills like rum and gambling. This was no doubt true in some cases (bars were plentiful in early America, just as now, and they hosted raucous evenings of cardplaying, cockfighting, and boxing), but it ignores the interplay of personal choices and broader, impersonal forces.

Many of the elites didn't believe in charity. As Eddy wrote in 1819 at the opening of New York's Bank for Savings, "the unconditional and indiscriminate relief of the indigent increases the amount of poverty.... By inducing [the poor] to rely on gratuitous and undeserved assistance, it destroys their sense of dignity and self-respect, degrades them in their own estimation, and reduces them to the abject condition of idle indifference and daily dependence."

Savings banks were meant to be the answer. They appealed to wealthy Americans' almost evangelical faith in individual responsibility and up-by-your-bootstraps grit, and to reformers' ideas about the "correct" forms of spending and consumption. Not coincidentally, once poor people had been "taught" to be thrifty and save, the public burden of paying for all those paupers might be alleviated. That never quite happened; we've always maintained some form of government-sponsored welfare in this country. But even though it never fulfilled its early promise, savings banking did catch on. It spread like a brush fire through young America and has lived on as "a favorite American institution of self-improvement," as the historian Stephan Thernstrom once wrote. In 1820, there were 10 savings banks in the United States with $1.1 million in funds.

Thirty years later, the country boasted 108 banks with assets of $43 million, and by 1899, 987 banks held over $2 billion in the names of almost 6 million depositors.

Rags to Riches in the New America

On the morning of November 4, 1825, throngs gathered along the banks of the Hudson River, the natural border between New York and New Jersey. They were waiting for a flotilla of boats that had come all the way from Buffalo—the first boats ever to sail the just-completed Erie Canal, which had been eight years in the making.

As the vessels passed into New York City, cannons sounded to announce their arrival. One by one, the ships glided along, each with streamers and banners fluttering in the wind behind it and a full brass band on board. The *Seneca Chief* carried De Witt Clinton, governor of New York and an early champion of the canal, along with ash from Detroit and Buffalo, white-fish from Lake Erie, and flour and butter from Michigan and Ohio. Further behind was *Noah's Ark,* decked out, naturally, with two eagles, two fawns, some "creeping things," a bear, and a menagerie of other woodland creatures from the western states.

The ships all formed a circle at Sandy Hook, New Jersey, the southernmost point of New York Harbor. There, after a brief speech commemorating the "wedding of the waters," Governor Clinton pulled out two green kegs filled with Lake Erie water and dumped them into the Atlantic Ocean. Then his friend, Dr. Samuel Mitchill, uncorked thirteen bottles of water and emptied those too into the sea below. They had been collected from some of the world's greatest rivers—the Nile, the Gambia, the Ganges, the Indus, the Thames, the Seine, the Rhine, the Danube, the Mississippi, the Columbia, the Orinoco, the Amazon, and La Plata. It was a symbolic act, but its meaning was clear: America was open for business.

The completion of the canal in 1825 ushered in America's "market revolution," an economic growth spurt that integrated once-isolated parts of the country into a national and international market economy. The canal introduced the Great Lakes region and much of the American interior to world trade, reducing freight rates and times by more than half. Ships plied the Mississippi and Ohio rivers, delivering factory goods to the western states and returning east and north with agricultural produce and raw materials. State governments improved their roads and cleared the way for railroad companies to expand their networks. With all of these transportation innovations, the fabric of the eighteenth-century economy — based on household self-sufficiency, bartering, and neighborhood exchange — slowly disintegrated. By 1860, the United States was the second largest industrial power in the world, eclipsed only by Great Britain.

A vocal minority at the time protested that the "progress" of the market revolution took place on the backs of black slaves (whose uncompensated labor helped keep American exports cheap) and Native Americans (whose lands had been confiscated during the westward expansion). Some observers, both native and foreign, commented disapprovingly on the expansive age and the rampant materialism it seemed to spawn. The poet William Ellery Channing lamented the new values of the "money-getting, self-seeking, self-indulging, self-displaying land."

But most people preferred to enjoy the good times while they had them. Consumers especially benefited from the expansion of trade, finding a surplus of choices to satiate every longing. Instead of advertising just "blankets," the Boston retailer T. D. Whitney boasted of his stock of "down quilts, exposition quilts, Marseilles quilts, American quilts, German quilts, crib quilts, berth quilts, eiderdown quilts, American blankets, summer blankets and crib blankets." Jordan, Marsh and Company, the Boston dry goods store that opened in 1841, rehabilitated the villainess of the French Revolution when it advertised its Marie Antoinette brand of black silks, "confidently recommended by us for its wearing qualities, softness of finish, and richness of color."

Ads for beauty potions, ointments, and skin creams proliferated all over the country; Ring's Vegetable Ambrosia for Gray Hair could be gotten at the local druggist; and Professor Gardner, the "New England Soap Man," promised that his lather cleaned skin and teeth *and* could make grease stains disappear from linen. Drapes and feather beds, men's suits and woolen rugs, all items once made at home or custom-ordered from local artisans, were now mass-produced and ready on demand.

With commerce on the rise, more and more capital sloshed through the American economy. Because the markets rewarded anyone who could produce in scale, companies merged and consolidated. Larger factories displaced the small home workshops that once characterized manufacturing industries. White-collar businesses—the banks, insurance agencies, and brokerages that kept the wheels of commerce greased—grew as well. As a result of these developments, the nature of employment in America changed radically. All the factories, shipyards, railroads, and front offices of the new economy needed workers, and they drew young men away from the small communities where they'd been reared. These men generally commanded a higher income at their new wage jobs, but they surrendered the independence they'd once enjoyed as farmers or craftsmen.

It was an era of displacement, change, and fortune building, and it helped to spawn nineteenth-century America's most potent cultural ideology: the promise of upward mobility. The United States offered riches to any man who worked hard, saved his money, and kept his eye "on the main chance."

This idea had drawn settlers to America from the very beginning; even the Puritan John Cotton in 1630 acknowledged that many of the pilgrims bound for America had embarked on the dangerous journey for economic opportunity as much as for religious freedom.

From the early 1800s, these notions of self-invention and personal advancement seeped more deeply into the story Americans told about themselves, ultimately becoming a core element of our national folklore at home and abroad. In a speech at Union College in Schenectady in 1839, the businessman Robert Stickney told students that "the aspiring youth, however low he may walk in the vale of poverty," could achieve just as much wealth and success as "the sons of fortune in the palaces of the wealthy and the great." In 1849, observing the pace of growth in northern industrial cities like Lowell, Massachusetts, one writer noted that "he who five years ago was working for wages, will now be found transacting business for himself, and a few years hence, will be likely to be found a hirer of the labor of others."

Statements like these obscured the reality that a young man's family legacy at Harvard or his father's business connections in most cases still trumped a poor boy's peerless work ethic. But the sentiment in them was immensely powerful, and they were repeated over and over. Phrases like "self-made man" and "architect of his own fortune" popped up everywhere as shorthand for the most admired archetype of America's emerging individualistic, dollar-hunting culture. "In this country," declared the Philadelphia author Timothy Shay Arthur, "the most prominent and efficient men are not those who were born to wealth and eminent social positions, but those who have won both by the force of untiring personal energy."

And what was the secret to success? The prescription hadn't changed much since Franklin's day. Frugality and industry would help any young man get ahead. A multitude of conduct books and didactic novels were published in the mid-1800s to guide the ambitious upstarts who were setting out from their farms and villages to make it in business. Titles like *On the Formation of Business Habits* (1835), *Worth and Wealth: Maxims for Merchants and Men of Business* (1857), *How to Get Rich; or the Money Maker's Manual* (1867), and Horatio Alger's *Ragged Dick,* all of them bestsellers, offered advice on everything from how to apply for bank credit to behavior and etiquette questions, like how to hold a fork and what times to call on customers. Most of all, they drilled into young men lessons of morality, thrift, and sobriety.

The books were filled with fatherly warnings, especially on the subject of money. In them, the moral discourse of money constantly intersected with the economic discourse of vice. Cities were dangerous places, filled with temptations. Gambling, drinking, prostitution, fraudulent business practices: any of these might seduce even the most well-meaning naïf. "Demoralization flows into a city through the channels of commerce," warned Edward Fletcher in his 1849 book, *The Temptations of City Life; A Voice to Young Men Seeking a Home and Fortune in Large Towns and Cities.* Fletcher's solution, of course, was to work hard and be frugal.

Every penny saved was one less penny that went to the racetrack, the tavern, or the brothel. And having a reserve of cash would give young men the security and confidence required to thrive. "We presume that it needs no demonstration to prove that the saving of money is as essential as getting it, for the attainment of a permanent independence," wrote Edwin Freedley in his 1852 bestseller, *A Practical Treatise on Business.* "This is one of those self-evident truths that meet with a ready and universal assent. It is even a truism that it is as physically impossible for money to accumulate without saving, as for a leaking vessel to hold water. There is no income so large that cannot be got rid of, and no sum so small, that an able-bodied, industrious man may earn in this country, that will not suffice, so long as he remains single, to lay the foundation of an independent fortune.... An excellent judge of good wines, or a connoisseur in rare dishes, may calculate with certainty that his pockets will become slim in exact proportion as his belly grows round. In a word, prosperity without economy is an impossibility."

On the surface, it sounds like Franklin. But there was one essential difference. Franklin encouraged young tradesmen to earn "a competence," a modest income appropriate to a public-spirited republican, which allowed them to live happily and independently. Freedley and his cohort generally had a different goal in mind: getting rich. The aspirations of the nineteenth century had largely outgrown those of the Revolutionary patriots.

"To Live Content with Small Means"

One group of Americans continued to hold on to the vision of modest livelihood. In fact, even as the spectacles of new wealth captured Americans' imaginations, there was a flowering of philosophies that exalted the rhythms of the simple life. This was in some measure a backlash to the raw ambition and greed unleashed by the market revolution. It was also a tribute to the charisma and charm of two very different personalities.

Ralph Waldo Emerson and Henry David Thoreau were friends and intellectual brothers, and they were at the center of the Transcendentalist movement that took root in Concord, Massachusetts, in the 1830s and 1840s. Unlike some of their contemporaries—the moral reformers behind the temperance and antipauperism societies of the period—the Transcendentalists didn't believe in imposing a way of life onto anyone. Instead, they advocated a deeply spiritual and deeply personal version of thrift, a way of life built around the notion of material simplicity. And they welcomed anyone who was willing to commit to a personal regime of self-denial and the pursuit of intellectual and spiritual truth. As the Unitarian minister William Henry Channing put it: "To live content with small means; to seek elegance rather than luxury, and refinement rather than fashion; to be worthy, not respectable, and wealthy, not rich; to study hard, think quietly, talk gently, act frankly.... This is my symphony."

Emerson was born in 1803 and raised in a poor household after his minister father died of tuberculosis. He later credited this early poverty with teaching him to find pleasure in books and in following the meanderings of his insatiably curious mind. When his first wife died, leaving Emerson a generous yearly income of $1,200, he was able to devote himself to long walks ("In the woods is perpetual youth," he once wrote), contemplation, writing, and lecturing. He preached a form of rigorous self-reliance, one based not on the grasping ambition of the emerging capitalists but on the virtues of what the English poet Wordsworth called "plain living and high thinking."

Like Benjamin Franklin, Emerson argued that thrift begat independence, that a life of simple needs could be devoted to intellectual exertion or public service. "Economy is a high, humane office, a sacrament, when its aim is grand; when it is the prudence of simple tastes, when it is practiced for freedom, or love, or devotion," he wrote in 1841.

On some days, as he wrote, Emerson could look out his window and see Henry David Thoreau raking and pruning trees on his land. Emerson had taken in his young friend when Thoreau needed work and a place to live. The arrangement allowed the two men to engage each other every day in the lofty work of self-knowledge and truth seeking. These philosophers shared with their Puritan forebears a stringent belief in self-discipline and the subjugation of material or sensual desires. But they parted company with Puritans on the topic of work. Whereas the Calvinists exalted work as a vehicle for discipline and a means of avoiding idleness, Thoreau believed work crushed a man's soul, kept him chained down, and obstructed his natural instincts for freedom. "The mass of men lead lives of quiet desperation," he famously wrote in *Walden,* his best-loved book.

The publication in 1854 of *Walden* hardly caused a stir. But the book later established the Harvard-educated Thoreau as America's most visible advocate of voluntary simplicity, a reputation that remains mostly untarnished today. Fed up with the artifice and insubstantiality of the society he saw around him, Thoreau decided to seek a more authentic life. He built himself a cabin on a bit of Emerson's land near Concord, and lived there for two years and two months, recording his thoughts and insights into the journals that would become *Walden.*

We now know that Thoreau wasn't quite as monkish as the book suggests. He walked into town for almost-daily doses of conversation and happily accepted regular deliveries of his mother's pies. But Thoreau asserted that he'd found his own prescription for contentment, writing that "a man is rich in proportion to the number of things he can do without."

He recognized, however, that not everyone was cut out for the solitary and outwardly simple life of the mind. Thoreau was emphatic on this point. Forced one day by a rainstorm to take cover in a poor woodsman's unkempt hut, Thoreau lectured his hosts, an Irish immigrant named John Field and his wife, on the virtues of building one's own cabin (rather than renting, as the Fields did) and of going without coffee, butter, fresh meat, and other provisions. If they would learn to do without these pricey items, Thoreau explained, they wouldn't have to work so hard. But the Fields were unmoved by Thoreau's suggestions, and the philosopher concluded that some people simply were not capable of recognizing the benefits of the simple life: "Through want of enterprise and faith men are where they are, buying and selling, and spending their lives like serfs."

Thoreau's afternoon with the Fieldses suggests that while Transcendentalism appealed to radical thinkers who hoped their ideas might persuade some Americans to throw off the yoke of materialism, theirs was a very cultured and genteel asceticism. Transcendentalists weren't connecting with people who were struggling to get by in the capricious landscape of nineteenth-century capitalism. Emerson and his peers mostly understood that the greatest change they could hope to enact would be to encourage the middle and upper classes, the people who made up the audience for their writings and lectures, to question their own getting and spending.

The Transcendentalists' ideas did capture the imaginations of a great number of Americans. But while Thoreau actually lived out a version of the simple life in his cabin in the woods, few others were interested in following his example. As the economy continued its explosive boom-and-bust growth and standards of living rose, many Americans were content merely to purchase some token of the simple life and admire it on their walls. Paintings of rural scenes, depicting humble farmers and their apple-cheeked children, were popular among the upper classes at midcentury. These images idealized America as a pure, uncorrupted Garden of Eden, full of cheerful, simple people engaged in tasks like bargaining for a horse, attending a country auction, or tilling fields. They reflected the sentimental view Americans wanted to have of themselves, as the frugal and industrious republicans Jefferson and Adams had canonized, not the reality of their increasingly market-oriented lives.

★　　★　　★

IT WAS A self-image that was becoming harder and harder to support. In truth, the social fabric of the United States was fraying from the stress of economic change, industrialization, immigration, urbanization, and rancor over the most pressing question of the day, the future of slavery in the Southern states. When war finally erupted after Lincoln's victory in the 1860 presidential race and the South's subsequent decision to secede from the Union, the nation endured four years of slaughter. By the end, 600,000 soldiers were dead, and so was the American slave system. Nearly 4 million blacks were suddenly free.

Most freed slaves owned no land and had worked only as unskilled laborers. Their economic prospects were dim. What was the solution? To many freedmen and their supporters, the route to prosperity was a plot of land, on which the former slaves could raise their own families, control their own labor, and profit from their hard work. It was the old republican dream of the yeoman farmer, independent and free, a dream finally, hopefully, available to America's sizable black population.

As ever, savings banks were a crucial component of this vision, a necessary institution to help freed blacks realize the prosperity they had been denied through all the years of the market revolution. In 1865, a group of former slaves along with some Northern friends established the Freedmen's Savings and Trust Company in order "to find a means of elevating the newly emancipated race which would train its members in habits of thrift and economy, and which, by encouraging them to save their earnings, would aid them in securing a stronger position in the social order."

In 1867, the bank put out a booklet with a short piece entitled "Reasons Why You Should All Put Money in the Savings Bank":

1. *Because it is your surest way to get a start in life.* Thousands of rich men would have been poor all their lifetime had they not used the Savings Bank.

2. *Because being your own masters, it is your duty to provide for your settlement in life, for your families, for sickness, and for old age.* You can in no way do this so well as by a monthly deposit in a good Savings Bank.
3. *It teaches you the value of money,* and prevents you from spending it foolishly.
4. *You should use this bank because it is conducted by your best friends,* and it is hoped you will, ere long, help to conduct it yourselves; and being authorized by Congress, and approved by the President of the United States, it is the safest place for your money.
5. *It gives you character.* As soon as you become worth a little money or property, every one begins to respect you and ask your advice.
6. *It is a good example of thrift to your children,* whom you will desire to see respected and prosperous citizens. They will be sure to imitate your example.

Thousands of depositors responded to these appeals, some handing over just a few pennies at a time. Most accounts never topped $50, but to their owners, these reserves represented a toehold of integration into the economy and a means for managing their financial affairs, whether remitting money to distant relatives or saving up to purchase a home.

That dream crumbled in 1874. The bank failed after its directors, caught up in the speculative bubble of the time, made disastrous investments in real estate and railroads. Half of the sixty-one thousand depositors never got even a penny of their money back.

The bank's message of self-respect and economic advancement found a new and fuller expression, however, in the work of a former slave, Booker Taliaferro Washington. Born in 1856 on a plantation in Franklin County, Virginia, Washington was in many ways the black counterpart of Benjamin

Franklin, with the kind of success-against-all-odds story that seemed both to confirm the promise of America and also, by its very exceptional quality, to call all the myths into question. By dint of his rather awe-inspiring determination and perseverance, Washington attended the Hampton Normal and Agricultural School in Hampton, Virginia, where he earned his room, board, and tuition working as a janitor in the early mornings. He caught the eye of Samuel C. Armstrong, the school's founder, who later recommended the twenty-five-year-old Washington to be principal of the newly formed Tuskegee Normal and Industrial Institute in Tuskegee, Alabama.

At Tuskegee, Washington perfected his vision of "self-help," a go-along-to-get-ahead form of black empowerment and education that he became both loved and reviled for. What freed blacks most needed, Washington believed, was not political representation or restitution for their years of suffering, but a useful education in agriculture and the trades, and the good manners to fit peacefully into a white-led society. "We wanted to teach the students how to bathe; how to care for their teeth and clothing. We wanted to teach them what to eat, and how to eat it properly, and how to care for their rooms," he wrote in his autobiography, *Up from Slavery*. "Aside from this, we wanted to give them practical knowledge of some one industry, together with the spirit of industry, thrift, and economy, that they would be sure of knowing how to make a living after they had left us."

At the heart of Washington's self-help movement were the same values—once radical, now increasingly bourgeois—that had fueled the Revolution. Hard work, sobriety, frugality, humility, honesty—these were the keys to success and independence, Washington assured his students.

Washington's pedagogy was rooted in his own experience of advancement and in the frustrations he witnessed among his less farsighted brethren. As a child, he recalled, he was teased by other students for wearing a hand-sewn hat rather than a factory-made one. "I have always felt proud, when I think of the incident, that my mother had strength of character enough not to be led into the temptation of seeming to be that which she was not—of trying to impress my schoolmates and others with the fact that she was able to buy me a 'store hat' when she was not. I have always felt proud that she refused to go into debt for that which she did not have the money to pay for." Years later, he noted, some of the same boys who once taunted him "have ended their careers in the penitentiary, while others are not able now to buy any kind of hat." In his travels around Alabama before taking up the Tuskegee post, Washington stayed with families he met along the way, and despaired at the heedless consumption he saw among poor farmers who had bought expensive ornaments on credit. "On one occasion when I went into one of these cabins for dinner, when I sat down at the table for a meal with the four members of the family, I noticed that, while there were five of us at the table, there was but one fork for the five of us to use. Naturally there was an awkward pause on my part. In the opposite corner of that same cabin was an organ for which the people told me they were paying sixty dollars in monthly installments. One fork, and a sixty-dollar organ!"

In his famous speech at the 1895 Cotton Exposition in Atlanta, the speech that brought him plaudits and a national platform, Washington expounded on the importance of the Protestant values: "We shall prosper in proportion as we learn to dignify and glorify common labor and put brains and skill into the common occupations of life; shall prosper in proportion as we learn to draw the line between the superficial and the substantial, the ornamental gewgaws of life and the useful. No race can prosper til it learns that there is as much dignity in tilling a field as in writing a poem. It is at the bottom of life we must begin, and not at the top."

Washington argued that thrift was critical to the advancement of his race and urged his students to save their money. Only when a person saves money can he buy a house and have the comfort and stability that leads to good health, he said. In a sermon called "A Penny Saved," published in 1902, Washington told his charges, "We cannot get upon our feet, as a people, until we learn the saving habit; until we learn to save every nickel, every dime and every dollar that we can spare."

In the same sermon, he said: "The possession of money, the having of a bank account, even if small, gives us a certain amount of self-respect. An individual who has a bank account walks through a street so much more erect; he looks people in the face. The people in the community in which he lives have a confidence in him and a respect for him."

Washington's rivals and critics saw him as an accommodationist, a patsy who told white audiences exactly what they wanted to hear—that blacks harbored no ill will toward whites, that they simply wanted the opportunity to participate in the American dream of upward mobility, that they needed only practical skills and a little forbearance, and they would become productive members of society. Whites, in turn, gave Washington millions of dollars to continue his work at Tuskegee. But Washington's pronouncements about the good relations between whites and blacks and the mutual reliance between the two communities were often exaggerated and they willfully denied the reality of life in the Jim Crow, post-Reconstruction South. Even as he was extolling Tuskegee's harmony with its neighbors and assuring his white benefactors that blacks appreciated every bit of their charity, successful black merchants and businessmen in the

South were frequently terrorized by whites who resented the parvenus' ability to buy luxuries formerly reserved for them. Washington's biographer Louis Harlan describes a white mob that chased a black family out of town because they had gotten "uppity" and bought a buggy and a piano; in Mississippi, a black grocery store owner was warned to sell his buggy and walk to work. Southern whites were not necessarily the benign allies and neighbors that Washington portrayed them as, and his prescriptions for success whitewashed a period of rampant racism and violence.

Every Penny "An Atom of Wealth"

After the Civil War, America's factories and natural resources were freed up, and the process of modernization gathered steam again. Immigrants from the hinterland and from abroad poured into cities. New technologies like the steam engine were transforming production, and the transcontinental railroad, completed in 1869, connected one end of the country to the other, unleashing yet another wave of growth in agriculture, manufacturing, mining, real estate, and just about every other American industry.

Industrialists and bankers, speculators and criminals, accumulated fortunes on a scale that rivaled the monarchs of Europe. Men like Cornelius Vanderbilt and Henry Clay Frick spent millions of dollars on costume balls, mansions, and trinkets. They competed to outspend and outimpress each other. At one New York City dinner, the host passed out cigarettes wrapped in $100 notes; each bill was monogrammed in gold with his initials. Mrs. Stuyvesant Fish held a lavish party for her pet monkey, dressing him up in a tuxedo. In pursuit of something new and different to electrify his friends, a midwestern millionaire held a "poverty social": guests were asked to arrive wearing rags and tatters, then were served scraps of food on wooden plates while sitting on buckets and boxes.

"They played being poor for one night and not one of them but joined in ecstatic praise of their host and his unusual ability to provide a sensation," wrote one journalist.

Ordinary Americans pored over accounts of Astor and Vanderbilt parties in the new "society pages" of the daily papers, and lined the sidewalks at charity balls and coming-out galas just to watch the well-heeled alight from their carriages.

The most obvious exception to the spirit of the age was Hetty Green. Even as the robber barons were building French-style châteaus on upper Fifth Avenue, Hetty was living in rooming houses, moving frequently in order to avoid paying property taxes. She sometimes did business in the Manhattan offices of Chemical Bank. There, she set up her papers at an old desk behind the counter. Bank employees later remembered her bringing with her a lunch pail filled with oatmeal, which she mixed with water and heated on the radiator. Thus she avoided paying for a restaurant meal.

Readers reveled in stories about Hetty's parsimony. Reporters followed her to her apartment and pestered her for interviews; sometimes she obliged, and in these conversations she showed off her lively wit and no-bull common sense. In 1899, she invited Leigh Mitchell Hodges, a journalist from *Ladies' Home Journal,* up to her apartment for an interview. He sat on her "shabby haircloth sofa" and asked her why she participated so little in the over-the-top society life enjoyed by most of New York's millionaires at the time. "As for society, I believe in it," she said. But "I'd get very tired of living in one of those great houses in New York, going all night and sleeping all day. They don't have any real pleasure. It's intercourse with people that I like."

Hetty's attitude was unusual. In general, it was a period of such excess and bloat among the wealthy that it was christened the "Gilded Age" by Mark Twain, a man who himself alternated between wealth and poverty. With a mix of sarcasm and sorrow (he too had been seduced by speculative ventures that later went sour), Twain asked in 1871, "What is the chief end of man?—to get rich. In what way? Dishonestly if he can; honestly if he must. Who is God, the one only and true? Money is God."

In 1899, Thorstein Veblen wrote that the conspicuous consumption of the day was practiced by what he called the "leisure class," which had become, in the advanced industrial age, the aristocracy of a nominally egalitarian America. This class—and the adulation bestowed on it by the groups beneath it on the social and economic ladder—represented a striking reversal of social currency from a century earlier, when, in the official cosmology of the Revolutionary heroes, industry and thrift had defined a man's reputation. Now, the less a man appeared to work, the more he was admired. The more he spent, the more he was exalted.

But as the economy wilted in the late 1890s, popular sentiment whiplashed against the swells. Muckrakers like Ida Tarbell wrote incendiary, sometimes thinly researched investigations of the odious business tactics behind the big fortunes, and many Americans lost patience with vulgar displays of wealth. When Cornelia Bradley-Martin threw a costume ball in 1897 that came to more than $300,000 (more than her husband's tax bill the previous year), New Yorkers were enraged. The city doubled the assessment on the couple's assets and the offenders soon quit the metropolis, running off to Scotland and returning to New York only once for a short visit years later.

DESPITE THE EXCESSES of the Gilded Age, thrift advocacy didn't die, not by a stretch. Thrift persisted, as the historian David Shi says, "as an attainable ideal on an individual basis and as a sustaining myth of national purpose." And it remained in some circles the always-longed-for corrective to poverty and urban depravity.

The message of reform and social activism, muted during the previous few decades, resurfaced with a vengeance in the Progressive Era. From about 1890 to 1920, Americans attacked social problems with a new energy and optimism. "Reform" was in the air, but it was an elastic concept and interest groups used the term liberally, mostly to advance their own agendas. Big business advocated an end to government interventions; politicians promised they would defeat corruption and patronage; altruistic educators and social workers applied themselves to eradicating alcoholism, crime, disease, and poverty.

One of those altruists was John Henry Thiry, a rare book dealer who had immigrated to New York City from Belgium in 1859. A lifelong bibliophile and autodidact, Thiry retired in 1873 with his wife and sons to a home in Long Island City, a Queens neighborhood just over the East River from midtown Manhattan.

In the last quarter of the nineteenth century, New York teemed with entertainments and pleasures befitting a world-class city: live theaters, nightclubs, cabarets, and prostitutes. Thiry was distressed to see his two sons throwing away their money first on sweets and chewing gum and later on cigarettes and vaudeville shows. When he lectured them on wise spending habits and harked back to his own frugal childhood in Belgium, his sons accused him of being old-fashioned. Conditions had changed, they said; the world had become one giant candy store, and they were just following the spirit of the day, sampling the confections the city was offering.

Thiry's sons were no different from other American boys. And that, he realized, was the problem. Savings banks were still a popular institution, but they were no longer advertised with the same sense of moral urgency that had attached to them earlier in the century. American children were not being taught how to save money. Instead, they were loosed on the world with a little change in their pockets and a buffet of temptations laid out before them.

Before long, Thiry was the founder and prophet of the school savings bank movement. Starting with just one school—Public School 4, in Long Island City—Thiry either personally started or inspired thrift education and savings programs in thousands of schools. By the time he died in 1911, more than 200,000 children around the United States had collected a total of $5 million by depositing their pennies, nickels, and dimes in local banks.

The "Thiry System" was ingeniously simple. Every Monday morning, the classroom teacher called the roll and invited each student, when her name was called, to bring her change up to the teacher's desk. The teacher noted the amount of each student's deposit, sealed the weekly total in an envelope, and brought it to the principal's office. An administrator then brought the school's total collection to a local bank, where the appropriate amount was credited to each child's account. The students received passbooks in which they could watch their money "grow," as they were introduced to the wonders of compound interest. According to Thiry, the whole collection process could take as little as fifteen minutes a week, hardly cutting into the time needed for reading, writing, and arithmetic.

School savings banks appealed to a generation of educators who, like the social workers and moral reformers of previous eras, looked around them and saw signs everywhere of the decline of modern civilization. Poverty, crime, alcoholism, violence, "sexual immorality" (which usually meant prostitution and teenage pregnancy)—these vices haunted city streets and might lurk in the hearts of even the most docile children. While Thiry and his followers sometimes talked in the most practical terms about the value of savings — noting that children could stash their cash for Christmas gifts, or that the bank account would encourage a boy to accumulate funds for a large purchase like a bike rather than fritter it away on theater tickets and soda — they often took off into flights of rhetorical excess, suggesting that savings accounts and thrift were cures for a range of moral dangers.

"The School Savings Bank is a relief measure for pauperism, a preventive to crime, a developing force for honesty, sobriety and peace. The boy and the girl who go out from public school with definite business knowledge and one or two hundred dollars of their own earnings and savings to their individual credit are not likely to become criminals or paupers," wrote Sara Louisa Oberholtzer, a Philadelphia writer and advocate who became Thiry's chief partner in spreading the gospel of school savings banking. Thiry himself argued that thrift taught children discipline and fortitude. "Every time Tommy, with money in his pocket, passes the door of the candy shop, he gains in strength that will later help him to resist the graver temptations of his manhood," he said in a 1911 interview.

As always, the rationale for saving was muddy, a cocktail of old-fashioned moralizing and get-ahead, free-market cheerleading. It reflected what the historian Lendol Calder calls the "Victorian money management ethic," the dominant view of how Americans should operate in the money economy of the late-nineteenth century. This mixture of Protestant asceticism and republican common sense held that money was not filthy or dangerous, but that it required self-control, restraint, and pragmatism. In its combination of economic theory and moral laws, it took cues from Adam Smith and early economic philosophers in making a distinction between "productive" spending (money invested in machinery, equipment, or necessary consumer goods) and "consumptive" spending (money wasted on frivolous things that are used up with no lasting economic benefit). All uses of money entailed consumption, but not all of it was consumptive—and the best kind of spending was the kind that could turn a bit of cash into even more.

So Thiry and his minions often spoke of the necessity of learning to build up capital for future opportunities, capital that could translate into productivity and investment.

> Capital of whatever kind is given for use and consumption. Thereby the importance of saving is emphasized, for the purpose of saving is to have more to consume. At this point saving as a mere end in itself should be sharply exposed. Animated by no higher motive, the desire to save inevitably gravitates toward the demoralizing passion of the miser.
>
> On the other hand, the system of school banking, which I still have the honor and privilege of advocating, imparts that higher motive. It raises before the pupil a standard of saving, ideally moral perhaps, yet wholly attainable because severely and practically economical. It teaches that no effort to produce can be efficient without capital, and that capital is impossible without saving; he who saves not his seed corn has already prohibited a coming harvest.

Reflecting a coldly utilitarian approach to both childhood and savings, he added, "The child is a unit among millions, and his penny is an atom of wealth."

Thrift advocates distributed lesson plans, wrote parables and songs for inclusion in textbooks, conducted essay contests, and stressed the importance of integrating savings education into every subject. Math class was an opportunity to discuss budgeting and compound interest; in English class, students might read *Stories of Thrift for Young Americans,* a book

of morality tales featuring virtuous mothers, hardworking
fathers, and children who learn, by example or hard lessons,
the importance of prudent spending and saving. In Duluth,
Minnesota, the thrift campaigner Lulu Grogan compiled nine
months of thrift lessons into a book entitled *Gateway to Independence*. September would be devoted to the value of school
banking, while March covered "Thrift in the Use of Clothing and Materials." Each month's lessons were illustrated with
a drawing and a little poem featuring the "Thrifties," an elfin
brother and sister. November's lesson shows them delivering
papers and raking leaves, with the caption:

> *The Thrifties all know how to work;*
> *They earn in many ways,*
> *And a part of what they earn is saved*
> *For they know that banking pays.*

After Thiry's death in 1911, Oberholtzer carried on his
work under the auspices of the Women's Christian Temperance Union, a reform organization that supported Prohibition
and focused primarily on public health issues. She lectured at
dozens of conferences every year, some as far away as Europe,
responded to inquiries from schools around the country, and
oversaw the publication of all the deposit envelopes, ledger
books, and other forms required to administer the savings
bank programs. She published annual statistics and a quarterly newsletter called "Thrift Tidings" from 1907 to 1923,
and she filled notebooks with her painstaking penmanship,
copying down aphorisms from thinkers such as Cicero ("Men
know not how great a revenue economy is") and the French
moralist Joseph Joubert ("Be saving, but not at the cost of
all liberality. Have the soul of a king and the hand of a wise
economist").

Oberholtzer also spent a good deal of time raising funds for her activities since, ironically, "There is no money whatever that I have knowledge of in Mr. Thiry's estate to aid in any such work. His estate was entirely bankrupt," as she noted in one letter to a publisher who was interested in producing her materials.

Like Thiry and Oberholtzer, Simon William Straus believed that all the ills of modern society could be cured by creating a nation of savers. Straus, a Chicago banking heir and real estate financier, founded the American Society for Thrift in 1914. He became famous for his élan as an innovator in the financial industry and for his penurious but ill-fated campaign against the practice of tipping waiters, bellboys, and other proletarians (realizing that opposition was useless, he gave up after a few years).

As a banker, Straus benefited every time someone deposited a dollar into his banks (along with his own firm S. W. Straus and Company, he founded the Franklin Trust and Savings Bank, named, naturally, after America's chief exemplar of frugality). Thrift was good for the soul, and for bankers especially it was good for business, too.

Seeing firsthand what frugality could accomplish—his own parents had achieved the American dream by living frugal, sober lives, Straus wrote—and also being in a business that relied on the saving impulse in great numbers of people, Straus was well placed to become a vocal proponent of thrift. He took to it with zeal, reasoning (unoriginally) that if he could awaken the thrift habit in millions of Americans, he could cure a full panoply of social ills. In a diatribe against thriftlessness and "its deteriorating effects on the individual," Straus wrote, "Like the slow growth of a cancer, it eats its way surreptitiously until it kills the will and impoverishes the character....It has a tendency to poison ambition, paralyze the will, torture the brain, and drive the individual to the abyss of total failure."

Thrift was the central element in Straus's moral and physical philosophy. It extended to the efficient use of time, the adoption of appropriate entertainments and temperate health habits, and even the correct method of chewing food. "Regard your physical health as a bounteous bank account," he wrote. "In our great cities people break down in health or reach premature senility because of late hours, loss of sleep, fast pleasures, and headlong, nerve-wracking methods of existence. Without regard to the laws of nature, we have been guilty of over-eating, have brought about ill-health, and have incapacitated ourselves for effective work by the improper mastication of our food. Your physician will tell you that a very large percentage of sickness, accidents, and deaths can be attributed directly to habits of physical thriftlessness."

The American Society for Thrift held its first meeting on January 13, 1914, at Chicago's City Club. There, Straus and five local reformers and businessmen wrote the society's mission statement, determining that it would "promote thrift among the people of the United States" through, among other things, "(1) Education in the principles of saving and economy [and] (2) Inquiry into and inspiration of the examples of other nations among whom thrift has a greater development and recognition as a fundamental need for individual and public prosperity, good citizenship and tranquility." Straus reached out to organizations that shared his goals, such as the National Education Association, with which he had a long association in connection with school savings banks and thrift education work.

THE AMERICAN SOCIETY for Thrift hit its apex a year before Hetty Green died, when it was invited to host a conference at the 1915 Panama-Pacific Exposition held in San Francisco to celebrate the opening of the Panama Canal. The exposition was a fantastical event, a world's fair–like love song to the wonders of modern technology, commerce, and development. The city spent $50 million (more than $1 billion in today's dollars) for the construction of a phantasmagoric collection of buildings on 635 acres of city land, in what's now the Marina section, on the northern tip of the city. Elaborately decorated halls testified to the triumph of modernity; jumbo sculptures of Greek gods and Mongolian warriors towered over the exposition's 19 million visitors. Amazingly, the buildings were primarily made of cheap plaster combined with sand and burlap fiber, designed to be dismantled and destroyed at the end of the nine-month fair.

The implicit theme of the exposition was prosperity. An Ohio exhibit showed a massive cornucopia with the words "The Land of Plenty" on it and thousands of ears of corn tumbling out of it. The "Ancient Oil Barons" were celebrated with an Egyptian-inspired edifice flanked by four gaudy dragon sculptures. A "Court of Abundance" consisted of a two-hundred-foot-tall tower nestled between barrel-vaulted arcades, all surrounding an enormous reflecting pool.

To Straus, having the AST represented at the exposition was a milestone. He lobbied successfully for California governor Hiram Johnson to declare the final day of the congress "Thrift Day," a time for the people of the state to give thrift "the hearty encouragement it deserves." He gathered hundreds of people to hear speeches and testify to the need for "systematic work along thrift lines." In his own address to the group, he exhorted his listeners to use every avenue to inculcate frugality, "for thrift is patriotism—the patient, plodding heroism that comes in the everyday life of our citizens."

But it's hard to gauge exactly what the American Society for Thrift accomplished at the exposition that seemed geared toward a different ideal entirely, or elsewhere during its fifteen-year history. In the five-volume *Story of the Exposition,* by Frank Morton Todd, Straus's International Congress for Thrift barely rates a single mention. Instead, Todd's books are devoted to the optimism of economic growth and the communications and transportation advances that were making trade and commerce easier for America's consumer society.

World War I would accomplish what Straus's efforts alone could not. The war forced a version of asceticism on the American people and inspired energetic campaigns to eliminate waste and promote savings in the form of war bonds and savings stamps. But by the 1920s, the danger had passed, the economy was roaring, and so were consumers' appetites.

Straus continued to proselytize on thrift throughout his life, but his words fell on the ears of a nation that was increasingly deaf to his message. In recognition of this fact, the AST's educational director, Arthur Chamberlain, noted with frustration in 1926 something that had long been true, that "To spend freely and to be wasteful, even, has in some quarters been considered a mark of distinction."

By the time Straus died of a blood disease on September 7, 1930, his work on thrift was barely a footnote in his obituary. The *New York Times* wrote that Straus had revolutionized real estate finance by introducing a newfangled mortgage bond and then underwriting some of the country's most famous structures, including New York City's Chrysler Building, the tallest skyscraper in the world when it was built. The *Times* obit noted that Straus had founded the American Society for Thrift and written a book about it, but even in 1930, when Americans regarded Wall Street with suspicion, the article extolled his business achievements and practically ignored his thrift advocacy. And in the *Historical Dictionary of the Progressive Era, 1890–1920,* a definitive collection of eight hundred articles on the important people and ideas of that period, neither Straus nor the society he founded, nor even thrift education and thrift activism in general, merited a mention.

HETTY GREEN — or, more accurately, her legend — had more staying power than Straus. Hetty died in 1916 not, as the *Guinness Book* wrote, from a fit over the virtues of skimmed milk. She suffered a stroke in April and passed away three months later. Her death was front-page news in papers all over the country.

A 1908 profile of Hetty had suggested she was grossly unhappy, living a drab and impecunious life. "In [Hetty Green's] safe is locked a pint of diamonds and one of the finest collections of pearls on earth," Mabel Potter Daggett wrote in *Broadway* magazine. "Yet the girl stenographer who takes her dictation probably has a lighter heart under a new spring gown, [and] the butcher from whom she buys chuck steak at twelve cents a pound has a better Sunday dinner."

But in memorializing Hetty eight years later, the newspapers were respectful, even admiring. The *New York Times* posted an editorial that said, "Probably her life was happy. At any rate, she had enough of courage to live as she chose and to be as thrifty as she pleased, and she observed such of the world's conventions as seemed to her right and useful, coldly and calmly ignoring all the others."

Hetty left a fortune of $100 million at her death — approximately $2 billion in 2009 dollars — which was split equally between her two children. Hetty's son, the eccentric and affable "Colonel" Ned Green, maintained relatively conservative investments but went to town with the interest he received from the principal. A year after Hetty died, he married a former prostitute and housekeeper named Mabel Harlow, and the two set sail on Ned's new 255-foot yacht. Then he built a palatial limestone-and-marble mansion on some land he'd inherited from his mother. He filled it with his collections of rare books, diamond jewelry, and pornography.

After Ned died in 1936, his portion of the family money went to his sister, the childless, widowed Sylvia. She lived a solitary life in New York City and Greenwich, Connecticut. When she died without heirs in 1951, her will was found, according to Hetty's biographer Charles Slack, "stashed with four bars of soap in a cabinet." In it, she gave away her $100 million estate to a haphazard group of beneficiaries, including New Bedford's public library, Columbia University, and a dozen or so relatives she hardly knew. She even gave $10,000 to a man she'd never met, the New York City parks commissioner Robert Moses, "in appreciation of his work creating public parkways," as the will said.

That was the end of Hetty Green's fortune. Unlike her contemporaries J. P. Morgan and John D. Rockefeller, she hadn't donated millions to libraries and universities to help rehabilitate her reputation or ensure that she'd live on in the future. Instead, Hetty's main claim to immortality remains her entry in the *Guinness Book of Records,* where the world's greatest miser is sandwiched between Shirley Temple, the world's youngest self-made millionaire, and the Bolivian bride Elena Patino, whose tin magnate father bestowed on her the world's largest dowry.

Chapter 3

"What Use Can a Woman Have for Arithmetic?"

Sarah Tabitha Reid's days were too long and never long enough. On a typical morning in the 1860s, the New Jersey farmwife woke up at four a.m., swept the kitchen floor, collected eggs, fed the family's chickens and turkeys, fetched water from the well, and made the fire—and that was all before breakfast.

The rest of the day was just as busy. Sarah lived a life of never-ending chores and backbreaking labor. In the afternoons, she churned butter, tended her vegetable garden, picked huckleberries, canned peaches, baked a dozen loaves of bread, made candles, gathered nuts, pounded and wrung out the washing, sewed shirts for her husband, William, battled the layers of dirt and ash that settled all over the house, and, of course, cooked all the meals for her family and their farmhands.

Yet she never quite seemed to get it all done. The days were so exhausting, she confided to her journal, that she longed for "that land of rest where sweet rest will never end."

Despite her unrelenting work, money was always tight at the Reid farm. William worked part of the year as a bricklayer in New York City to make extra cash, and Sarah scrimped everywhere she could. But they had nothing left over at the end of the month for conveniences or luxuries. Even a Christian duty like charity meant sacrifices at home. When Sarah wanted to donate money to a group of foreign missionaries, she stopped putting sugar in her tea and gave the savings—just a few pennies—to her local church.

Thrift was a way of life for rural women like Reid, as ordinary and unremarkable as the rising and setting of the sun each day. It was a virtue in the sense that families valued resourcefulness and frowned on wasteful spending. But more than anything, thrift was simply a requirement for survival on a small farm. Wives produced most of their families' essentials at home, conjuring soap out of food grease and fireplace ashes, rendering a cow's fat into tallow for candles, and drawing water from a well or stream in order to put a stew on the table. When the butter ran out, Sarah spent hours churning another batch and then kneading and pressing it into a solid consistency. When a sheet tore, she sat down in the evening and mended it after completing the rest of her housework. To make sure her family had enough food to get through the winter, she canned every last tomato, bean, and beet.

It was a life that required unimaginable effort and ingenuity. Corn husks were stuffed into sewn-up sheets to make mattresses; corncobs were dipped in tar and resin, then used as kindling. Housekeepers turned the remnants of burnt coal into fertilizer for their gardens or tossed them onto ice to make it less slippery. Did little Johnny drop a bowl and crack it? No matter. Women learned from childhood how to whip up homemade glues out of ingredients like linseed oil, steel filings, egg white, potter's clay, and even garlic juice. Not a piece of crockery was thrown out unless it was truly beyond repair—and even then, it was most likely ground down to a paste and used for fixing the next broken plate.

Fabric was reused and repurposed every which way. As

older kids outgrew their britches and shirts, women altered the castoffs to fit the next children in line. In this way, years of life might be squeezed out of a single garment until it no longer hung together, and even then its parts could be recycled into a quilt, a carpet, or, ultimately, bartered as rags to peddlers who then sold them to paper mills.

IN THE EARLY republic and through the nineteenth century, the vast majority of American women endured this kind of hardscrabble existence. Whether they were pioneers in Oregon, homesteaders in North Dakota, or, like Reid, farmwives in New Jersey, their lives were defined by scarcity and hard labor. These conditions fostered respect for even the most mundane belongings—a scrap of cloth, a sack of flour, a cord of firewood. When nearly every item the family used was the product of its own relentless work, no morsel of fat was wasted, no shred of fabric thrown out. These were women who didn't need to be lectured about thrift.

But as the population shifted into cities and towns, more families joined the urban middle and working classes. They relied on wage labor, participated in the money economy, and often enjoyed higher incomes and a higher standard of living. As a result, women's lives became unhinged from many of the farm chores that had once structured their days. Instead of churning butter, they began buying it at a shop; instead of going down to the stream to do their washing on Mondays, they sent it out to a washerwoman. They might still can peaches or bake bread, but they purchased their fruit and flour from a market in town and bought eggs from a farmer who came door-to-door once a week. The transition to town life freed women from some of their most arduous daily tasks, but it also stripped them of their position as key players in the household's economic life. In the city, women functioned as *consumers* of daily necessities — rather than as the *producers* — to a greater extent than ever before.

But did ladies know how to handle money? Could they figure out whether the butcher was cheating them? Should they pay cash at the dry goods store or keep a credit account? A slew of anxieties about women's new role in the market-place led Samuel Smiles, a Scottish reformer, to remark in his 1875 book, *Thrift,* "Some may say, 'What use can a woman have for arithmetic?' But when men marry, they soon find this out." According to Smiles and many other commenta-tors, managing the modern home required shrewd attention and a thrifty eye on all household expenses. "If women do not earn the family income, at least they have to spend the money earned," he wrote. "If the woman who has a household to manage be innocent of addition and multiplication; and if she fail to keep a record of her income and expenditure, she will, before long, find herself in great trouble.... The most worth-less unit in a family is an ill-managing wife, or an indolent woman of any sort."

How would women internalize the skills required to keep house in nineteenth-century America? Because of urban-ization and increasing geographic mobility, they'd moved away from the mothers and grandmothers who, at another time, would have passed along their knowledge to a new bride. So, as with young men seeking their fortune dur-ing the same decades, housewives turned to self-appointed experts in the labor of homemaking. For the next century or so, women were the recipients of volumes of suggestions, sermons, and scoldings about how to be frugal and budget judiciously. Exploring the content of this advice and how it changed over the years reveals much about how the role of both women and thrift changed from the 1800s up to the present.

Advice books, cookbooks, and housekeeping manuals sold

briskly during the nineteenth century and usually contained a hodgepodge of recipes, cleaning tips, sewing projects, "home apothecary" formulas, and home-decorating projects. Along with practical advice, most of these tomes doled out a heavy dose of moral prescription. Authors waxed on about how wives and mothers should serve as examples of virtue, kindness, cleanliness, and sober living. By glorifying women's domestic roles, these bromides also rationalized women's exclusion from the public spheres of work and politics. Historians later referred to this view as the "cult of domesticity," a conservative ideology that exalted women as angels of the hearth.

Thrift was built into the lives of rural women, but writers of the time believed it had to be explicitly stressed for the new urban consumers. So advice books, along with didactic novels and short stories, included admonitions and reminders to that effect, along with anxious warnings about female extravagance. In his 1859 conduct book *The Poor Girl and True Woman,* the best-selling author William Makepeace Thayer contrasted two friends, virtuous Mary and spendthrift Hattie. The young women were sitting together one day discussing their futures. "I think we ought to be frugal, though we have abundant means," Mary says, but Hattie has a different philosophy. "Enjoy it as long as it lasts, is my rule," she says. Predictably, within a few short pages, Hattie's husband is bankrupt and the family is destitute. "This is a theme of great importance to girls," Thayer concludes. "For the habit of extravagance, formed in early life, may utterly disqualify them to become the mistresses of families."

The majority of women's advice manuals were written for middle-class and affluent housewives and advised them on the tricky work of managing servants or the art of Grecian painting. One of the only exceptions was *The American Frugal*

Housewife, Dedicated to Those Who Are Not Ashamed of Economy, a plainspoken cookbook by the fervent abolitionist and writer Lydia Maria Child. Born in 1802, Child's ambition and intelligence overflowed the constraints imposed by her gender. She watched her older brother leave for Harvard to receive the education she herself craved, and she devoured books like *Paradise Lost* while still a teenager, then criticized Milton for his male chauvinism. At the tender age of twenty-two, she published her first novel, *Hobomok,* an instant success that featured a sympathetic portrait of an interracial marriage between a white woman and a Native American man.

Though born into a genteel home (her father owned a successful bakery), Lydia married a penniless and idealistic lawyer named David Lee Child in 1828. David was an erratic provider, at best. He earned a pittance at his law practice because of his penchant for taking on the cases of the downtrodden and oppressed. What little income he earned went to the causes he supported or to wild ventures he started in the service of his ideals. In 1836, David embarked on a quixotic quest to prove that northerners could produce sugar more easily and cheaply than slave-owning southern and Caribbean sugarcane growers. He studied beet farming for a year in Belgium and then returned home to put the plan into action. Problem was, his Massachusetts beet farm never turned a profit and in fact left the Childs deep in debt. Early on in their marriage, Lydia became the main breadwinner, a task she accomplished by parlaying her own experience of making ends meet into *The American Frugal Housewife.* It was an instant bestseller. Published in 1829, it went through at least thirty-five printings by 1850, when it fell out of favor largely because of Lydia's antislavery activism.

Child's prose contained none of the disquisitions on the joys of motherhood and the sacredness of the hearth that were so common in other advice manuals. Instead, she begins the book with some blunt instructions:

> The true economy of housekeeping is simply the art of gathering up all the fragments, so that nothing be lost. I mean fragments of *time,* as well as *materials.* Nothing should be thrown away so long as it is possible to make any use of it, however trifling that use may be; and whatever be the size of a family, every member should be employed in earning or saving money.
> "Time is money." For this reason, cheap as stockings are, it is good economy to knit them. Cotton and woolen yarn are both cheap; hose that are knit wear twice as long as woven ones; and they can be done at odd minutes of time, which would not be otherwise employed. Where there are children, or aged people, it is sufficient to recommend knitting, that it is an *employment.*

Later in the introduction, she notes: "Books of this kind have usually been written for the wealthy; I have written for the poor....I have attempted to teach how money can be *saved,* not how it can be *enjoyed.*"

No household task escaped Child's budget-cutting eye. Her chapter "Odd Scraps for the Economical" is a marvel, with hints on everything from exterminating bedbugs (an ounce of quicksilver mixed with two egg whites, and applied with a feather) to making straw mattresses to finding a cheap substitute for green tea (the youngest leaves on a currant bush). She recommends buying fresh eggs in large quantities, in early spring, and preserving them in a pail of water, coarse salt, and unslaked lime. "It is bad economy to buy eggs by the dozen, as you want them." Similarly, "Preserve the backs of old letters to write upon. If you have children who are learning to write, buy coarse white paper by the quantity, and keep it locked up, ready to be made into writing books. It does not cost half as much as it does to buy them at the stationer's." Butter is sweetest and cheapest in September and June, she says, so she tells readers to stock up, then pack it "in a clean, scalded firkin, cover it with strong brine, and spread a cloth all over the top."

Like most women of her era, Child had a basic understanding of how to treat just about any illness, usually with little more than the contents of her pantry. But Lydia-style thrift was not for the faint of heart. She recommends raw onion as "an excellent remedy for the sting of a wasp." A sore throat can be soothed by taking a warm stocking right off the foot and tying it around the neck. She suggests slathering earwax on chapped lips for a truly cheap—free, actually—nineteenth-century version of ChapStick. Diarrhea required no more than a piece of flannel dipped in brandy and sprinkled with cayenne pepper, then laid across the bowels. Even something as tough to shake as dysentery, it seems, could be brought down with a mixture of black tea, boiling milk, nutmeg, and sugar.

The book's substance is the recipes and suggestions that fill it, but Child wasn't one to keep her opinions to herself, so she turned it into a political statement as well. Living beyond one's means "is wrong—morally wrong, so far as the individual is concerned; and injurious beyond calculation to the interests of our country. To what are the increasing beggary and discouraged exertions of the present period owing? A multitude of causes have no doubt tended to increase the evil; but the root of the whole matter is the extravagance of all classes of people. We never shall be prosperous till we make pride and vanity yield to the dictates of honesty and prudence!"

Later, in a section titled "Hints to Persons of Moderate Fortune" (which was really an extended opportunity for Child to sound off on women's education, the state of the economy, and other issues), she writes, "A republic without industry, economy and integrity, is Samson shorn of his locks. A luxurious and idle *republic!* Look at the phrase!—The words were never made to be married together; every body sees it would be death to one of them." Had John Adams and Ben Franklin been alive to read Lydia's screed, it would have done the old patriots proud.

The first edition of *The American Frugal Housewife* sold out immediately. One reviewer wrote of the second edition, in 1830, "If the fact that a book sells, is any proof of its popularity, Mrs. Child has the honor of having written the most approved work of these 'hard times.'"

But not everyone loved Child's combination of down-home instructions and political philosophizing. An anonymous reviewer, writing in the genteel journal *Ladies' Magazine and Literary Gazette,* sneered at "the system of economy recommended," criticized Child for using "crude" terminology, and suggested that she include some recipes "on a more liberal scale" for wealthier women. The reviewer's main criticism, though, was that Child's unapologetic focus on economy amounted to a defense of miserliness and avarice: "We fear the effect of thus inculcating the *love* of *money,* that root of all evil, as a wise precept, in a book designed as a manual for young housekeepers."

The author of the anonymous review was likely Sarah Josepha Hale, the editor of *Ladies' Magazine.* Today Hale is best known as the author of the nursery rhyme "Mary Had a Little Lamb" and for campaigning to make Thanksgiving a national holiday. In 1830, she was already one of America's most influential female writers, and she would remain so for the next fifty years, as an editor, author, and standard-setter for American womanhood. But unlike Child, with her earthy practicality and passionate activism in favor of radical causes, Hale was deeply immersed in the cult of domesticity and its conservative dogmas. She stridently propagated the argument that women belonged in the separate sphere of the home, and what was probably her review of *The American Frugal Housewife* painted a picture of women as virtuously untouched by the stink of commerce and coin. The notice contains one of her most famous quotes: "Our men are sufficiently money-making. Let us keep our women and children from the contagion as long as possible."

From her magazine's criticisms of Child, one would think Hale demurred from any discussion of money or money habits. In fact, Hale was actually a lifelong promoter of thrift. But she was more interested in frugality as an ideology, one denoting virtue and respectability, than as a set of skills and strategies for getting by. "An extravagant woman can never be an amiable or lovable one. Too often she destroys the comfort of her home, if she does not ruin the fortunes of her husband. Economy is essential in a well-regulated household; no amount of wealth excuses waste, or renders waste attractive," she wrote in an editorial in *Godey's Lady's Book,* one of the most popular women's magazines at the time.

In 1839, Hale published her own cookbook, *The Good Housekeeper.* With chapter headings like "Hiring a Cook" and "Hints to Help" (that is, servants), Hale wasn't speaking directly to the poor and middling families who relied on Child's book. But even though she was generally reluctant to acknowledge the financial realities of struggling Americans, she did include a chapter called "Cheap Dishes." True to character, she made it clear that she had no sympathy for the poor, or even a real understanding of their lives, characterizing them as either alcoholic or irresponsible, or both. Instead, she spoke to those industrious families who, by dint of hard work and thrift, aspired to rise in the world:

> This chapter is *not* written for the *poor.* The two classes, which in our country constitute the poor, care little

for economy.—There is the miserable poor, usually made so by intemperance in drink; these seldom take any thought how they shall live, but cook whatever they can obtain in the readiest way; and there is the luxurious poor, who live on credit and by 'speculations;' these are generally most fastidious in appetite and careless of expense; they would be disgusted at the thought of a 'cheap dish.' It is not for such that I shall take pains to prepare receipts [recipes] for dishes combining the greatest economy of cost with the most nourishing and healthy materials—because it would be care and pains thrown away. But the rich, who intend to continue so, the thriving, who mean to be rich, the sensible and industrious, who love comfort and independence, the benevolent, who wish to do good—these classes all practice economy, and will not despise 'cheap dishes.'

While Child was practical to the core and sensitive to the hardships that American women faced, Hale remained steeped in a conservative ideology glorifying Calvinist morality and genteel womanhood. These dueling visions of domesticity were somewhat reconciled in the 1869 book *The American Woman's Home*, written by Catharine Beecher and Harriet Beecher Stowe. The authors were members of a famous American family—their father, Lyman, was a prominent evangelical minister, and Harriet had already published the bestseller *Uncle Tom's Cabin*—and this pedigree launched their book into the ranks of the most popular home-instruction manuals of the nineteenth century. It was dedicated "To the Women of America, in whose hands rest the destinies of the republic."

The Beechers did more than give advice on how to choose cuts of meat and clean curtains. To them, women's work had been marginalized by the economic and social changes of the market revolution, and they sought to restore women's self-respect and social position. While the early farmwife had been a critical partner in a family's survival and success—hauling water, processing staples like butter and cheese and grain, spinning wool for home use and barter—the housewife of the mid- to late-nineteenth century in many cases could no longer claim to be so useful. Industrial development and more sophisticated distribution and marketing had brought many labor-saving conveniences to homes. Running water, ovens, sewing machines, and crude laundry machines made women's lives easier, but they also drained some of the status out of housework, which was no longer regarded as arduous labor, integral to a family's survival.

So the Beechers presented housework as a job that was just as important as any man's. Men receive training for their professions, they argued; why, then, shouldn't women receive training in their primary work? The home might be a separate sphere, but it was no less important in the functioning of society. Housework was really "domestic science," the Beechers said, and it required the same kind of organization and businesslike efficiency that men used in their workplaces. They suggested that planning and outfitting one's home was more about engineering than it was about taste and fashion. Detailed drawings sketched out floor plans for the ideal home, designed to eliminate waste of energy and money: "The aim will be to exhibit modes of economizing labor, time, and expenses, so as to secure health, thrift, and domestic happiness to persons of limited means, in a measure rarely attained even by those who possess wealth."

While Harriet went on to write more novels, Catharine, headmistress of the Hartford Female Seminary in Connecticut, continued to advocate for a new system of formal education for girls that incorporated training in cooking, cleaning, and other skills of housewifery. These ideas formed the core philosophy behind the modern field of home economics.

The first classes in this new discipline were taught at Iowa State College in 1872 and then spread to other campuses. The collection of nutritionists, economists, sanitation engineers, reformers, and educators who were developing and teaching these courses around the country—among them some of the first female scientists in America—began gathering in 1899 at annual conferences held in Lake Placid, New York. They used their training to bring new importance to housework, lending it the imprimatur of science and moral philosophy in classes like Household Technology and Sanitary Chemistry and Biology. Beginning in 1900, instructors at Cornell University's College of Agriculture (and later at the newly created College of Home Economics) set up laboratory-like environments for teaching grocery purchasing and "mothercraft." They even rented babies from local orphanages. The infants—given nicknames like "Dicky Domecon" and "Edna Mae Domecon," for "domestic economy"—lived with students in practice apartments for up to two years before being given up for adoption. (Prospective parents were especially eager to adopt these babies who'd been raised according to the latest scientific standards.)

In 1908, practitioners boosted the field's credibility when they created the American Home Economics Association. "Home economics should find its way into the curriculum of every school because the scientific study of a problem pertaining to food, shelter or clothing...raises manual labor that might be drudgery to the plane of intelligent effort that is always self-respecting," wrote Martha Van Rensselaer, professor of home economics and codirector of the New York State College of Home Economics, in 1913.

The field's expansion dovetailed with the broader, growing belief that science could solve every problem of social and physical dysfunction, from crime to insanity to cancer. This was the era of phrenology and eugenics, and measurement, experimentation, and analysis were applied to every aspect of life, including swimming strokes, potato planting, and factory jobs. Theories about "scientific management" grew out of the work of the efficiency expert Frederick Winslow Taylor. Taylor revolutionized industrial production by breaking up every job into smaller and smaller tasks and studying the "time-motion" relationship of each (he even studied how water boys—the kids who brought drinking water to unskilled laborers at a factory or a construction site—could do their rounds more efficiently). The logical conclusion of this effort was the modern assembly line. According to critics, assembly lines dehumanized workers, turning them into machines who repeated a single task over and over and over again. But Taylor was lionized by economists and capitalists for wringing maximum productivity out of every "labor unit." His ideas were adapted for use by car companies (most famously by Henry Ford), shipbuilders, and steel mills.

In home economics, these ideas found their way into books with such titles as *Increasing Home Efficiency* and *The Efficient Kitchen*. Some advocates recommended time-motion studies of housework such as the "string plan," in which a child followed his mother around with a ball of string and unwound it as she went about her work, in order to measure the distance she covered. Housewives could then study their movement patterns and eliminate wasted motions and unnecessary steps.

The most extreme example of this genre was Christine Frederick's *Household Engineering: Scientific Management in the Home*. Frederick turned her Long Island home into a laboratory for testing new tools and equipment and furniture arrangements, calling it the Applecroft Experiment Station. Her 1920 book disassembled every household task into its most basic parts, and suggested ingenious ways to minimize the amount of time, effort, and money that went into a wife's duties. In an inefficient kitchen, for example, pots were in a closet in one corner and knives in a drawer clear at the opposite end of the room; getting potatoes ready to boil required five minutes and nineteen separate steps. In the efficient kitchen, though, the knife hung on a nail next to the cutting board and the pot sat on a shelf nearby; the same task was pared to just three minutes and eight steps.

Like the Beechers before her, Frederick emphasized that homemaking was just as important—and required just as many skills—as a man's work at the office. Therefore, women should approach every task like a CEO setting up his company's next factory. There was the weekly menu, for instance—a complex project requiring forethought and strategy. If she planned well, a woman could create the correct leftovers for the following days' meals, and save on time and cooking fuel. Scalloped potatoes one night become creamed potatoes the next night, all from the same batch of cooked potatoes. Add a little water to the tomato aspic from Sunday dinner, and *voilà*—tomato soup for Monday lunch. In Frederick's world, there should be no such thing as "leftovers," only "planned-overs."

Women should also save fuel by turning the heat off as soon as their pot of water began to boil, Frederick said. And don't discard the water that the vegetables boiled in! Instead, she recommended using it as the base for sauces, thereby conserving both water and nutrients.

IN ITS BEGINNINGS, home economics emphasized sewing, cooking, and other skills necessary for a life with few modern conveniences, but as society at large changed, so too did home economics. By the late nineteenth and early twentieth centuries, the model of home production, even the urban housewife's truncated version, was a quaint anachronism. A thousand small changes, and millions of individual decisions, combined to bring about a revolution in how Americans produced and purchased goods. The trend of urbanization continued and so more families participated in the market economy; women handled money more frequently than at any other time in the past. At the same time, industrialization begat mass production techniques, making it easier and sometimes cheaper for women to buy clothing and food rather than make it themselves. Instead of canning vegetables at home, wives bought canned goods at the store; instead of buying fabric and sewing her own dress, even a working-class woman could pick out a ready-to-wear frock at the local department store.

Providing extra inducement were the alchemists of the burgeoning advertising industry. After World War I, factories were making sheets and bread and appliances in greater quantities than ever before. Who would buy all this stuff? Manufacturers called on ad agencies to bring consumers to their goods. The wizards on Madison Avenue responded with newspaper spreads and radio spots promising that their clients' products were better, safer, more healthful, more delicious, and more reliable than anything women could make at home. As early as the mid-1800s, advertisers were arguing over who really influenced household buying decisions: husband or wife? By the 1920s, it was conventional wisdom that women controlled the family budget; so manufacturers and admen aimed more and more of their messages, even for major items like homes and then cars, at these home economists.

Meanwhile, innovation was changing the retail landscape as well. Department stores like Wanamaker's and Gimbel's, F. W. Woolworth's national chain of five-and-dime stores, and mail-order companies like Sears opened up new ways of shopping and made goods more accessible to even the remotest housewives. Food shopping had once entailed visits to the butcher, the vegetable market, and the grocery store, where all the products remained behind a counter until a clerk came and filled the order. But modern supermarkets emerged in the 1910s and 1920s. Offering self-service and every ingredient under a single roof, they introduced a whole new and impersonal way of stocking the American pantry.

The surfeit of merchandise brought its own dilemmas for women. Which crackers were best? What kind of detergent was appropriate for the new washing machines? Was store-bought milk safe?

These questions were ready-made for the second and third generations of home economists, who made it their business to teach women how to evaluate goods and make informed purchases. High school home ec teachers brought their classes to local stores to inspect merchandise and discuss the basics of smart shopping. Citing a Columbia University study, Christine Frederick pointed out in 1920 that women purchased 96 percent of all dry goods, 87 percent of all "raw and market foods," and 48.5 percent of all hardware and house furnishings. Given their authority over the family's spending, she argued, women must be absolutely scrupulous in planning and accounting for every penny. She recommended an elaborate record-keeping system involving index cards and double-entry bookkeeping.

"Never before in the history of the family have the burdens of purchasing been placed so heavily on woman's shoulders," she wrote. "*To become a trained consumer is ... one of the most important demands* made on the housekeeper *of today.*" That meant reading government crop reports and checking commodity prices in the newspaper so that "the observant consumer" can buy her groceries "to advantage." If drought or heavy rains had ruined the Idaho potato crop, for example, then women should buy a winter's worth of spuds early, before prices rose. If the wheat crop was hit by blight, she said, "buy a barrel of flour at once."

For all her attention to economizing, Frederick and most other advice writers of the 1910s and 1920s displayed no skepticism toward the retailers—the "merchants of desire," as one historian calls them—who promised the new consumers a fantasy life of ease, convenience, and quality. If anything, home economists enthusiastically embraced twentieth-century marketing methods. Frederick herself worked as a consultant for manufacturers and advertisers and unapologetically promoted the brave new world of modern consumption. In her 1929 book *Selling Mrs. Consumer,* an instruction manual of sorts for businessmen seeking to attract female customers, she disparaged the kind of thrift that American women had practiced before the "machine and power age" emancipated them. "We held on to what we possessed too long, made too few changes, tried to get too much out of a purchase, and denied ourselves too much. We were, really, *merchandise hoarders,*" she wrote. The key to a healthy American economy, she added, is "creative waste": "There isn't the slightest reason in the world . . . why, for instance, bread crusts and left-over portions of breadloaves should be on the conscience of Mrs. Consumer because she doesn't make a bread pudding or French toast out of them, as foreign housewives do. Or hash out of yesterday's roast beef. Or dust cloths out of old undergarments; or pantaloons for son out of father's cast-off suits—and so on *ad infinitum.*" It was a 180-degree reversal from the official dogmas that had dominated advice to women a hundred years earlier.

From the 1920s onward, home economics turned its attention to such issues as product safety and quality control, and to turning American wives into educated, discerning consumers. Home economists continued to play a critical role as bridges between corporate America and the "female buyer." They set up laboratories for testing brand-name appliances like ironing boards, mattresses, and ovens, and often took consulting gigs, offering their design and marketing advice. At the same time, they showed women how to purchase and use the new products that lined store shelves. Students at Cornell's College of Home Economics in the 1930s and 1940s, for instance, received instruction in buying and applying makeup and reading the labels on food cans.

These shifts reflected not just changing standards for the field of home economics, but the fundamental transformation of American society as a whole. Home ec teachers still emphasized economy and efficiency. But the appeals to women's frugality had little to do with abstinence or household production of a family's essentials. Instead, the message revolved around "wise buying" and participating wholeheartedly in the revolution of prosperity and abundance. "Change is in the very air Americans breathe," Christine Frederick wrote in *Selling Mrs. Consumer,* "and consumer changes are the very bricks out of which we are building our new kind of civilization."

Chapter 4

Cheap Jews and Thrifty Chinese

In 1885, a theater group in New York debuted a new comic play by Frank Eugene Chase called *A Ready-Made Suit.* The play revolved around a woman who is charged with polygamy after marrying nine men in quick succession. During her trial, two Jews described as "eminent jobbers in secondhand clothes" appear in court to testify. As one of them explains to the jury, they both married the defendant on the same day because "ve dinks if ve can get von vife between us, dot vill be less expensive."

The crowd no doubt roared in appreciation of the joke. They certainly would have understood the subtext. By this time, the image of the stingy, grasping Jewish merchant or pawnbroker was a familiar one in American popular culture, a staple of dime novels, variety shows, humor magazines, and newspaper editorials. It's one that remains with us today, hardly dulled by age or political correctness.

For instance, there's the popular joke about how Moses received the Ten Commandments from God: One day God appears to a Babylonian and says, "I have a commandment. I'd like to give it to you." The Babylonian says, "What is it?" God says, "Thou shalt not steal." The Babylonian says, "Well, no thanks." So God goes over to an Egyptian and offers him the same deal. When the Egyptian hears what the commandment is, he also turns it down. Then God meets Moses and says, "I have a commandment for you." And Moses says, "How much is it going to cost me?" "Nothing," says God. "Fine," says Moses, "I'll take ten."

There are countless variations on the theme. Why did the Jews wander in the desert for forty years? Because one of them dropped a nickel.

What's a Jewish dilemma? Free pork.

And the truly vulgar: Have you heard the one about the Jewish pedophile? He's the guy who said, "Hey kids, go easy on the candy."

JEWS AREN'T THE only ethnic group to have been branded with the scarlet letter *C*. Go back in history and you'll find a glut of accusations—often muffled in humor, sometimes loosed with open contempt—by one group that its neighbors or adversaries are cheap or miserly or obsessed with money and accumulation. The English viewed the Scots as hopeless cheapskates (the Irish were written off as drunks and spendthrifts). The Dutch have a long reputation for being tight with cash; Ben Franklin himself popularized the rhyme "The thrifty maxim of the wary Dutch, is to save all the money they can touch." In America, Yankees—members of old families of New England—were both admired and reviled for their legendary thrift. Scandinavians, Germans, and Japanese were tagged as parsimonious by American writers, and Westerners used up a great deal of ink describing the frugal ways of Chinese living both in China and abroad.

Why have so many ethnic and national groups been cast in the role of the world's tightwads? The late Harvard psychologist Gordon Allport once said that stereotypes are projection screens for modern man's anxieties, and this one is no different. The stereotypes of cheap Jews and thrifty Chinese — two of the most enduring examples — reveal more about the people broadcasting them than they do about the real lives and practices of Jews and Chinese people. They tell us about the social, political, and economic worries that vexed Americans as they commiserated over a lost job with friends, or headed off to the mines for work, or spent their week's earnings at the grocery store. And they tell us about the complicated emotions that hovered under the surface in a free-market economy of winners and losers. Emotions like envy, resentment, admiration, fear, and, perhaps most of all, ambivalence — ambivalence about the promises of equality and opportunity and meritocracy that were advertised as the American dream.

These emotions bobbed up and fixed themselves to the waves of immigrants who came to the United States in the nineteenth and early twentieth centuries. Native-born Americans watched Jews and Chinese gain a fragile economic foothold in their adopted country and interpreted that success as a threat to their own property and job opportunities.

IN 1845, A time when Americans were founding benevolent societies to cure every possible social ill, a humor piece in the weekly New York City newspaper *The Spirit of the Times* asked its readers, "Why don't we have a Society for Ameliorating the Condition of the Jewed?" Referring to the Lower East Side lane known for its Jewish secondhand dealers, it went on, "That is a question which one who buys his clothing in Chatham Street asks us to propound."

"The Jewed," of course, were the imagined honest Christians who had been bilked by the city's Jewish merchants. By the 1840s, the term *to jew* was already common slang in

America, meaning "to bargain or haggle." The three-letter verb contained a long history, hundreds of years of mental and political contortions that created an airtight link between Jews and money.

How do you trace a stereotype as old and potent as this one? In an *ex post facto* sort of way, anti-Semitic Christians over time have dredged up Jesus's expulsion of the money-lenders from Jerusalem's temple, or Judas Iscariot's decision to go to the high priests and ask them what they would give him if he betrayed Jesus. The priests promised him thirty pieces of silver, and for those coins Judas delivered the son of God to his future killers. These examples have been presented everywhere from European ballads to American spirituals as evidence that Jews will sell out anyone for a proverbial buck.

But stereotypes are forged under specific and concrete conditions. The specter of the mercenary, deceitful, money-obsessed Jew emerged sharply during the medieval barbarism of Europe in the twelfth and thirteenth centuries, a period when many of the worst Jewish stereotypes unfolded: the Jew as devil, the hook-nosed Jew, the Jew as vicious or lascivious or a Christ killer.

Jews came to dominate the moneylending business during that era, though not wholly by choice. Excluded by edict from the powerful Christian craft guilds, they were unable to pursue trades like stonecutting, glassmaking, or metal-work. Farming was risky for a people who were often chased off their land. And the Catholic Church's injunction against usury—Luke enjoined Jesus's followers to "lend, hoping for nothing again," later interpreted as a warning against lending money at interest—prohibited Christians from entering that lucrative profession while leaving it wide open for Jews. Across Europe, Jews in the Middle Ages seized the opportunity, partly to gain some political leverage as a shield against the virulent anti-Semitism of the time.

But their participation in moneylending—always one of the least sympathetic of professions—made them easy targets of resentment. Jews found themselves in symbiotic but severely imbalanced relationships with European kings and barons. As creditors, these "court Jews" helped finance the royals' building projects, military escapades, and extravagant spending. But the Jews were dependent on those very customers for protection from anti-Semitic mobs, and from laws and Church decrees condemning or curtailing their activities. Even worse, the Jews knew that an unhappy royal could simply choose to expel them, as Philip Augustus did in France in 1182 (he invited them back in 1198). It was a delicate and tenuous partnership, but because of it, a stereotype flowered of Jews as obsequious, cowardly, subservient, happy to do the dirty work of hated rulers. When they collected debts, too, they stirred up hostility. Pope Innocent III complained in the early thirteenth century that Christians were losing their patrimony to the lenders: "Our heritage has been turned over to strangers, our houses to outsiders." Over time, more and more kings agreed with the Church and imposed harsh taxes and restrictions on the moneylenders' profession. From a contemporary vantage point, we can view the lenders as productive members of society who made possible the building of early modern cities and civilizations. But to Gentiles in the medieval period, they were little more than despised parasites.

The figure of the usurious Jew reached its apogee in about 1596 with the appearance of Shylock, the tragicomic moneylender at the heart of *The Merchant of Venice*. Shylock, of course, famously demanded his payment of a pound of flesh from Antonio, the eponymous merchant, who finds himself unable to repay a loan. Shakespeare's Shylock is a complex, multifaceted character, both sympathetic and reviled, a victim and a villain. But the figure has carried an enormous amount of currency in the four centuries since he first appeared on stage, turning up in the most casual and the most poisonous forms of anti-Semitism. American dime novelists used the phrase "old Shylock" as shorthand for low-dealing, miserly Jews. And the Nazis seized on *The Merchant of Venice* as a propaganda tool in Germany, broadcasting it on the radio and staging multiple productions — all nuance drained out — after Kristallnacht in 1938.

SHYLOCK REMAINS, TO this day, the most enduring Jewish stereotype to surface in history or literature, and he may be just who Peter Stuyvesant was imagining when, in 1654, he tried to deport twenty-three Jews who had recently arrived in New Amsterdam (now New York City) from Portuguese-occupied Brazil. Stuyvesant, the director of the Dutch West India Company in New Amsterdam, petitioned his superiors in Holland for their removal, condemning them as "a deceitful race" worshipping at "the feet of Mammon." The home office denied Stuyvesant's request, along with all of his later attempts to restrict Jewish immigration and activities.

As Jews, mostly from Germany, began arriving in the United States in greater numbers after 1825, they brought the commercial skills they had honed in Europe. They eventually displaced the Yankee peddler as an American mainstay. "With the dispersion of Jewish peddlers and shopkeepers throughout the country," says the historian John Higham, "the European tradition of the Jew as Shylock came to life. To a segment of American opinion, the Jews seemed clothed in greed and deceit."

By and large, Jews received a warmer welcome in America than just about anywhere else in their diasporic travels. A country founded on religious freedom and secular law was bound to offer them a greater degree of autonomy and protection than Europe had. And in fact, it did. The old persecutions still followed them, but usually in a muted and nonviolent form. Their presence in America elicited a more complicated mix of emotions than elsewhere, too — perhaps because the traits for which Jews were reviled in Europe were among the ones most admired and applauded in the unabashedly commercial society of nineteenth-century America, traits like enterprise, ambition, deal-making prowess, a good head for numbers, and an understanding of trade and finance. Part fact and part fiction, the image of Jews as consummate moneymakers was in some ways an excellent calling card in the New World.

Some editorialists celebrated the Jewish presence in America. In 1851, a writer in Syracuse, New York, remarked that "the Jewish population comprises some of the most industrious and frugal of our citizens," and he hoped the building of a synagogue would encourage "others of the same creed" to settle there. Nine years later, the New York business journal *The Shoe and Leather Reporter* published an article stating that, while Christians were quick to blame their own failure on these immigrants, the Jew has "by economy added to the strength and material wealth of the country.... Jew traders of the South and West have done much by their accumulated savings to form a reserve in hard times."

There was a downside to Jews' perceived financial acumen, too, though. As the historian Michael Kammen wrote about the ambiguities of the nineteenth-century American character, "In America, to be 'shrewd' was to be admired and condemned at the same time," and Jews, collectively and individually, absorbed insults, tirades, and actual persecution over their perceived economic success and the activities of individuals who reflected badly on the whole group. During the Civil War, for instance, Jews were frequently condemned as smugglers and profiteers, accused of orchestrating the black market for Southern cotton (in truth, there were Jews among the black-market speculators, but they were a distinct minority; most were Gentile merchants from the Union states). On December 17, 1862, General Ulysses S. Grant issued Order 11, expelling all Jews from the areas under his control on grounds of economic subversion. Lincoln reversed that order several weeks later, aggrieved that his own general had endorsed such blatant anti-Semitism. (As Lincoln's general in chief Henry Halleck wrote to Grant, "The President has no objections to your expelling traitors and Jew peddlers which I suppose was the object of your order, but as it in terms proscribed an entire religious class, some of whom are fighting in our ranks, the President deems it necessary to revoke it.") But when Henry Adams, the novelist and Boston Brahmin, wrote in 1893 that "with communism I could exist…but in a society of Jews and brokers, a world made up of maniacs wild for gold, I have no place," he expressed an age-old stereotype that had already blossomed on American soil.

This stereotype can be found in its baldest, most cartoonish form in the cheap dime novels that were ubiquitous in mid- to late-nineteenth-century America. These books told sensational tales of urban crime, outlaw culture, the Wild West, and glory on the high seas or the battlefield. They cost just 10 cents, naturally, and, though literary critics disparaged them, dime novels were hugely popular among the working class. A single publisher like New York–based Beadle and Adams could distribute dozens of titles a year, selling millions of copies over just a few seasons.

Dime novels were ideologically conservative and racist in nature. They appealed to white natives or white immigrants (some series were written for Irish or German audiences) and transmitted ethnic caricatures of all kinds to people around the country, many of whom had probably never met a Jew or an Arab or an Asian in their lives. The Jewish characters invariably spoke in a crude European accent and often bore comic appropriations of unmistakably Semitic names, like Silverheimer, Grabbenstein, and Swindlebaum. *The Miser's Heir,* penned by Peter Hamilton Myers in 1854, tells of a peddler and moneylender named Hakes: "The old man, whose features and occupation proclaimed him a Jew, and whose speech told that he was a German, was sitting, spiderlike, in the back part of his den, watching for prey." Hakes later explains "the Jewish ten percent": "I gif him one thousand now, he gif me ten thousand when he ish a man."

Oppenheim, a character in the 1888 dime novel *Lone Hand in Texas,* is described as a miserly "typical Jew." Albert Aiken's 1884 tale *The Genteel Spotter* includes Moses Cohenstein, an old pawnbroker and fence for stolen goods. *Gold Plume, the Boy Bandit,* by Prentiss Ingraham (1881) tells of a Jew who has come west to cheat miners and is forced to buy a round of drinks for everyone just to save his skin.

One of the most revealing characters in these types of novels is the outwardly poor but secretly rich Jewish peddler or pawnbroker. These men lived in shabby homes and wore torn, ill-fitting clothes. But behind the doors of their hovels, all was opulence and luxury, fine furniture and decadent meals. Joseph Holt Ingraham's 1845 novel, *The Clipper-Yacht; or, Moloch, the Money-lender!,* was a popular tale set in London's Jewish quarter. "Wretched as some of their shops and the habitations above them for their families were, they were far richer than they seemed, and many of them had thousands of pounds loaned at usurious interest to the merchant and the noble." Mordecai Fezenzac, the Jewish banker in Sylvanus Cobb's *The Mameluke; or, the Sign of the Mystic Tie* (1852), is an ugly old man "bowed down by the weight of tyranny and the everlasting sin of his race." But inside his "mean, dilapidated looking house" is a "splendidly furnished apartment."

The authors of these books and, perhaps, the readers they were writing for, might have believed that a Jew could never be poor; even if he looked the part, he must be secreting his money away and simply "crying poor" so he could continue to cheat and overcharge his Gentile customers. These characters exemplified a common fear: that Jews wielded too much influence over American commercial life and were getting rich from cunning and dishonesty. They also reveal Americans' inability to square the prevailing Jewish stereotypes with the fact that many of the supposed money-grubbers actually lived in poverty or in conditions known to most working-class families, laboring in factories for a meager subsistence wage.

THE CHARACTER OF the obsequious and avaricious Jew, like all stereotypes, was woefully exaggerated and largely untrue. It required the gross flattening out of reality—a reality in which many Jews struggled, worked hard to gain a modest hold on success, and generally lived unassuming, respectable lives. If the image of the Jewish peddler—his hooked nose preceding him as he trudged along forest paths and country roads, his alert eyes looking out for the next naïve customer—suggested a cunning deal-maker, the reality of that life, as transmitted through a few surviving diaries, shows a more complex picture.

Abraham Kohn left his home in Bavaria, Germany, around 1841 to join his brother in New York. Kohn was educated and well-read, but he was attracted by the twin promises of religious freedom and economic opportunity that had drawn immigrants to America ever since the Pilgrims blazed the trail. In the diaries he kept from 1842 to 1843, Kohn exposes the hollowness of the one-dimensional character—good or bad, cunning or honorable—circulated by many non-Jews at the time. "O, that I had never seen this land, but had remained in Germany, apprenticed to a humble country craftsman! Though oppressed by taxes and discriminated against as a Jew, I should still be happier than in the great capital of America," he writes soon after arriving. "There is woe — threefold woe — in this fortune which appears so glamorous to those in Europe. Dreaming of such a fortune leads a man to depart from his home. But when he awakens from his dreams, he finds himself in the cold and icy night, treading his lonely way in America."

One night, while fretting over a stretch of bad business, Kohn asks himself, "Why must I worry? No, gold shall not drive me to misery. May the devil have the banknotes and let me have a book to read that I may be of good cheer!" But his days of schlepping along a circuit of thrifty farm families in the Midwest, trying to make a few sales a day, wore him out. "Accursed desire for money, it is you that has driven the Bavarian immigrants to this wretched kind of trade! No, I must stop this business, the sooner the better."

Kohn did stop peddling a year or two later, but he didn't return to Bavaria, nor did he forsake his profession altogether. His was a classic story of immigrant success. Like many peddlers before and after him, he saved up some capital and opened a small clothing store in Chicago. He also helped found a local synagogue and became active in local politics, eventually rising high enough in the Illinois Republican party to meet Abraham Lincoln.

BY 1877, APPROXIMATELY 250,000 German Jews lived in America. Their arrival in the preceding decades had coincided with America's industrial and market revolutions, creating conditions particularly well suited to individuals with experience in trade, commerce, and finance. A number of Jewish businessmen and bankers prospered mightily, founding or expanding some of the country's most successful manufacturing firms, department stores, and investment banks.

But the success of men like the retailer Julius Rosenwald, of Sears, Roebuck, and the banker Jacob Schiff did not give them entrée into the exclusive precincts — the country clubs, summer resorts, and charity galas — of America's old Protestant elite. Instead, wealthy Jews found themselves excluded under a new pretext. In newspapers and the cocktail conversations of "polite" society, they were branded as vulgar and ostentatious, coarse and materialistic, "tasteless barbarian[s] rudely elbowing into genteel company," says one historian.

This was brought into relief in June 1877, when the eminent banker Joseph Seligman and his family were denied a room at the elegant Grand Union Hotel in Saratoga Springs, New York. (The manager blamed a recent downturn in business on the presence of "Israelites," and so he decided to stop accepting Jewish guests.) Despite an uproar of protest from Jews and some Gentile defenders, the "Seligman incident" gave other establishments cover to practice the same restrictions. In July 1879, Austin Corbin, the president of the Manhattan Beach Company, owner of several Coney Island hotels, told a reporter from the *New York Herald,* "Personally I am opposed to Jews. They are a pretentious class who expect three times as much for their money as other people. They give us more trouble on our road and in our hotel than we can stand. Another thing is that they are driving away the class of people who are beginning to make Coney Island the most fashionable and magnificent watering place in the world. . . . They are a detestable and vulgar people." Turning to his brother, Corbin looked for agreement. "What do you say, eh, Dan?" His brother replied, "Vulgar? I can only find one term for them, and that is 'nasty.' It describes the Jews perfectly."

It was the old Shylock image, recast for the Gilded Age. At

a time when the Vanderbilts were building their ersatz Versailles in Newport and the gluttonous railroad investor "Diamond Jim" Brady ate seven lobsters at a sitting and regularly mashed a pound of caviar into his baked potatoes, Americans both celebrated and debated the excesses on display. Disgust, envy, and resentment mingled with admiration and appreciation for capitalism's victors. Successful Jews became convenient screens on which to project some of those emotions. "In an age of parvenus the Jew provided a symbol of the parvenu spirit," writes John Higham. "Anti-Semitic discriminations subjected him to a discipline that native Americans could not so easily impose on themselves."

The image of the social-climbing Jew, out of his league but aggressively clamoring after respectability, showed up in humor magazines like *Puck* and *Judge*. In a *Puck* story called "Instructive Exercise," the fictional Mr. Goldheimer sends his son to a gym where he exercises on a pole shaped like a dollar sign. When the young man tells his father that he heard money can't buy happiness, his father replies, "It's not the money, it's the interest." A 1901 cartoon from *Life* magazine shows Jews clumsily trying to master upper-crust activities like polo and tennis. These same media outlets preached assimilation for immigrants and denounced the "clannishness" of Jews, yet the overall message was ambiguous: Jews should become Americanized, but not too rapidly; they were clannish but too eager to invade the WASP's cultural sanctuaries; they were greedy and materialistic but also bookish; they were miserly but also ostentatious and vulgar. These elements couldn't quite be reconciled; instead, they remained muddled together, deployed selectively to criticize and neutralize threats to the old social hierarchies of the time.

It's no surprise too that these expressions of anti-Semitism crystallized in the 1880s, 1890s, and early 1900s. In these decades more than a million Eastern European Jewish immigrants arrived in the United States. Most came from Russia, where violent pogroms were making life unbearable for Jews. They were largely poor and uneducated, a world apart from the German Jews who had arrived in America long before and achieved some measure of assimilation, even if incomplete. The idea that hordes of hungry new immigrants were moving into American cities added to the elite's sense that it was being overrun and populated its anxieties with what one historian has called "visions of inundation."

IN THE LATE nineteenth and early twentieth centuries, a new variation on the theme of the money-worshipping Jew emerged. It was the ominously labeled "international banker," a reference to European families like the Rothschilds and the Lazards, who, according to some observers, controlled the great fortunes of the world and dominated the international economy. This figure was a favorite demon of non-Jews at both ends of the political spectrum: he was condemned by the rural radicals and urban laborers of the populist movement as an amoral money broker intent on stripping away the common man's protections and traditions, and also by anti-Semitic industrialists who saw Jewish bankers as obstacles to their own consolidation of power.

An 1884 pro-socialist tract noted that "our era may be called the *Jewish* age. The jews [sic] have indeed had a remarkable influence on our civilization. Long ago they infused in our race the idea of one God, and now they made our whole race worship a new true God: the Golden Calf.... 'Jewism,' to our mind, best expresses that special curse of our age, Speculation."

Henry Ford was perhaps the most famous of the anti-Semitic industrialists in the first quarter of the twentieth century. He became convinced during World War I that a cabal of Jewish bankers had instigated the conflict mainly to encumber European governments with high-interest loans. Partly to air these views and partly to shore up circulation at his ailing newspaper, the *Dearborn Independent,* Ford commissioned a ninety-one-part series of inflammatory articles called "The International Jew: The World's Problem." The stories were patchworks of myth, anecdote, generalization, and ghost story. "The Jew is the world's enigma," said the introductory article, on May 22, 1920. "Poor in his masses, he yet controls the world's finances." The following month, Ford started printing excerpts of a favorite (but at that point largely unknown beyond a small circle of Jew haters) anti-Semitic bogeyman, *The Protocols of the Learned Elders of Zion,* which were purported to be the minutes of a meeting of Jewish elders, at which they described plans for world domination. *The Protocols* were eventually discredited as a forgery.

Under threat of lawsuits and boycotts from American Jews, Ford apologized for these activities in 1927. But by then, thanks to his efforts and a variety of other means—magazine articles about Jewish millionaires, political cartoons, dime novels—the notion of Jews' economic hegemony was firmly entrenched in the culture. In 1933, researchers published a study of Princeton undergraduates' perception of Jews. Out of eighty-four possible traits, "shrewd," "mercenary," "industrious," "grasping," "intelligent," "ambitious," and "sly" were those that respondents used most frequently to identify Jews. In later studies at Princeton, Jews were also classified as "aggressive" and "materialistic."

The Jews had plenty of Gentile defenders during these years, some of them highly placed. But even their friends were unable to sidestep the old stereotypes, trapped within the same lexicon of admiration, caricature, and contradiction that distinguishes anti-Semitic statements. Thus, the sympathetic author Herbert Eaton was able to say with equal conviction in 1879 that Jews were assiduously frugal but also so captivated by jewelry that the word was named for them:

> If a Jew makes a dollar, he lays by at least, one-
> half that amount, safely. Perhaps more. This is not
> an occurrence, but an almost universal rule of this
> people.... Carlyle says: "Whoever has sixpence is
> sovereign over all men to the extent of that sixpence,
> commands cooks to feed him, philosophers to teach
> him, kings to mount guard over him to the extent
> of that sixpence." This truth seems to be indelibly
> impressed upon the mind of the Hebrew. The
> principles of frugality are inherited, and increase rather
> than diminish with age. The Israelites are necessarily a
> money-getting people.

Later, on the same page: "Jewelry takes its name from this people, and with it they decorate themselves to a great extent. Their love for the beautiful and valuable is a peculiar attribute which has descended with them from generation to generation."

And in an assertion practically designed to stoke fear among the old WASP elites, he writes, "It being a rule that a Jew should be rich, it follows that without money he is not so highly esteemed among his own people. Everyone expects to see a Jew become rich. It is safe to say, that within the next century two-thirds of the wealth of the United States will be in the hands of the American Hebrew." He ends the essay with the following wish: "Would that all Americans were as wise as a serpent and as cautious as a Jew."

These kinds of ambiguous, perhaps ambivalent tributes weren't rare. In a speech delivered across the country in the

1870s called "The Scattered Nation," the North Carolina governor and later U.S. senator Zebulon Vance celebrated the Jewish presence in America and extolled the Jews' penchant for education and economic success. "I have never seen an adult Jew who could not read, write, and compute figures," he said, "*especially the figures.*"

ARTHUR HENDERSON SMITH was twenty-seven years old when he arrived in China in 1872 as a Christian missionary. Smith, a Civil War veteran and recent graduate of Beloit College in Wisconsin, didn't know it at the time, but he would go on to spend the rest of his life, until his death in 1932, as a self-styled bridge between the United States and the opaque and enigmatic Orient. In his life in Shandong Province, he attempted to translate Western mores and Christian beliefs to his Chinese hosts. And in books and articles, he tried to explain the "inscrutable" Chinese to American readers back home.

Smith's book *Chinese Characteristics,* published in 1894, was one of the earliest and most influential (and, as later critics pointed out, most distorted) surveys of Chinese culture written for an American audience. It was organized according to various traits Smith had observed among his adopted countrymen, qualities like "Politeness," "The Absence of Public Spirit," and "The Talent for Misunderstanding."

In Chapter II, "Economy," Smith refers to the locals' "simple diet" of "rice, beans in various preparations, millet, garden vegetables, and fish," and notes that "the Chinese are pre-eminently economical," especially in contrast to the home country:

The populations of new countries are proverbially wasteful, and we have not the least doubt that it would be possible to support sixty millions of Asiatics in comparative luxury with the materials daily wasted in a land like the United States, where a living is easy to be had. But we should like to see how many human beings could be fattened from what there is left after as many Chinese have "eaten to repletion," and the servants or children have all had their turn at the remains! Even the tea left in the cups is poured back into the teapot to be heated again.

Smith waxes further about the Chinese diet with some combination of appreciation, curiosity, and censure:

Doubtless it will appear to some of our readers that economy is carried too far, when we mention the general practice to eat *all* of these animals as soon as they expire, no matter whether the cause of death be an accident, old age or disease.... Dead dogs and cats are subject to the same processes of absorption as dead horses, mules and donkeys. We have been personally cognizant of several cases in which villagers cooked and ate dogs which had been purposely poisoned by Strychnine to get rid of them. On one of these occasions someone was thoughtful enough to consult a foreign physician as to the probable results, but as the animal was "already in the pot," the survivors could not make up their minds to forego the luxury of a feast, and no harm appeared to come of their indulgence!

Readers at home may have been disgusted by these tales, but by the time Smith's book appeared, Americans had already heard stories of Chinese people eating cats, dogs, and even rats as a means of saving money so they could accept lower wages than other workers. The thrifty Chinese, able to subsist on a fraction of an American worker's income, was a stock character from the 1860s onward, and it was one of the most potent images behind the anti-Chinese sentiment that overtook the West Coast and ultimately the U.S. Congress in the late nineteenth century.

On January 24, 1848, the foreman of a California entrepreneur named John Sutter came across what looked like shiny rocks in the water near a lumber mill he was building for Sutter. Testing revealed that the rocks were gold. Fearing that his plans for an agricultural empire would be wrecked by a flood of prospectors, Sutter tried to keep his discovery quiet. But rumors spread and within months, thousands of men around the world were gathering provisions and preparing to make the trip to the pioneer town of San Francisco. The California gold rush had begun.

Word of the "golden mountain," or *gam saan,* quickly reached China, prompting the first major wave of Sino-American immigration. Over 90 percent of the immigrants were men, and most hoped to work in California for a few years, strike it rich in the gold mines, and then return to China to live out their lives as wealthy landowners. Few actually realized that dream; like the majority of the "forty-niners," the Chinese immigrants found it wasn't so easy to get rich. Most followed the same path as Ah Louis, an eighteen-year-old from Guangzhou who arrived in America in 1856 and went to the Oregon gold fields to claim his *gam saan.* Louis struck out there, but rather than return home to China, he found work as a laborer and then settled permanently in California. So did most of the other Chinese gold seekers. Many were too poor even for passage home and stayed unwillingly, while others embraced American frontier life and stuck around to pursue whatever opportunities they could find. Ah Louis was in the latter camp; he opened a small shop in San Luis Obispo that catered to the area's Asian workers, selling everything from rice to opium (which was legal until 1915).

Between 1849 and 1882, approximately 250,000 Chinese came to the United States. In the beginning, there were no federal or state restrictions on who could come to America; politicians were happy to welcome new arrivals, since western expansion and industrialization demanded an abundant supply of workers and settlers. White Americans—some native-born, some from Ireland, Italy, and other European countries—also tolerated the Asian arrivals, at first. Building railroads, clearing land, digging coal mines—these were labor-intensive activities that required a steady stream of young bodies, and there was plenty of work to be had.

Entrepreneurs and capitalists were happy to exploit the Chinese immigrants' labor. Chinese men were the primary labor force, most famously, for the Central Pacific Railroad, which in 1863 began building the western portion of the first transcontinental line. When some observers questioned whether Chinese men were too small and fragile for the heavy labor of railroad building, the Central Pacific cofounder Charles Crocker responded by saying, "They built the Great Wall, didn't they?" Soon after, Leland Stanford, president of the Central Pacific and later governor of California, reported to Congress that "as a class they [Chinese] are quiet, peacable, patient, industrious and economical...they soon become as efficient as white laborers. More prudent and economical, they are contented with less wages." Chinese workers were indeed paid lower wages than their mostly Irish counterparts, but they weren't necessarily "contented" with the situation; they called a strike in 1867 and won better working conditions, but no wage increases.

By 1857, the economy and the mood in the western states had turned sour. The most accessible gold deposits had been stripped by then, and once those were gone, white Americans began agitating against the foreigners who had come to America for their share of the dream. Latin American and Chinese prospectors bore the brunt of this animosity as victims of "Foreign Miner" taxes, along with physical violence and mob attacks.

During this time, California, now in bust mode after the gold boom, was home to scads of what one historian called "unemployed and disappointed men." They found an easy scapegoat for their troubles in the burgeoning Chinatowns in cities like San Francisco, Sacramento, and Los Angeles. The year 1870 marked the beginning of an official anti-Chinese movement, with labor unions organizing the first large demonstrations against "cheap Chinese labor," a phrase that would become the rallying cry for a generation of exclusionary policies.

The rhetoric of the anti-Chinese forces was unambiguous: Chinese men were taking jobs away from white workers, underbidding them, thanks to what seemed like an almost inhuman willingness to work long hours (they could survive on one or two hours of sleep a night, the story went) and eat little more than rice and rodents. Conferences were convened, statistics were collected, opportunistic politicians piled on. The California State Senate conducted an investigation of the "political, economic, and moral consequences of Chinese immigration" and released a famous report in 1878, endorsing the foregone conclusion that such immigration was indeed a great evil. According to testimony included in the report, *coolies* (the term derives from the Hindi word for *day laborer;* it was used as early as the 1600s by European merchants in India) could survive on 15 cents a day while the average white laborer required $1.75 to $2.00 per day, and at least $2.50 if he was supporting a family.

Other immigrants, then and now, scrimped and scraped in their first years in America, sacrificing everyday comforts in order to save money, get ahead, and send cash back to the home country. But no other ethnic group at the time was tarred as thrifty — *thrifty* being a real insult in this case — quite like the Chinese. Why were the Chinese seen as a greater economic threat than, say, the Mexican and Irish laborers who also moved to California in great numbers during the same period?

Part of the answer lies in the constellation of myths and half-truths that clung to the Chinese and made them seem especially contemptible to Americans. In the minds of many whites, the Chinese were tainted with the stench of criminality and cruelty, branded as a wily and shrewd race with no "Christian" morals or feelings. (By contrast, Mexicans endured a reputation for being lazy and unambitious, "thriftless vagabonds" in the words of one observer during the period). News articles that trickled into the United States from China depicted the country as a germ-infested slum, a place of cruel and immoral practices, and a haven for idol worshippers, drug smugglers, opium addicts, polygamists, and gamblers. Ill-informed medical reports suggested that China was teeming with wicked diseases, and that Chinese people spread their contagions to everyone they met. An 1872 newspaper headline read, "White Lepers in San Francisco — A Pest Brought from China." Newspapers also reported on the infamous *highbinder tongs,* secret gangs of Chinese immigrants who engaged in nefarious activities, such as operating prostitution rings composed partly of women who had been kidnapped from the home country.

In addition, Chinese immigrants were simply more exotic, more foreign, than the European and Hispanic newcomers that Americans were used to. Many Chinese men shaved the hair at the front of their heads and wore the rest in a long braid, called a queue, that dangled down their backs. Their everyday clothes looked to Americans like loose pajamas and were topped off by broad-brimmed straw hats or skull-caps. They walked California's streets in soft fabric slippers. Their language was unintelligible to English speakers. Their staple food was rice, not bread or potatoes, and they had little taste for the slabs of meat that crowned the archetypal American dinner plate. They used chopsticks instead of forks. The Chinese were unrecognizable, *inscrutable* to native-born Americans, and made for a blanker canvas on which to paint Americans' fears and fantasies.

One typical report, written in 1877 by the New York congressman Edwin Meade, said that the Chinese worker's dinner was usually a bowl of rice mixed with a piece of pork or fish; "besides, it is not exaggerated that he will feed upon the meanest kind of food, including vermin. His dress, now so well known, consists of the cheapest quality, without under-garments or any of the accessories which we consider quite indispensable to a complete raiment. His rent is barely nomi-nal. He occupies a small room in common with twenty to fifty others, platforms being raised so as to economize space to the fullest extent. Coolie lodgings literally resemble a box filled with herrings."

In contrast, Meade and many other nativists asserted, the American worker required a higher standard of living. While most Chinese laborers arrived alone, with no families to sup-port, the American worker needed the manly nourishment of meat and bread, as well as a house of his own with "sepa-rate rooms for his grown up children of different sexes," and money to support his church, his children's schools, and all the other institutions required by a modern republic. "Not only substantial food, comfortable clothing, and decent house-hold accommodations are necessary to him, but his family must be supported in a respectable manner, and schooling and religious training be provided for his children. These latter have become essential and are the glory of our race and nation.... Coolie labor means to white labor starvation, alms-houses, prisons filled, and lastly, capital wasting itself. Liberal wages and white labor mean prosperity for all classes and progress in the ways of Christian civilization."

As with the Jews, few whites were able to face up to the ironies of the situation: outsiders, not Americans, were best embodying the virtues upon which the republic had been founded. Benjamin Franklin's and John Adams's vision of a nation of frugal, industrious individuals found its greatest expression in the hungry, ambitious immigrants who came to America. Americans had forsaken their early valorization of thrift. Now, thrift was seen as threatening (at least when practiced by outsiders)—threatening to the "standard of living" that had by then come to define America's identity and place in the world.

As the historian David Tucker astutely points out, the arguments of Meade and countless politicians, labor leaders, and editorial writers represented a complete reversal of the old system of values. By defending an "American standard of living" (a topic which absorbed sociologists and economists at the time), these leaders redefined American-ness in terms of consumption, not the old rubric of republican thrift.

As Tucker also notes, fears of "race suicide lurked behind all discussions of the standard of living." To nervous whites, China's massive population ensured a relentless stream of immigrants whom they feared would undermine every beloved American tradition, from Christianity to social mobility to democracy itself. "To any one reading the testimony which we lay before the two houses it will become painfully evident that the Pacific coast must in time become either American or Mongolian," reads the *Report of the Joint*

Special Committee to Investigate Chinese Immigration, which was commissioned by Congress in 1876.

> There is a vast hive from which Chinese immigrants may swarm, and circumstances may send them in enormous numbers to this country.... While conditions should be favorable to the growth and occupancy of our Pacific possessions by our own people, the Chinese have advantages which will put them far in advance in this race for possession. They can subsist where the American would starve. They can work for wages which will not furnish the barest necessities of life to an American. They make their way in California as they have in the islands of the sea, not by superior force or virtue, or even industry, although they are, as a rule, industrious, but by revolting characteristics, and by dispensing with what have become necessities in modern civilization.

THESE NATIVIST APPEALS culminated in Congress's passage of the Chinese Exclusion Act of 1882, the first law ever passed restricting immigration to the United States. Mindful of the importance of trade with China, legislators barred Chinese laborers, but continued to allow merchants as well as students. The law was set to expire after ten years, but it was renewed in 1892 and again in 1902, when officials voted to make it permanent (it was finally repealed in 1943).

Not satisfied with these victories, nativists agitated for more exclusions. Even after the Chinese "threat" had largely subsided—Chinese immigration slowed dramatically after the 1882 act, from about fourteen thousand per year to about four thousand—they turned their attention to other ethnic groups that supposedly posed a danger to the American way of life. When a movement grew, again in California, to add Japanese to the list of unwanted nationalities, Teddy Roosevelt claimed in his 1905 State of the Union address to support an open immigration policy. But he later wrote that the California legislature was right in its protest against Japanese immigration, "for their very frugality, abstemiousness, and clannishness make them formidable to our laboring class."

The trope of the thrifty immigrant was a powerful one indeed. And yet it was also a flexible one, endlessly accommodating new information and new fears without ever losing its grip. As Chinese people moved farther into the country's interior, setting down roots with laundries, restaurants, and other low-capital, work-intensive ventures, the popular image became less about "cheap labor" and more about shrewd business practices and careful spending. Newspaper articles entitled "Chinese Thrift" and "Frugality of Chinese" both lauded and condemned (often in the very same story) their work ethic and their deftness with money. In 1909, the *Fort Worth Star-Telegram* reprinted a small notice from the *Siamese Weekly News* in Thailand. Under the headline "Thrift of the Chinese," it read: "With their wonted acute perception of the possibilities of things, the Chinese have taken advantage of the anti-mosquito campaign in the French concession to enrich themselves. One of the methods adopted to destroy the embryo nuisances is to pour kerosene on the waters of the various creeks and pools, and as a consequence most of them now carry a surface covering of oil. The Chinese, who do not view the work in the same light as the foreigner, have recently commenced skimming the creeks of the floating oil and using it to their own purposes."

In the United States during these decades, the Chinese were sometimes referred to as the "Jews of the East," an analogy that was already common in other parts of the world, especially Southeast Asia. Since the 1500s, Chinese pirates, traders, sailors, and others alert to opportunity had settled in the lands that would become Thailand, Vietnam, Malaysia, and Singapore. Like Jews, they were often forbidden from owning land, and so they remained in or gravitated to trades like retailing and banking. As early as the seventeenth century, the link between the so-called Chinese character and economic qualities like thrift, hard work, and commercial savvy was firmly established. In 1634, the British traveler Sir Thomas Herbert published a book describing the Chinese propensities both for gambling and earning back their losses; the Chinese traders in Sumatra and other lands, he wrote, were "too subtle for young merchants, oftimes so wedded to dicing, that, after they have lost, their whole estate and wife and children are staked; yet in littel [sic] time, Jew-like, by gleaning here and there, are able to redeem their loss." Two and a half centuries later, another British adventurer, Isabella Bird, commented that the Chinese in Malaya were "quick-witted for chances, markedly self-interested, purpose-like, thrifty, frugal, on the whole regarding honesty as the best policy, independent in manner as in character, and without a trace of 'Oriental servility.'" A later visitor to Java commented that the Chinese merchant "could as soon leave off breathing as leave off buying and selling"; even his thoughts might be "noted in figures."

Predictably, Chinese settlers' role as the commercial class in their host countries angered many natives. In 1914, King Rama VI of Thailand published a pamphlet called "Jews of the Orient," in which he denounced what he saw as the disproportionate wealth and influence of Chinese brokers and speculators. He called them "vampires" who suck out the "life-blood" of their customers, the unfortunate and hard-working Thai people. Even worse, he wrote, the Chinese sent their ill-gotten gains back home to China; at least Jews, having no country of their own, spent their lucre in the country where they earned it.

As with Jews, Chinese in America eventually became identified with a jumble of often contradictory traits. In the American popular imagination, they were at once abstemious and ostentatious, shrewd and opportunistic, but also poor and degraded, thrifty savers but status-conscious philanthropists and spenders. According to some accounts, they were uniformly honest; in others, they cheated and connived, happily taking advantage of Chinese and non-Chinese customers alike. All of these images relied on a need to generalize and define, to neutralize unknowns, and to resist economic competition. And these stereotypes have long lives, popping up even now in unexpected ways and places; on the streets of Honolulu today, the slang term *pake* is used both as a noun for "Chinese person" and an adjective meaning "cheap." And a *chang* is a cheapskate, a term derived from a common Chinese surname.

WHY DO THESE stereotypes persist? There are the historical conditions that brought them into being and made them so potent in the first place. Then there's the incontrovertible and slightly discomfiting evidence: is it any coincidence that Jews and Chinese are among the most economically successful ethnic groups to have established themselves in America, according to data from the U.S. Census and the Pew Forum on Religion and Public Life? Which leads to other knotty questions: are they successful because they're thrifty or are they labeled thrifty (derisively, admiringly) because they're successful?

Historians have surmised that immigrants tend to be a self-selecting group of ambitious individuals; they're strivers and risk takers, the kind of personalities that generally succeed wherever they are. In the particular cases of Jews, there was the added circumstance of being frequently despised in the countries they considered home. They sought out protection and security by making themselves economically indispensable, as moneylenders or traders or retailers. Money was also the means for escape from hostile lands (whether Inquisition-era Portugal or Nazi Germany); it was good sense to make sure your assets were plentiful and liquid. In Art Spiegelman's graphic novel *Maus,* the artist's father Vladek, a Holocaust survivor, tells his son, "Always I saved—just in case."

Jews and Chinese themselves seem conflicted, ambivalent really, about their own ability to "compute figures," as Zebulon Vance said, to save and succeed. It elicits a fusion of pride and embarrassment. And so the stereotypes pop up in ethnic groups' self-perceptions, too, extending the lives of what might otherwise have been treated as outmoded or racist ideas. The Yiddish vaudeville shows of the early 1900s usually included the stock character of the fast-talking shyster or the secondhand dealer in his mismatched coat and pants. Jack Benny's show in the 1940s and 1950s portrayed him as a skinflint who gets a huge laugh when a mugger sticks him up and says, "Your money or your life!" Benny takes a long pause and then, when prodded with the gun, yells exasperatedly, "I'm thinking!" And just last year at a stand-up performance I attended, a Jewish comedian mentioned the time his mother asked him to buy Sweet'N Low. "What?" he asks her, "Did the restaurants all go out of business?"

An old fable from China, adapted for Chinese American audiences, tells of a miser who was dragged to the mountains by a tiger. The man's son picked up his bow and arrows, ran after them, and was about to shoot, when suddenly his father cried out, "You aim better so that not to damage his skin. Otherwise we won't get a penny for it!" And in the one-woman show *Aliens in America,* the writer Sandra Tsing

Loh describes growing up with an exuberant German mother and a stingy Chinese father who drinks his tea from a cracked glass beaker, uses a cereal box as a briefcase, and hitchhikes to save on gas. Her parents' personalities merged, she says, in a disastrous family vacation to Ethiopia, "the one place where adventure and economy meet."

Such self-deprecations may operate as a defense against the cruelties of outsiders or as some kind of shorthand for a minority-group identity forged partly from the ordeal of assimilation. But when Jack Benny showed off his elaborately protected money vault to friends, he was reproducing, bolstering, and poking fun at the stereotype of the cheap Jew all at once.

Ira Glass, host of the radio program *This American Life,* referred in a couple of segments to his family's schema of "book Jews" and "money Jews." His mother, he says, was appalled that he aired this delineation on national radio. But the comment points to a final irony of the ethnic experience with cheapness and frugality. For many immigrants, extreme frugality (often coupled with extreme poverty) was the path not to Revolutionary-era yeoman independence, but to the kind of conspicuous consumption that the United States has come to represent. Immigrants (Jews, Chinese, and others) usually don't scrimp and save in order to have a simple cottage in the woods; they do it to have a big house on a fancy block (or to send their kids to Ivy League schools so *they* can ultimately have a big house on a fancy block). Like the rest of their adopted countrymen, they are caught in the American yo-yo swing between frugality and extravagance. And yet, trapped inside multiple and sometimes contradictory stereotypes, they cannot always spend their way to membership in the mainstream of American society.

Chapter 5

"Use It Up, Wear It Out, Make It Do, or Do Without"

By the beginning of the twentieth century, the swanky Willard Hotel at the corner of 14th Street and Pennsylvania Avenue was already Washington, DC's, unofficial center of power. Representatives from the Union and Confederate states met there in February 1861 in a doomed last-ditch effort to prevent the Civil War. That same month, threats on Abraham Lincoln's life were so credible that a detective smuggled the president-elect and his family into the hotel at dawn a couple of weeks before he took office. Lincoln set up camp in the Willard for ten days, holding staff meetings by the lobby fireplace until his March 4 inauguration. A few days after the family checked out, the new president paid the $773.75 bill with his first White House paycheck.

In 1901, the Willard family tore down their five-story building and replaced it with a magnificent twelve-floor "skyscraper" in the Beaux-Arts style of the French Second Empire. It was designed by Henry Janeway Hardenbergh, whose pen had also sketched New York's Plaza Hotel and the original Waldorf-Astoria. The grandeur of the Willard's facade matched the outsize marble columns and soaring ceilings inside. It was only fitting for a place where congressmen, ambassadors, and lobbyists feasted on beluga caviar and lobster Newburg, both at a steep $1.50 a serving in 1912. Surveying the outrageous prices at the Willard's tobacco stand a few years later, Woodrow Wilson's vice president, Thomas Marshall, allegedly said to a companion, "What this country needs is a good five-cent cigar."

So it was ironic that in November 1917, the Willard played host to a "frugality dinner" with a self-consciously stripped-down menu and a message of patriotic austerity. The evening was organized by Wilson's Treasury secretary William McAdoo and by Frank Vanderlip, the new chairman of the War Savings Committee. The guests were businessmen from around the country who had agreed to lead state chapters of the committee, and they dined that night not on lobster or cherries jubilee but on chicken, vegetables, and ice cream. The meal cost $1.50 a plate instead of $5 for the usual six- or seven-course banquet dinner, the *New York Times* reported the following day. "The serving of chicken is in keeping with a desire to conserve beef for army use.... Conservation of cigars was practiced, for instead of placing two or three beside the plate of each diner, a box was passed. No limit was placed on the number that each guest might take, but one was the unofficial allotment a man."

As the diners lit up after the meal, Vanderlip rose and announced a new campaign to raise $2 billion in war financing through the sale of 25-cent Thrift Stamps and $5 War Savings Certificates.

"There could be no finer inspiration than the group of men who are sitting around this table," he began. "You are men of large affairs, from nearly every state in the Union, who at the request of the Secretary of the Treasury, have closed your desks and come to Washington to devote yourselves to one of the great undertakings of the war."

You are called upon to point out the tremendous value of saving the pennies as well as the dollars. [Americans] will begin to save, and they will save in a way which will not only release great sums for the use of the Government, but will establish habits of thrift which will lay the foundations for the future greatness of America.

... What this will mean in conserving the resources of America is inestimable. What this will mean in the future economy of America is incalculable.

Victory can only be won by the valor of our soldiers, combined with the intelligent use of our resources.... There is no more important movement in America today than this movement for savings and economy.

A bit melodramatic, perhaps. But there was truth in Vanderlip's message. The United States had already been loaning millions of dollars to Allied forces and shipping tankers full of meat and grains to Europe to prevent mass starvation among civilians. On April 6, 1917, when the United States officially entered World War I, the American commitment to the conflict grew exponentially. Inflation had spiraled upward in the previous decade. Now, thanks to even greater demand, President Woodrow Wilson feared that prices would jump further and that American reserves of money, supplies, food, and raw materials would quickly be tapped out.

In a message to the public a few days after the declaration of war, he called on citizens to economize in all areas: "This is the time for America to correct her unpardonable fault of wastefulness and extravagance. Let every man and woman assume the duty of careful, provident use and expenditure as a public duty."

When Wilson asked Americans to sacrifice their vaunted standard of living to the larger cause of the war, he was speaking to a nation that had transformed over the preceding fifty years into the most sophisticated consumer society in history. The changes are staggering to consider. In those five decades, cars had replaced horses and buggies, refrigerators were pushing out iceboxes, and the nation's dusty roads had been paved over with asphalt. New railway lines crisscrossed the country in every direction; boys and girls born on rural farms streamed into cities, helping to animate a sense that modern life thrived in these dynamic urban centers.

Small-town culture wasn't dead by any means. But it had been eclipsed by the prosperity of the times. Despite occasional stretches of economic recession, Americans' incomes and consumption rose steadily over the fifty years after the Civil War. By the 1910s, more Americans had more money in their pockets and more places—nickelodeons, automobile showrooms, department stores, supermarkets, P. T. Barnum's circuses—to spend it. Men who had watched their fathers' backs bend from years of hard farm labor and women who had once been responsible for grueling tasks like washing the family's clothes by hand felt liberated by the abundance of the new America, and they increasingly viewed self-denial as an anachronism left over from the joyless Puritan days.

But the next three decades would remind even prosperous Americans that they hadn't kissed hardship good-bye. Two world wars and a catastrophic economic depression stripped away some of the optimism and ebullience that had come to define the nation. These events forced Americans to retrench from their expectations of limitless abundance and recover their parents' and grandparents' talent for low-cost survival. They also forced the country to reckon with the role of thrift—as a national virtue and as a practical way of life—in twentieth-century America.

★   ★   ★

WHAT DOES IT take to fight a war? In the early days of the
U.S. military effort, the federal government estimated that it
would need to purchase 45 million tons of copper, 11 million
barrels of cement, 6 million pounds of wool, and 20 million
pairs of leather shoes, along with a steady supply of surgical
scissors, canvas tents, men's underwear, lumber for barracks,
beef, coffee, arms of all sizes, airplanes, warships, hospital
beds, chemicals, surveying instruments, and catgut for closing up wounds. All of this, Treasury Department officials
believed, would cost several billion dollars. The question was,
where would Uncle Sam get the money?

President Wilson and his advisers quickly decided they
would raise the lion's share of the war funds as loans from the
public rather than as higher taxes or newly printed currency.
Treasury Secretary McAdoo was a student of history, and he
had scrutinized the work of Salmon P. Chase, his counterpart
in Lincoln's cabinet during the Civil War. Chase had borrowed from the public to pay for the war, just as McAdoo
planned to do. But Chase's "public loan" was offered only to
wealthy individuals, and sold only through large banks and
brokerage houses. Not very public at all, McAdoo thought.

He was determined to do things differently, opening
up sales of the $50 and $100 bonds from the start to every
American, the more the better. In this decision, he was as
shrewd as any battlefield commander. By democratizing war
finance, the Treasury could tap into far more cash: not just
the savings of the wealthy, but also the $20 bills hidden under
farmers' mattresses, and the modest nest eggs stored in dresser
drawers around the country.

The secondary benefits were just as important. Bond sales
would soak up Americans' discretionary dollars, the money
they would normally be spending on gewgaws like cuckoo
clocks, electric irons, and tennis rackets. Crucially, those
foregone purchases meant more labor and raw materials could

be diverted into supplying and outfitting soldiers. Allowing Americans to literally "buy in" to the war effort would also give every individual—men too old to fight, women with sons and husbands on the front—a greater stake in victory. "Any great war must necessarily be a popular movement," McAdoo declared. "It is a kind of crusade; and, like all crusades, it sweeps along on a powerful stream of romanticism."

In 1917, the Treasury Department added 25-cent Thrift Stamps and $5 War Savings Certificates to the mix so that cash-strapped workers and schoolchildren could participate as well. McAdoo tapped Vanderlip to run the campaign. It was an inspired choice. Born poor on an Illinois farm, Vanderlip dropped out of college and worked as a lathe operator before joining the *Chicago Tribune* as a business reporter. A friend, the banker and political appointee Lyman Gage, recruited him to work in government, and from there Vanderlip went on to become vice president, and then president of National City Bank, the precursor to today's Citigroup. As a banker and a privately frugal man, he was a great zealot for the cause of thrift. He hoped, as he explained at the Willard Hotel, that the war savings movement would put the brakes on Americans' growing materialism. "We are a nation of spenders and we must learn to economize. It is unpatriotic to spend money for anything but necessities....Men engaged in producing luxuries should cease at once as a patriotic act," he later told a gathering of business editors in New York.

Retailers were reluctant to support the effort, beginning as it did right before the Christmas selling season. But Vanderlip simply told executives from Sears and Montgomery Ward, "We want to spoil as much Christmas trade as possible. Those of you who are in merchandising are shocked, no doubt. That is the lesson of thrift we have to learn."

McAdoo and Vanderlip enlisted the advertising industry in their crusade. Over the previous few decades, these masters of persuasion had been fine-tuning their understanding of the American consumer, helping corporations sell everything from soap to cigarettes to automobiles. Now, the war cabinet decided, they would help the American government sell patriotism, self-denial, and thrift.

George Creel, the master adman running the federal Committee for Public Information, marshaled a first-class propaganda campaign for selling war bonds and stamps. Pamphlets asked: "Have you helped your country by investing in the war loan, or have you helped Germany by keeping your money in your pocket?" and "Do you realize that it is an expression of disloyalty to decline to contribute to this loan?" The insinuation of guilt was constant: "Your countrymen are giving their lives; you are only asked to lend your money" and "If necessary, wear old clothes, old boots, old dresses; eat, drink, and smoke less and then borrow against your future savings to invest in this patriotic necessity."

At a dinner on November 9, 1917, at New York's Café des Artistes, Vanderlip called on the most celebrated illustrators of the day, men like Charles Dana Gibson and Howard Chandler Christy, saying, "We want posters and we want them now. We don't want inspiration. We want the concrete thing to place in the windows of America." The artists fell into line. They formed an unofficial club called the Vigilantes, with Gibson as their chief, and generated hundreds of designs that fairly exploded off the paper they were printed on. Lurid images—bleeding soldiers, women being bayoneted or carried off by "Huns," starving children—underscored the urgency of bond and stamp sales. One advertisement told Americans to "Lick a Stamp and Lick the Kaiser!"

While volunteers plastered posters onto the walls and windows of restaurants, laundries, post offices, schools, and shops, Creel pioneered the use of "Four-Minute Men," a domestic army of seventy-five thousand civilians who took the stage at cinemas and plugged war bonds in the amount of time required to change a movie reel. Eventually they fanned out beyond the theaters, bringing their message to farm auctions, schools, and union halls.

Volunteers organized thrift clubs and war savings societies. Celebrities joined in. Ring Lardner wrote a jingle:

> *There was a foolish man,*
> *And he bought a foolish block*
> *Of Yaki Hula common,*
> *And foolish mining stock.*
> *And now he dines on field mice,*
> *And pals with other tramps,*
> *Which never would have happened*
> *If he'd bought War Savings Stamps.*

Teachers too were called on to do their part. Piggybacking on the school savings plans designed by John Thiry and Sara Louisa Oberholtzer and already in wide use, Vanderlip suggested that all patriotic educators should harness the system toward the sale of war stamps and certificates. "The school teachers are the rallying ground for the best beloved possession of a country—its children," he said. "To the teachers belong the splendid privilege, the solemn duty of rallying them round the flag. . . . We must save money that we may save lives. The educators of America enjoy no greater privilege than that of being able to teach this lesson to the nation."

Vanderlip also received enthusiastic support from the Young Men's Christian Association, which in 1917 began organizing an annual National Thrift Week in January, falling, naturally, around Ben Franklin's birthday. During Thrift Week, museums sponsored exhibitions about Franklin, and bankers welcomed groups of schoolchildren into their vaults, where kids could eyeball stacks of cash and hear all the reasons why they should open a savings account and add to it for the rest of their lives. The YMCA also distributed prewritten sermons to ministers in the hope that they would use the Sunday of Thrift Week to preach the gospel of frugality. "Thriftlessness—debt—mars and stains the soul," went a typical sermon.

However virtuous the ends, the tactics McAdoo and Vanderlip employed were sometimes extreme. Some of the official speeches handed out to Four-Minute Men by the Committee for Public Information were filled with stories of German atrocity, sometimes true and sometimes exaggerated to froth up patriotism. According to one, "Prussian Schrecklichkeit (the deliberate policy of terrorism) leads to almost unbelievable besotten brutality. The German soldiers... were often forced against their wills, they themselves weeping, to carry out unspeakable orders against defenseless old men, women, and children....For instance, at Dinant, the wives and children of forty men were forced to witness the execution of their husbands and fathers. Now, then, do you want to take the *slightest* chance of meeting Prussianism here in America?" At a rally, McAdoo said, "Every person who refuses to subscribe or who takes the attitude of let the other fellow do it, is a friend of Germany and I would like nothing better than to tell it to him to his face. A man who can't lend his government a dollar and twenty-five cents per week at the rate of four percent interest is not entitled to be an American citizen." Senator Warren G. Harding called the loan drives "hysterical and unseemly."

THE THRIFT MESSAGE didn't end with the loose change in Americans' pockets. It extended to a medley of activities, inspiring a renewed (but short-lived) vigilance about waste and resource conservation. Families revived the old recycling traditions of the farm and peddler days as Americans who had gotten used to the expectation of ever-greater abundance adjusted to a new regime of scarcity.

Under its wartime director, Herbert Hoover, the Food Administration called for voluntary retrenchment (Hoover felt that rationing smacked of the very authoritarianism that Allied armies were fighting in Europe). He instituted Wheatless Mondays and Meatless Tuesdays, helping the United States send nearly 10 billion pounds of beef, grains, and other products across the Atlantic to soldiers and civilians. He also chided Americans for their wasteful habits. Like so many politicians before him, he invoked the half-mythical pedigree of American thrift. "Go back to simple food, simple clothes, simple pleasures," he urged. "Pray hard, work hard, sleep hard, and play hard. Now is the time to lay your double chin on the altar of liberty . . . if we are selfish or even careless, we are disloyal. . . . We need [to] get back once more to the old-fashioned home, the kind of home in which many of us older folks were raised, where . . . the waste of foods, as we were taught by our mothers, was sin. . . . Can we not all of us . . . help spread that sense of sin?"

This was an old language, the Calvinist language of condemnation. But like McAdoo and Vanderlip, Hoover was fluent in the idioms of advertising, persuasion, and emotional appeal. "The world lives by phrases," he declared, and he too commissioned the fast talkers of Madison Avenue to write hundreds of slogans and jingles. These filled the airwaves and appeared on posters, restaurant menus, even chewing gum wrappers. "Don't let your horse be more patriotic than you are—eat a dish of oatmeal!" shouted one. "If U fast U beat U boats—if U feast U boats beat U," declared another.

Pamphlets explaining the principles of conservation and food substitution were printed in French, Spanish, German, Italian, Swedish, and Yiddish for the country's non–English speakers. The media jumped into the effort as well. "Do not permit your child to take a bite or two from an apple and throw the rest away," admonished *Life* magazine. "Nowadays even children must be taught to be patriotic to the core."

The American housewife was on the front lines of this war against waste and extravagance. It was she who was supposed to prepare Macaroni with Peanut Butter, Cottage-Cheese-and-Nut Roast, Victory Bread, and Conservation Soup (made of potatoes, onions, milk, and ketchup, according to a cookbook published in 1918 by Miss Farmer's School of Cookery in Boston). Hoover asked women to sign pledge cards promising "to carry out the directions and advice of the Food Administrator in the conduct of my household, insofar as my circumstances permit." A massive volunteer corps spread out through towns and cities to collect the signatures. First Lady Edith Bolling Wilson posted her pledge card in a window of the White House.

Posters urged women to find substitutes for the beef and sugar that had long been staples of the family table; cookbooks suggested meals based on fish, fruit, vegetables, and eggs, the products that were too perishable to be sent overseas. Recipes circulated for cottonseed sausage—three parts meat to one part cottonseed—and a syrup made of mesquite beans. Nothing should be wasted, admonished the Food Administration: "Catch the carp; buy the carp. Cook the carp properly and eat it. Eat the roe; can the roe. Make carp jelly," came one directive.

Housewives were told to sift through their waste: Fatty acids could be salvaged for soap, fruit pits and nut shells could be saved for the carbon used in gas masks. The rest could be composted for pig feed and fertilizer. The National War Garden Commission pressed Americans to plant their own vegetable plots. More than 5 million families complied, freeing up, by one estimate, over $500 million worth of vegetables to be sent to troops overseas. And with their homegrown food savings, of course, the gardener could afford an extra $50 or $100 war bond.

VANDERLIP REGARDED ALL these thrifty activities as nothing less than the stirrings of a fundamental reformation of American character. He and his aides at Treasury were convinced that war gardens and conservation and, especially, their own savings-stamp and loan drives, could do more than finance the battle against Germany; they believed the campaigns could permanently revive the tradition of frugality in America.

Even when the war drew to a close, Vanderlip and McAdoo urged Wilson to keep the Savings Division's work alive. Wilson did, and for the first year after the armistice, the agency's budget remained high at $3.5 million and it employed more than a hundred people.

The postwar Treasury secretary, Carter Glass, commissioned a new thrift curriculum to be taught in schools, with lessons for first graders (math problems asking how many nickels and dimes a child needed to buy a 25-cent Thrift Stamp) up through high schoolers (English essay assignments with titles like "The First Time I Ever Admired Savings").

Officials also partnered with community groups like the National Education Association, which maintained a Committee on Thrift Education; one article by the committee chairman listed candy, chewing gum, coffee, and tea as wasteful luxuries. The organizers of National Thrift Week, including YMCA and Treasury Department officials, redoubled their efforts. In 1922, they announced plans to enlist 500,000 Americans in a national budget league with a set of ten basic principles, including "Work and earn," "Make a budget," "Carry life insurance," "Own your home," and "Pay your bills promptly."

Some appeals clung to a fundamentalist version of thrift, harking back to the Puritan days of John Cotton and Cotton Mather by casting thrift as a moral virtue and a matter of character. But other parties, like the Thrift Week promoters, attached their appeals to more modern language, making the case for thrift in terms of efficiency and scientific management. Bankers, in particular, tried to be pragmatic. They stepped away from the notion that self-denial itself was a virtue and instead accommodated themselves to the reality of the American consumer society. They talked about "management of the business of living" and recommended saving as the route to acquisition, a rationale for consumption. In 1920, the American Academy of Political and Social Science devoted a whole issue of its journal to "The New American Thrift." One article began with the statement that "thrift is a means to the best life for individual and family," but then went on to rationalize the purchase of pricey luxuries. "Expensive consumption goods may furnish the goal that stimulates saving, for example: buying a watch; expensive wearing apparel such as furs or jewelry; [and] special house furnishings, such as furniture of finer quality, pianos, phonographs, paintings, etc." Philo Publicus, the republican who had railed against extravagance in colonial times, would have been appalled at this marriage between thrift and luxury. Back in his day, thrift was a moral concept at the heart of the ideal of living a modest, independent life. Now it meant wise money management in the service of a constantly rising standard of living.

THE APOSTLES OF thrift—the pragmatists as well as the fundamentalists—found themselves, more and more, shouting into the wind. Even during the war, economists and corporate leaders had begun to worry about what would happen after it was over. The army, they knew, would stop demanding so many tents, blankets, and tanks; European trading partners would go back to making their own stoves and textiles and wouldn't need so many U.S. exports. American manufacturers had expanded their operations dramatically to meet the insatiable requirements of war. They had built new factories, invested in expensive equipment, and hired millions of workers. With glass imports from Belgium cut off, the spectacles firm Bausch and Lomb had begun to make glass for periscopes, field glasses, and range finders. The Remington gun company of Bridgeport, Connecticut, had spent $12 million on a new facility for making small arms. Shipyard employment had jumped from 50,000 workers to 350,000. Machines hummed twenty-four hours a day. This productivity was terrific for economic growth; gross domestic product rose 20 percent in 1917 and 27 percent in 1918. But it also raised the specter of a severe recession once the guns fell silent. The mechanics of "conversion"—moving as seamlessly as possible from a wartime economy to a peacetime economy—weighed heavily on the minds of bureaucrats who were eager to avoid a downturn and business owners who wanted to maintain their high wartime profit margins.

In this light, the old virtue of thrift began to look more and more suspicious. In classical economics, savings—the result of individuals' self-denial and thrift—formed the necessary pool of funds from which corporations borrowed when they needed to build a new factory or hire more workers. But the war had so inflated America's manufacturing capacity that business interests began to see consumption, not savings, as the key to maintaining stability and growth. Corporations feared that if consumers internalized the war's scarcity message and withheld their cash even after the battles ended, corporate profits would suffer permanently.

Thrift, many businessmen believed, was an antiquated habit that didn't speak to the conditions of a consumer-driven, industrial economy. Thomas Edison, inventor extraordinaire and a shrewd businessman as well, told a convention of phonograph dealers in 1918 that "the urge to possess luxuries will do more to speed up production than all the prize contests, bonus plans, and proclamations that can be devised. The laziest and most nonproductive man in the world is the man whose wants are simplest." Toward the end of the war, retailers in nearly every city put placards in their windows telling shoppers it was "Business as Usual" and warning them to "Beware of Thrift and Unwise Economy." Newspapers published antisavings editorials under pressure from their merchant advertisers, in the hopes of getting the country spending.

Americans did. After the war, according to one Louisiana retailer, lumberjacks in his state were "living high, buying $3,000 autos, silk shirts for $10 and $12, and neckties for $5, while their wives and daughters wear hats costing as high as $20, and silk hose for $2.50. I have actually run out of silk hosiery at that price at our commissary store, the demand for high-priced goods being greater than that for the plainer kinds." Prices for food, clothing, and other essentials quickly shot up 116 percent over prewar prices, a combination of pent-up demand from consumers, a credit squeeze, and a drop in production. Every constituency blamed someone else; farmers pointed their fingers at manufacturers, manufacturers accused unions of making excessive demands, unions called strikes and condemned corporate greed, and everyone blamed the government (but then bridled at any price or wage controls the Feds tried to impose).

Consumers were furious about the raging inflation, and they punished manufacturers by consuming less. Even after spending began to return to normal in 1920, though, businessmen warned vigorously about the dangers of underconsumption. A group of New York City manufacturers organized the

National Prosperity Bureau in 1921. They warned Americans that prices had sunk as low as they ever would, so they should shop now before inflation started creeping up again. In the posters they sent around the city, Uncle Sam sat astride a hurtling train above the words, "Full Speed Ahead! Clear the track for prosperity! Buy what you need now!" Henry Ford had once sat on the Central Committee of the War Savings Division, but now he condemned thrift, too, saying frugal men "shrivel body and soul. Economy is waste. It is waste of the juices of life, the sap of living." He told young men, "Spend your money on yourself, get all the experience you can. Don't try to save money and be a miser."

Pyrex and Promises

By 1922, the inflation crisis had passed. Prices fell to manageable levels and a sense of optimism overtook the country. To elites and strivers, the years after the war were a time of ebullience and acquisitive aspiration, a period infused with the "contagious feeling that everyone was meant to get rich," says the historian William Leuchtenburg.

Washington went along with it. President Calvin Coolidge looked the part of a simple New England farmer and he praised simple virtues like thrift and sobriety. But in office, he championed America's commercial orientation. At a dinner in 1925, he announced that "the chief business of the American people is business," and in fact, cross-pollination between government and private enterprise guaranteed that corporate interests would be protected and furthered. The banker and industrialist Andrew Mellon served as secretary of the Treasury for most of the 1920s under the Republican presidents Warren Harding, Coolidge, and Herbert Hoover. In the tradition of what we now call "trickle-down economics," he engineered a series of tax cuts that brought rates on the wealthiest Americans' incomes down from 65 percent to 20 percent. President Harding also supported the evisceration of the American labor movement, which, for the first time during a period of prosperity, saw membership fall during the 1920s. "Never before, here or anywhere else, has a government been so completely fused with business," crowed the *Wall Street Journal*.

The twenties were, in a sense, a second industrial revolution. The innovations of the previous few decades—electricity, assembly lines, mechanization—along with vastly increased production capacity from the war years were brought to bear on manufacturing, resulting in an unprecedented range and quantity of new consumer goods.

Products like Pyrex glass bowls, cellophane, oil furnaces, rayon, and plastic altered the most mundane details of family life. Highways and improved railroad technology allowed wholesalers to ship lettuce, cherries, and tomatoes across the country. For the first time, Americans came to expect fresh fruit and vegetables in any season.

Egging on these transformations were the Mad men on Madison Avenue. Whether crude or sophisticated, their techniques were tailor-made for an optimistic audience willing to accept that eternal youth really might be hiding in a jar or that the right brand of cigarettes was an essential prop in the drama of sexual seduction. "We grew up founding our dreams on the infinite promise of American advertising," says the main character in Zelda Fitzgerald's novel *Save Me the Waltz*. "I *still* believe that one can learn to play the piano by mail and that mud will give you a perfect complexion."

Of course, Americans needed money for all of these delights. No cash? No problem. Buying on credit became easier and—most important—morally acceptable during the decade. The historian Lendol Calder dates the shift to 1926 and 1927, when a number of onetime critics of installment credit renounced their earlier opposition. In those years, the American Bankers Association and the American Federation of Labor released reports noting that consumer debt had "a proper place" in the economy. And in the July 1926 issue of *American Magazine,* a popular middle-class monthly that had long advocated conservative spending, a reader called "H.L.F." wrote in with his story of endless marital arguments over money. Eventually, he and his wife decided to burn their "budget book." As it went up in flames, he writes, he shouted to his son, "There she goes, Bobby! And maybe your college education and your whole future has gone with her; but we can't help it!" As he told other readers, "We have been free ever since."

One of the clearest indicators of the new attitude was also the most subtle. In 1925, General Motors asked the prominent economist E. R. A. Seligman to conduct a serious study about installment credit. The final report was published in 1927. In it, Seligman systematically deconstructed the old Victorian distinction between "productive credit" (money invested in machinery, equipment, or necessary consumer goods) and "consumptive credit" (money spent on frivolous things that are used up, destroyed, and "consumed" with no lasting economic benefit). According to Seligman, all credit was productive since it stimulated economic activity. To strip away the disapproval implicit in the phrase "consumptive credit," he introduced a new term to the financial lexicon: "consumer credit." After the report came out, a *New York Times* reviewer declared that the sin of installment buying had been "absolved by a high priest of the academy."

Retailers, manufacturers, and small-loan companies seized on Seligman's conclusions. One 1928 ad for the East Coast department store Goldman's juxtaposed the images of a businessman gazing out the window at his smoke-spewing factory and a stylish lady in a full-length fur wrap. "A factory or a fur coat (...both of them may be bought on credit)," says the ad. "What is the difference in these transactions? Nothing—Except size!" These ads were effective. Surveying the American landscape of the 1920s, the President's Research Committee on Social Trends remarked on "the new attitude towards hardship as a thing to be avoided by living in the here and now, utilizing installment credit and other devices to telescope the future into the present."

It was the Roaring Twenties. Pleasure was the pursuit of the day, personified by the fox-trotting flapper with a cigarette in one hand and a bootleg cocktail in the other. Facile interpretations of Sigmund Freud's work gave urban sophisticates a rationale for sexual experimentation and freedom. Movies, jazz clubs, country drives, and vacations to Miami rose up to fill the leisure time made possible by labor-saving inventions like vacuum cleaners, refrigerators, and canned foods.

The Treasury Department's Savings Division was essentially dead by around 1924, defunded by Congress and President Harding. "Thrift education never had a chance in peacetime," says the historian David Tucker. "So many interests were offended by a government program against buying that the program had long ceased to have any real support." And despite the best efforts of bankers to maintain the culture of saving, deposits as a portion of national income began to decline in 1926. The sober savings account increasingly lost out to more glamorous alternatives, like spending for pleasure and investing in the fast gains of the stock market.

Indeed, the greatest expression of the decade's optimism was the Dow Jones Industrial Average. It seemed immune to vertigo, rising higher and higher until even cautious office clerks and restaurant waiters jumped in, or made plans to (banks allowed anyone to buy a few shares "on margin"). How long could a man afford to stay out after watching his neighbor's stake in General Motors double from 1925 to 1928? These small investors joined the large corporations and superrich individuals who took their business profits—profits earned at the expense of workers whose wages rose at about half the pace of productivity—and sank them back into the market. Speculation was rampant; stocks levitated on little more than vapors, the casual assumption of nonstop growth. In September 1929, the market dropped, then rose, then wobbled again. On October 24, now known as Black Thursday, the plunge began in earnest. A record 13 million shares traded hands in a fit of panic selling. The share prices of corporate powerhouses like General Electric, Westinghouse, and U.S. Steel were eviscerated. By the following month the industrials index had been slashed in half, from a high of 452 points in September to November's low of 224. At the bottom of the market, in July 1932, it would fall to a trough of 58 points.

The Great Hangover

The October crash bankrupted many investors and destroyed confidence in the business leaders who had once seemed so heroic. The idea of business itself as an essentially benevolent force was now off the table. Instead, the fundamental weaknesses of the underregulated, probusiness economy were finally revealed: corporations had invested too heavily in expansion without raising wages enough to sustain demand for all the new products coming off the assembly lines; income distribution was severely skewed toward the wealthy due in part to a regressive tax system; the nation's banking system was broken and ineffectual.

The crash revealed an even darker truth: despite the flashy 1920s images of Gatsby et al., many Americans still lived in poverty, having missed out on the decade's gains. In 1929, the Brookings Institution reported that 60 percent of the nation's 27.5 million families lived on less than $2,000 a year, barely able to provide for basic necessities. Yet they were inundated with fantasies of the good life, a life that could be had for "just a dollar down." From 1920 to 1926, consumer debt nearly doubled, and household debt as a percentage of income rose from 4.7 percent to 7.25 percent. Meanwhile, families hadn't put aside any money for the inevitable rainy day. When the jobs that kept working- and middle-class families afloat began to disappear early in the Depression, so too did the trappings of their American dream.

If Americans adopted thrift during World War I out of patriotism, they reprised the experience of self-denial during the Great Depression out of desperation. Just two months after Black Thursday, employers had tossed several million people out of work. In December 1930, the Metropolitan Life Insurance Company estimated that 24 percent of its policy-holders were unemployed; who knows how many more had stopped paying their policies and remained uncounted. "You cannot help feeling sorry for the stars and nebulae many light years away who still have the year 1930 coming to them," eulogized the *New York Times*. In the first few years after the crash, an average of 100,000 men and women lost their jobs every week, driving the unemployment rate to 25 percent. Some of the unlucky ones scraped out a living by way of the International Apple Shippers' Association. Faced with a glut of Northwest apples, the organization arranged to sell them on credit to jobless men, who took up posts on street corners around America, off-loading the apples at 5 cents apiece. Others lined up outside employment agencies, hoping for a day's work hauling boxes or demolishing old buildings.

Families adopted other strategies, some drastic and some negligible, to get through the lean years after the crash. For many of them, the Depression exposed a hard truth about their vaunted standard of living: it wasn't sacred, it wasn't handed down by God, and it wasn't guaranteed. These lessons left emotional scars on an entire generation of Americans. It also instilled in them a sense of caution and humility about those "infinite promises" Zelda Fitzgerald had written about.

The memoirist Robert Hastings lived the American dream as a child in 1920s Illinois. Even on a miner's salary, his father had acquired a house and car, ordered new city services like water lines and waste disposal, and treated his family to the occasional dinner out. But the mine closed soon after the market tumbled. "With no dependable income, we cut back on everything possible. We stopped the evening paper, turned off the city water and cleaned out our well, sold our four-door Model T touring car with the snap-on side curtains and isinglass, stopped ice and milk delivery, and disconnected our gas range for all but the three hot summer months," writes Hastings in his book *A Nickel's Worth of Skim Milk: A Boy's View of the Great Depression.* "Looking back, I find it amazing what we did without. A partial list would include toothpaste (we used [baking] soda), toilet paper (we used the catalog), newspaper or magazine subscriptions, soft drinks, potato chips and snacks, bakery goods except bread and an occasional dozen of doughnuts, paper clips, rubber bands, and restaurant meals. We had no water bill, no sewer bill, telephone bill, no car expenses—gasoline, tires, batteries, licenses, insurance, repairs—no laundry service, no dry cleaning (we pressed woolens with a hot iron and a damp cloth), no bank service charge (no bank account), no sales or income tax."

Hastings's parents planted a garden, and "a typical spring meal was a big pan of lettuce wilted with hot bacon grease and vinegar, finely chopped and mixed with green onions and tiny radishes." A winter dinner might be milk gravy and biscuits; when milk was scarce, his mother made a barely edible "water gravy" out of bacon drippings, flour, salt, and water. If bread lasted long enough to become stale, it was steamed until it got soft and hot, then dipped in gravy.

Desperation drove many to thrift and more than a few people into wild gambles. Eric Sevareid, the future broadcast journalist, joined the bands of men who moved to California hoping to live off the dregs of the last gold discoveries. "We were more like scavengers," he later recalled to an interviewer. "The hope of finding gold, which almost none of us ever did, was more of an excuse to live in the hills where life was cheap, than anything else."

Commodity prices lurched downward and consumer spending dried up, leaving farmers, business owners, and even some large corporations unable to pay back their bank loans. As a result, 40 percent of the nation's banks collapsed between 1929 and 1933, wiping out the life savings of millions of Americans.

WHAT DID THE government do to stem the crisis? With the benefit of hindsight, we can say that President Hoover and the Federal Reserve didn't do nearly enough—or did the wrong things altogether. This isn't surprising; until the Depression, there was almost no such thing as "economic policy." Politicians and even economists mostly believed that business recessions were natural and self-correcting, and they saw little need to take decisive action. According to economic theory as understood at the time, a slowdown in investment should lead to a surplus of money, as savings accumulate in banks. That surplus should, theoretically, lead the "price" of money—interest rates—to drop, thus giving firms greater incentive once again to invest. *Voilà*—the recession corrects itself. But in the early 1930s, investment never picked up; instead, that first crash in the fall of 1929 led into one year after another of unemployment and misery. For the most part, economists and policymakers were baffled.

As in so many past crises, many leaders returned to the

kind of Puritan moralizing they had abandoned during the booming twenties, when America's prosperity had seemed boundless. "People will work harder, live a more moral life," Treasury Secretary Mellon said after the Depression started. A president of the National Association of Manufacturers said in 1930 that the downturn was a result of workers' moral turpitude, rather than any flaws in the economic system.

What little the government eventually did often made the problems worse. Hoover was committed to a balanced budget, so he raised taxes in 1932, which further depressed spending. Measures that were intended to protect American businesses, such as the Smoot-Hawley tariffs on twenty thousand imported goods, had the opposite effect; other nations retaliated with their own protections, and world trade contracted by 65 percent.

A few American economists, such as William Trufant Foster and Waddill Catchings, suggested that government stimulate the economy with strategic spending on public works, but their theories had little impact until John Maynard Keynes, the brilliant British polymath, came along with his incisive diagnosis for the ailing economy. Keynes showed that as long as corporations expected demand to remain low, they had no reason to invest even when money was cheap. Thus, contrary to popular thinking at the time, the economy could find an equilibrium—a low-production, high-unemployment equilibrium—and stay there indefinitely.

Keynes's analysis was revolutionary in many ways. For one, he used psychology to help explain the leaps and dips of the economy. Concepts like *confidence* and *expectations* had never been applied to business cycles before; economists had simply believed that firms responded automatically to the levers of supply and demand, and that these adjustments kept the economy on a jagged but ultimately upward-trending path. Keynes showed that low expectations were actually a powerful force capable of paralyzing all commerce. Second, he made the most convincing argument that government needed to "prime the pump," as he liked to say, and jump-start the economy during recessions. If businesses were too nervous to invest, or even worse, if they were so scared they were laying workers off, then public investment—putting people back to work building bridges, paving roads, and teaching kids—would have to do the trick. This would have been heresy in an earlier era, when politicians considered balanced budgets almost a God-given commandment. But as the Depression dragged on, deficit spending began to look downright seemly.

In Keynes's theory, demand was the engine of growth. Henry Ford would hire engineers and designers and assembly-line workers only if he believed families were sitting at their dinner tables planning their next car purchase. Arrow Shirts would hire sewers for its garment factories—and buy the cloth made by other workers—only if it thought men and women were flush enough to replace their old clothes. According to this feedback loop, the key to business investment—which in turn meant job creation and overall economic health—was demand, which was just another word for consumption. Only the prospect of future profits would motivate companies to invest.

In his *Treatise on Money,* published in 1930, Keynes put it this way:

> It has been usual to think of the accumulated wealth of the world as having been painfully built up out of that voluntary abstinence of individuals from the immediate enjoyment of consumption which we call thrift. But it should be obvious that mere abstinence is not enough by itself to build cities or drain fens.... It is enterprise which builds and improves the world's possessions.... If enterprise is afoot, wealth accumulates whatever may

be happening to thrift; and if enterprise is asleep,
wealth decays whatever thrift may be doing.

Thus, thrift may be the handmaid and nurse of
enterprise. But equally she may not. And, perhaps,
even usually she is not. For enterprise is connected
with thrift not directly but at one remove; and the link
which should join them is frequently missing. For the
engine which drives enterprise is not thrift, but profit.

This was a shocking reversal of traditional theory, which
held that savings created the pool of funds that made business investment possible. Keynes argued the opposite: in a
sophisticated financial system, where money moves quickly
between players and banks can even borrow from other banks
to finance their loans, companies have ready access to funds.
Thus, Keynes said, it is investment that leads to savings, since
only investment (and the prospect of higher profit) creates
jobs, which increases incomes, which leads to higher savings.
This idea — that higher savings lowers the economy's total
output (and thus, that thrift is a private virtue but a public
vice) — became known as the "paradox of thrift."

During a Depression, especially, the tendency to save was
disastrous in Keynes's view. He wasn't alone; academics and
businesspeople fretted about consumers' reluctance to spend.
More often than not, of course, it was because people didn't
have the money to buy in the first place. Americans weren't
hoarding their money; they simply didn't have any. In 1929,
private citizens had saved $3.8 billion out of their annual
incomes. By 1932, that number had fallen to zero, and Americans were actually spending down the savings they'd put
away in better years. (Or they were taking out loans just to
get by. Between 1929 and 1931, cash lending, often by shady
payday-loan outfits, nearly doubled.) Many workers too had
been stung by the earlier orgy of easy credit and reckless

spending; once the economy turned down, unemployed and underemployed Americans watched men from the bank come to claim the homes and cars and washing machines they'd bought "on time." Those with money *were* afraid to spend, and with good reason—in a time when one in four Americans was out of work, no one knew when the pink slip might land on his own desk.

Still, in Keynes's consumption-driven theory, thrift was the enemy of economic growth. "Whenever you save five shillings, you put a man out of work for a day," he pronounced in a 1931 radio address to his fellow Britons. He urged them to set aside their fears. "You will do yourselves good—for never were things so cheap, cheap beyond your dreams. Lay in a stock of household linen, of sheets and blankets to satisfy all your needs. And have the added joy that you are increasing employment, adding to the wealth of the country because you are setting on foot useful activities, bringing a chance and a hope to Lancashire, Yorkshire, and Belfast."

Keynes published his most influential book, *The General Theory of Employment, Interest, and Money,* in 1936. It elaborated on all of these ideas, with the benefit of some hindsight on the Depression. On the paradox of thrift, he wrote that "up to the point where full employment prevails, the growth of capital depends not at all on a low propensity to consume but is, on the contrary, held back by it." In other words, thrift doesn't always promote economic growth; in a faltering economy, it holds it back.

In 1932, Americans brought their anger and desperation to the polls, and flipped leadership into the hands of the Democrats, Franklin Delano Roosevelt beat Hoover by a landslide, and his party took over both houses of Congress with large margins. Keynes's message resonated with

FDR's policy experts; men like Federal Reserve Chairman Marriner Eccles, the lawyer and later Supreme Court justice Felix Frankfurter, and the influential economist Alvin Hansen boosted Keynes's profile. Frankfurter even set up a meeting between Keynes and President Roosevelt at the White House in 1934. (Neither man came away particularly impressed; FDR later told his labor secretary, Frances Perkins, that Keynes "left a whole rigamarole of figures. He must be a mathematician rather than a political economist." Keynes countered by telling Perkins he had "supposed the president was more literate, economically speaking.")

FDR was also torn between Keynes's prescriptions for deficit spending and his own desire to balance the budget. He never wholly supported the idea of massive public-works spending. Instead, he viewed it as a necessary evil to cure rampant unemployment, and Keynesian theory became the backbone of many of Roosevelt's New Deal programs. In the first hundred days of his administration, FDR and the Democrats passed fourteen major pieces of legislation that became the foundation of the New Deal. The National Recovery Administration and the Agriculture Adjustment Act propped up prices; agencies like the Work Projects Administration and the Civilian Conservation Corps put millions of Americans back to work so they'd have the money to start spending again.

Controversy remains about the efficacy of the New Deal. It relieved suffering by bolstering employment—between 1933 and 1937, unemployment dropped from 25 percent to 14 percent—and creating much-needed protections for Americans with programs like Social Security and unemployment insurance. Congress also created the Federal Deposit Insurance Corporation, guaranteeing bank deposits of up to $2,500 and restoring Americans' confidence in savings banks. The economy as a whole improved for a few years. But a new recession in 1937 pushed the unemployment rate back up to 19 percent.

Still, the 1930s marked the beginning of a long-term enshrinement of consumers as the new saviors of the American economy—the global economy, even. It displaced the old cosmology that put corporations at the center of the economic universe. "I believe we are at the threshold of a fundamental change in our popular economic thought," Roosevelt said during his 1932 presidential campaign, predicting that "in the future we are going to think less about the producer and more about the consumer." Policymakers and economists took the message to heart, and so did business leaders, retailers, marketers, and consumers themselves.

This was a radical shift. Consumption had been reframed: shopping wasn't just about personal gratification anymore; it was a patriotic act with national consequences. Roosevelt's National Recovery Administration, the agency created to get the economy back on its feet during the Depression, trumpeted the new worldview in its campaigns to revive American business: "When you buy cigars you help provide income for farmers, labor, salesmen, dealers, and yourself. Buy now," its display cards read. The NRA also gave consumers seats on various advisory committees alongside representatives from business and labor.

WHAT FINALLY PULLED the country out of Depression, however, was not Roosevelt's New Deal or economic theories. It was another war.

By the late 1930s, Japanese aggression against China, and Hitler's incursions into Austria, Czechoslovakia, and Poland, had led to full-scale war in Europe and Asia. At the outset, the United States maintained military neutrality, but it lent its financial and diplomatic support to the Allied powers of

Britain and France. Once again, the need for weapons, munitions, and other supplies lit up American factories, offering millions of workers their first steady employment in as much as a decade.

After Japanese planes bombed Pearl Harbor on December 7, 1941, and the United States officially entered the conflict, production demands skyrocketed. American factories couldn't seem to make enough airplanes, trucks, tanks, ships, guns, bullets, and explosives, along with tents, uniforms, and other wartime provisions. Years of overcapacity and oversupply gave way to the prospect of colossal shortages, and Roosevelt had to figure out how to minimize them.

Wilson and his deputies had relied on patriotism and voluntarism to compel ordinary Americans to trim their spending and conserve resources during World War I. But the United States had changed. During the twenties, many Americans surrendered to the pleasure principle: sexual liberation, easy credit, instant access to goods. The Depression may have interrupted the upward arc of prosperity, but as the economy improved in the 1930s, Americans came to believe those hungry years had been an anomaly. They were eager to live well again. And now they had the money to do so—outfitting the Allies, and then American forces, put money back in every worker's pocket. The pent-up demand of all these newly thriving Americans convinced FDR that the only way to enforce restraint was through mandatory rationing. He and his minions set out to persuade Americans that thrift was once again back in style. Failing that, he would simply compel them to follow along.

The president authorized the War Production Board, the agency tasked with coordinating the flow of wartime resources, to ration consumer goods, and early in 1942, the WPB's Office of Price Administration began limiting access to rubber, sugar, meat, canned goods, coffee, butter, and other products.

In books and pamphlets, the OPA's Consumer Division made the case for rationing. One of them, *The Consumer Goes to War: A Guide to Victory on the Home Front,* proclaimed that "democracy lives or dies in our home towns."

"Our rich land of 'plenty' has become a land of 'scarcities,'" continued the author Caroline Ware, one of the country's leading wartime consumer advocates. "We have had too little money to buy the goods we were able to produce; now we have too much. We have been a wasteful people; overnight we must become savers. We have struggled to 'keep up with the Joneses'; now both we and the Joneses must 'keep down.'...We must fight today for survival. As individuals we must give up our accustomed ease, perhaps walk long and wearying distances, face actual hardships, empty larders, cold houses. In fact, to exist we must learn to be good consumers. At the same time, by being good consumers we make our contribution to the war effort."

Women were pressed into action. Volunteers held community canning workshops and once again asked housewives to sign the Consumer's Victory Pledge. It read: "As a consumer, in the total defense of democracy, I will do my part to make my home, my community, my country, ready, efficient, and strong. I will buy carefully. I will take good care of the things I have. I will waste nothing."

Winifred Raushenbush, a social activist and writer, penned *How to Dress in Wartime,* a breezy handbook for enduring sacrifice with style. "[Chairman of the War Production Board] Donald M. Nelson...tells us to expect severe privation before the war is over. This does not mean that you must become dowdy; not even if clothes are rationed, as they almost certainly will be eventually. There is neither virtue nor patriotism in dowdiness, in or out of uniform. Nobody wants it, not even the big bad bureaucrats in Washington." She recommended "summer austerity frocks"—dresses made with a minimum of fabric—and suggested that "because the number of colors, shades, and prints available will, in time, be somewhat reduced, it would be a very sound idea for you to collect a few accessories in colors that are especially becoming to you.... Color in clothes will add a great deal to general morale."

Posters and pamphlets ballyhooed the effort with the slogan "Use it up, Wear it out, Make it do, or Do without." One placard showed a housewife with a sassy look in her eyes. "I'm Out to Lick Runaway Prices," she declared. "Let's All Follow the 7-Key Plan to Hold Prices Down":

1. Buy and hold War Bonds
2. Pay willingly our share of taxes
3. Provide adequate life insurance and savings for our future
4. Reduce our debts as much as possible
5. Buy only what we need and make what we have last longer
6. Follow ration rules and price ceilings
7. Cooperate with our government's wage stabilization program.

The WPB was especially keen to limit consumption of rubber, and it was brought under ration rules for the first time in 1941. The Japanese controlled much of the Pacific, cutting off 97 percent of rubber imports to the United States. Secretary of the Interior Harold Ickes organized a massive rubber scrap drive. One of the first things he did was requisition all the rubber floor mats in his own government office building. According to the historian Richard Lingeman, "This brought a bristling reply from the Buildings Department, which pointed out that it owned the mats, so they were not Ickes' to donate; besides, they were needed to keep people from slipping on the marble floors. The next time Ickes was at the White House, he spied a rubber floor mat, rolled it up, and gave it to his chauffeur with instructions to drop it off at the nearest rubber salvage depot."

There was plenty of petroleum to go around, but the WPB rationed it, too, to reduce wear and tear on rubber tires. Speed limits were reset at thirty-five miles per hour. And the pastime of pleasure driving, so recently taken up by Americans in the new age of the automobile, was banned outright in January 1943. Cars should be used only when absolutely necessary, Roosevelt declared. Government snoops recorded the license plate numbers in the parking lots of nightclubs and racetracks and then threatened the car owners with confiscation of their gas ration stickers.

Rules, however, beget rule breakers. No matter how loud or how ubiquitous were the calls for patriotic self-denial, a black market, sometimes called "Mr. Black," thrived around each rationed item. Some of these markets were controlled by gangs and organized crime rings; others were small operations run by otherwise legitimate businesses, like a butcher putting aside some extra meat for a favorite customer. Authorities investigating these crimes found everything from counterfeited ration cards to back-of-the-truck cash sales of rationed foods. A study published after the war revealed that one in five businesses received warnings about illicit dealings, and one in fifteen actually faced charges. By the summer of 1944, more than one thousand people had been convicted of illegal gasoline sales. In answer to a Gallup Poll question near the end of the war, 25 percent of respondents said they thought it was okay to patronize black marketeers occasionally.

FDR knew what was going on. In his 1944 State of the Union address, delivered during a moment of high frustration and war fatigue, he admonished the people. "If there ever was a time to subordinate individual or group selfishness to the national good, that time is now. Disunity at home—bickering, self-seeking partisanship, stoppage of work, inflation, business as usual, politics as usual, luxury as usual...these are the influences which can undermine the morale of the brave men ready to die at the front for us....Overconfidence and complacency are among our deadliest of all enemies."

IN THE FACE of wartime realities, Keynes himself recognized that consumers needed to pull back. When World War II loomed in Europe, he knew government spending would become the engine for growth, and that private citizens in a war economy—or any full-employment economy, for that matter—actually needed to save in order to put the brakes on inflation and finance new investment. He designed a plan for compulsory savings in England, and wrote, in a 1939 *London Times* article introducing the plan, "In the new circumstances, it [savings] will again serve a social purpose and private prudence will coincide with the public interest." To Keynes, thrift was only anathema in certain circumstances. In a robust economy, he believed, citizens should find a healthy balance between spending and saving.

In the United States, there was no compulsory savings plan, only a very successful effort to once again sell war bonds. As in the First World War, the bonds not only financed the military campaign, but also soaked up excess income that might otherwise be spent on consumer goods (a situation that would have sparked inflation and raised demand for scarce raw materials). Ads for the bonds were ubiquitous, commandeering the airwaves and newspaper space, and period graphics are instantly recognizable today. Norman Rockwell contributed illustrations to the drives and Irving Berlin wrote the song "Any Bonds Today?," which became the theme for the National Defense Savings Program.

The Hollywood War Activities Committee put together a tour called "Stars Over America," sending 337 celebrities out to drum up bond sales. The German-born Marlene Dietrich cajoled thousands into offering their savings in the fight against her home country; Hedy Lamarr offered kisses for $25,000 and raised $17 million. As Bette Davis boarded the train to begin her tour, she tartly offered, "I think it is outrageous that movie stars have to wheedle and beg people into buying bonds to help their country. But if that's the way it is, I'm going to squeeze all I can out of everyone." Over the course of eight loan drives, U.S. citizens purchased more than $156 billion in war bonds—worth roughly $1.8 trillion today.

But unlike those in World War I, the bond sales weren't harnessed to any kind of long-term thrift campaign. Quite the opposite, actually. Instead, following the harrowing experience of the Depression and the rise of Keynesian ideas about the importance of demand, economists fretted over the possibility that Americans would save their way into another postwar depression. As had happened before, they stirred up excitement about postwar spending, reminding the folks at home that, without the stimulus of $250-million-per-day military expenditures, the fate of the U.S. economy would be in their hands. It was a message that Americans took to heart, paving the way for a world defined by shopping malls, shiny kitchen appliances, and the dream of a two-car garage.

Chapter 6

Lively Golf Balls and Two-Ford Freedom: The Postwar Years

In September 1943, almost two years after the United States entered World War II, the department store Macy's bought a full-page ad in the *New York Daily News,* with the words "What We're Fighting For" splashed across the top in big letters.

Ostensibly, it was a pitch for the Third War Loan Drive. But instead of trumpeting the role that thrift played in winning the war, the retailer promised a different set of rewards for the purchase of all those bonds and savings stamps. "We're defending Democracy....But we're also fighting for a lot of little things," it said.

> We're fighting to be able to take home dozens of bars of chocolate—and come back for more....We want to be permitted to take a taxi to Brooklyn....And what fun to step up to a drug counter and buy a tube of toothpaste—without swapping it for an old wrinkled tube!...
>
> We men are fighting for the right to have cuffs on our pants, or leave them off—as the fancy strikes us....We want to be permitted to buy thirty pairs of shoes a year—even if we can only afford three!...And

how about the return of those lively golf balls that'll go
a mile[?]

"Little things, yes," the retailer gushed, "but each one a
definite part of American life!"

It was a masterly piece of ad copy. What reader, deprived of
those treats — chocolate bars and taxicabs — during the long
years of the Great Depression and World War II wouldn't have
found his appetite whetted for the coming days of prosperity
and peace?

In fact, the Macy's ad was typical of appeals made in the
wartime years. Even before the conflict ended, leaders of
all stripes were wringing their hands over the possibility of
a postwar depression. When fighting ceased, there'd be no
more orders for tanks and uniforms — and, on top of that,
millions of young soldiers would return home to reclaim the
civilian jobs they'd once held, leading to high unemployment. Diagnosticians predicted a long and painful transition
back to a peacetime economy.

To forestall the seemingly inevitable, politicians, Wall
Streeters, and corporate marketing departments called for a
massive adjustment in the American economy: if war was no
longer to be the engine of prosperity, they said, then consumers would have to pick up the slack. Taking a page from
history's playbook, they framed spending as an economic
imperative — the only way to avoid another devastating
depression was for Americans to open their wallets and climb
aboard the Consumer Express.

"Only if we have large demands can we expect large production," wrote the economist Robert Nathan in his 1944
book, *Mobilizing for Abundance*. "Ever-increasing consumption
on the part of our people [is] ... one of the prime requisites for
prosperity. Mass consumption is essential to the success of a
system of mass production."

Like Macy's, advertisers prepped Americans for the all-out shopping spree that would arrive with the peace. The rationing and recycling that consumers were enduring was just temporary, they were told; after the war, manufacturers would reengineer their machines and workforces to produce the cars and vacuum cleaners of the future. "Ordnance Today, Washers Tomorrow," the Easy Washing Machine Company promised. A magazine spread for Royal typewriters, under the headline "What This War Is All About," told Americans that a victory against fascism would give them the right to "once more walk into any store in the land and buy anything you want."

And when the war ended in 1945, shoppers flooded into stores for the silk ties and steaks they'd long denied themselves. With veterans' benefits, many young families bought single-family homes in the suburbs and then outfitted them with drapes, sofas, bedroom sets, barbecue grills, and lawn mowers. In 1945, Americans drove 69,500 new cars off dealers' lots. The following year, the number leapt to 2.1 million and hit 6.7 million in 1950. These cars weren't cheap, either; even low-priced Chevys and Fords cost about $1,300, or nearly half an average family's annual income.

Federal programs greased the transition to a consumer economy. The Employment Act of 1946 explicitly charged the government with responsibility for promoting "maximum employment, production, and purchasing power." Through innovations like the GI Bill and the Federal Housing Administration, Washington guaranteed new mortgages and set off the biggest residential construction boom of the twentieth century.

Thanks to the combination of public initiatives and private spending, the savings rate plunged from a wartime high of 26 percent in 1944 to just 4 percent in 1947 and the much-feared recession never arrived. One key lesson of the period was this: the shopping patterns of ordinary Americans could exert a decisive influence on economic trends. "Nothing is more important than the inclinations of the consumer," the editors of *Fortune* wrote in the early fifties. "His 'habits' have accordingly become a major preoccupation of American economists."

George Katona typified this new breed of economists and market researchers. These professionals tracked consumers' purchases and expectations, interviewing them about which appliances they planned to buy in the coming year and whether they preferred shredded wheat or oatmeal for breakfast. Katona had arrived in the United States from Germany in 1933, a Jewish refugee with a background in psychology and economics. After a brief career on Wall Street, Katona taught at the New School for Social Research. In 1946, he was appointed the director of the University of Michigan's Survey Research Center, where he combined his academic interests in the emerging field of consumer behavior. Under Katona, the center's monthly index of consumer confidence garnered terrific influence among corporate executives and policymakers. Even now it's one of our most closely watched measures of economic health or malaise.

According to surveys conducted in the early 1940s, Americans felt grateful that wartime wages allowed them to sock away cash. As Katona later wrote, respondents said they would use those reserves for "legitimate" uses, such as a down payment on a house or helping them get through another depression. They didn't expect to spend down their savings on daily living expenses or even for automobiles and household appliances.

But surveys done after the war revealed a new mood in America. "There was change from war to peace," he observed.

"A survey conducted early in 1946 revealed that the desire to spend and to acquire consumer goods had become much stronger and the desire to save weaker."

Katona recorded these attitudes and he celebrated them, too. He painted an image of Americans as thoughtful and optimistic consumers who, through their intelligent analysis of market conditions and their own needs, would use their spending power to moderate inflation and keep the economy on an upward trajectory. Americans' confidence in the future, he wrote, represented "the heart of the psychological climate in which prosperity flourished."

This optimism helped fuel the spending boom of the following years. In a 1952 survey, even as the Korean War raged on, 56 percent of Americans surveyed by Katona's group said that "financially, we're having good times now" (only 26 percent said times were bad). According to one interview subject, a leather harness cutter in a small town in Georgia, "Farmers have greater income than ever before—they are using more machinery and producing more at a lower cost. Everyone seems to have more money—wages generally seem to be higher and a person can buy most anything he wants. There are no big shortages. Another thing is the amount of building that's going on now. This shows that people either have money or credit and either one indicates good times."

The Federal Reserve's 1953 Survey of Consumer Finances found that consumers had "a confident attitude concerning their financial positions" and planned to purchase automobiles and "major household durable goods in large volume this year." Spending on those durable goods—large electronics like television sets and washers and dryers—were especially significant. While spending on food, clothing, and rent were always fairly steady, it was the consumption of nonessential home goods that economists believed would propel the economy's robust upward trend.

These survey results indicated a profound shift in the American value system. While the Victorians had maintained a distinction between "productive" and "consumptive" spending, that distinction was irrelevant by the end of World War II. Economists and politicians no longer recognized any difference between the purchase of a mattress and the purchase of a fur coat; both transactions contributed to the gross national product and kept employees on the payroll. A dollar spent on one was the same as a dollar spent on another. The most important thing was that those dollars be spent.

Indeed, Paul Mazur, a partner at Lehman Brothers, argued that a rising standard of living was the critical driver of the American economy. "We are a nation that *consumes* its way to property, security, prosperity, and freedom," he wrote in his 1953 book, *The Standards We Raise*. "Moreover, we are compelled by the dynamic character of economic relationships to continue to do so at an ever-increasing rate. Our society can keep itself stable only by *not* stabilizing its standards of living. Our economy leaves us no alternative to *spending* our way to prosperity, to *elevating* ourselves into security."

The advertising industry had already become adept at selling products; now merchants and government agencies called on it to sell an economic philosophy that placed consumption at its center. According to the critic Vance Packard, a forty-five-voice chorus in Detroit "cried out 500 times a week over television and radio: 'Buy days mean paydays...and paydays mean better days....So buy, buy!...Something that you need today.'" Meanwhile, the Advertising Council launched a campaign to create "Confidence in a Growing America." And when young women requested *Brides* magazine's handbook for newlyweds, they were told that by shopping for brand-name products to outfit their new homes, "you are helping to build greater security for the industries of this country...what you buy and how you buy is very vital in your new life—and to our whole American way of living."

This message came from all sides, even from those who were supposed to help young families prepare for their future. In 1959, a syndicated personal-finance columnist admonished readers that "if you decide to save, pay off debts, you help slow down business. If you decide to buy cars and appliances enthusiastically, you put a glow on the entire country." And in 1960, President Eisenhower told Americans that continued prosperity required consumers to "perform their economic function."

The elevation of the American consumer wasn't just a gambit to keep the economy moving forward. It was an essential component of the reigning anti-Soviet political ideology as well. Less than a year after Germany surrendered to Allied forces, Winston Churchill referred to the "Iron Curtain" that had descended between the Soviet Union and the West. The relationship between the United States and the Soviet Union calcified into a new kind of conflict, a cold war fought out through proxies, veiled threats, and a fast-moving arms race. In the context of this war, politicians and eminent thinkers conflated democracy with capitalism, and capitalism with consumerism, until, through a sleight of logic, consumerism itself was widely identified with democracy. The two were one and the same. According to Paul Mazur and much of the political and business establishment, the consumer lifestyle was an expression of freedom and a critical bulwark against Communism.

"The world is apparently choosing between the ideology of the slave state and the ideology upon which that American way of life is based," Mazur wrote. "The slave state has given as the fulfillment of its economic promises an unbroken period of low standards of living. Concurrently, America has given its free citizens the opportunity to win and to hold, with infrequent breaks of business depression, a standard of material well-being that offers an average family what only the aristocracy of old would have had as its privileged right. It is a standard of living that many of the bureaucrats of the Politburo would probably be happy to accept in trade for their own."

Or, as William Levitt, the founder of the new suburban Levittowns, put it more succinctly, "No man who owns his own lot and house can be a Communist. He has too much to do."

ALONG WITH THE political and economic rationales for the new religion of consumerism was an emotional one: pleasure was not only permissible, but psychologically healthy. The early Americans had imagined life as a long grind of duty and faith, with rewards deferred until a glorious afterlife. That view was largely obsolete by the middle of the twentieth century. The rewards of hard work and worldly success were meant to be savored in this life—in a European vacation, a condo in the Sun Belt, three-olive martinis, a gleaming Chrysler in the garage.

Prominent psychologists like Ernest Dichter and the felicitously named Smiley Blanton assured their clients and a broader American audience that consumption was a means of creative expression and self-discovery. Puritanism was old-fashioned and outdated, they said, backing up their claims in the vocabulary made popular by Sigmund Freud. Self-denial was evidence of "repression"; thrift was "neurotic" and suggested that a person was incapable of enjoying life.

The Austrian émigré Ernest Dichter—like Katona, an exiled Jew who embraced the open spirit of his adopted country—used the new technique of "depth interviews" to reveal individuals' subconscious associations with products.

In one of his first American assignments, for Ivory soap, he showed up at YMCA gyms and canvassed women about why they take baths. In the process, he uncovered an erotic element in his subjects' experience, later writing that baths were "one of the few occasions when the puritanical American was allowed to caress himself or herself." At the Institute for Motivational Research, the marketing firm Dichter founded in 1946, he built a thriving business interpreting consumer behavior for a roster of other clients, including Chrysler, Esso (now Exxon), and Dupont.

Dichter viewed cars, washing machines, cigarettes, and frozen dinners as articulations of Joe and Jane America's hopes and dreams. Shopping was a creative activity, therapeutic even, a way for men and women to understand themselves and show the world who they really were. "Buying is often an excellent way to get out of a rut," he wrote in his 1947 book *The Psychology of Everyday Living*. Thirteen years later, he told his readers that "every time we go out, we do so really to prove to ourselves that we have the power to express our innermost desires by the selection of a specific type of merchandise."

Dichter saw that Americans maintained an inner resistance to the message of liberatory consumption. Thanks to the tradition of Puritan morality and the official valorization of thrift and restraint, they held on to an atavistic shame when it came to matters of self-indulgence. Dichter exhorted citizens not to be weighed down by what he called the "burden of the good life": "We are ashamed of our thick carpets, good food and enormous cars.... What has become imperative for us is to revise our morality. Hedonism, as defended by the old Greeks, has to be brought to the surface again. We have to learn to forget the guilt of original sin.... We have to learn to accept the morality of the good life." He told his followers, "In the promotion and advertising of many items, nothing is more important than to encourage this tendency to greater inner freedom and to give moral permission to enjoy life through the use of an item, whether it is . . . a speedboat, a hi-fi set, or a sports jacket."

Freud's disciple Smiley Blanton, a pop-psychology pioneer who had been analyzed by the great man himself, equated spending money with loosening up, dropping inhibitions, and saying "no" to the airless repressions of American Calvinism. In 1959, Blanton plugged his vision in the book *Now or Never: The Promise of the Middle Years,* aimed squarely at well-to-do Americans who were searching for some kind of psychic emancipation.

"Are you making life drab by denying yourself or your family ordinary pleasures on the grounds of being prudent?" he asked, adding that the miser "always has an array of arguments to justify his penny-pinching. A depression is at hand. The value of the dollar is steadily shrinking. His wife doesn't know how to manage money. His children are potential spendthrifts. If all else fails, he will fall back on the ancient and incontestable statement: 'Money doesn't grow on trees, you know!'"

To Blanton, thrift signified deprivation and uptightness, a triumph of the authoritarian superego over the freewheeling id. He explained stinginess with a watered-down version of Freud's anal retentiveness theory. The "condition" originated in early potty training, which Blanton called "a child's first serious conflict with authority." If parents were too harsh or severe, or even too lavish with their praise, during this delicate process, he said, the child resents their intrusion and refuses to cooperate. "He will delay, he will withhold, he will not 'give.'" These tactics become transferred, later in life, to the adult's dealings with money, operating as "invisible forces . . . depriving him of happiness."

Blanton said he didn't advocate profligacy or carelessness

when it came to spending. "But there is something both pathetic and exasperating about people who refuse to live up to anything approaching their means. They are really fugitives from living."

THE BURNING QUESTION, for leaders in every field, was how to encourage Americans to drop those fugitive ways and surrender to the enticements of the consumer society.

Part of this transformation was natural, an outgrowth of pure demographics. When soldiers returned from the war, they flocked to city halls and churches with the sweethearts they'd left behind. Marriage rates skyrocketed after 1945, and the baby boom that started about nine months after the armistice sent pram factories and infant-clothes manufacturers into overdrive.

All these new families translated into demand for new homes and the sofas and bedroom suites to furnish them. The construction and furniture industries mushroomed. Suburban developments popped up in former hayfields, connected to cities by new highways that, in turn, increased automobile sales. The rise of suburbia had some unintended consequences too. Women who'd left their cities, friends, and extended families spoke of feeling lonely and isolated. Shopping came to replace the constant socializing that went along with crowded urban living. When the *Chicago Tribune* conducted a marketing study in the 1950s, one third of the women surveyed called their shopping trips "fundamentally social." The supermarket manager and the salesgirl behind the counter at the dress shop in the new shopping center became substitute friends for women who were otherwise confined to the house most of the day.

In a 1956 television ad called "Two-Ford Freedom," an attractive young wife in a fitted dress and pearls talks on the phone with a friend and agrees to meet her at two o'clock. Then she tells the camera, "Three weeks ago, I couldn't have accepted that invitation. Like so many people, we live in the suburbs, and Dave needs the car every day for business. When he was gone, I was practically a prisoner in my own home....But that's all changed now. Three weeks ago, we bought another Ford....It's a whole new way of life. Now I'm free to go anywhere, do anything, see anybody any time I want to."

Prosperity also drove an increasing emphasis on style. In the 1800s and through the first few decades of the 1900s, corporations divided their customers into two markets: the "class" market, for the few families that could afford the very best, and an undifferentiated lower market, which consisted of families who needed only functional products and cared little for style. That model shifted in the 1940s and 1950s. Thanks to fast-rising wages and the redistribution of incomes, more and more Americans rose up into the middle class. They had money to spare; now they too could keep up with the latest styles. The "mass" market emerged, as manufacturers catered to families that demanded both style and affordability. The editors of *Fortune* wrote in 1955, "Suburbia is becoming the most important single market in the country. No longer does the city dweller, male or female, set the styles. It is the suburbanite who starts the mass fashion—for children, hard-tops, culottes, dungarees, vodka martinis, outdoor barbecues, functional furniture, picture windows and costume jewelry."

A new word also began to appear regularly in the pages of trade journals and on the lips of politicians and economists: *obsolescence*. Civic leaders worried that Americans would satiate all of their wants and needs and that they'd have no appetite or room for the new goods rolling off assembly lines. Fears of saturation dominated business periodicals. The answer to this problem, many believed, was to make sure consumers discarded and replaced their purchases as quickly as possible.

Obsolescence could take a few different forms. Functional obsolescence meant innovations that brought real improvement, like better car engines or longer-lasting lightbulbs. This was simply called progress and no one quibbled with that. But more and more manufacturers, taking a cue from the auto industry, also used fashion as a form of obsolescence. They promised pizzazz, style, novelty, *excitement*. Is your wife bored at home? Perhaps she's just tired of her old appliances. Buy her a new refrigerator in pink or olive green! Furniture retailers encouraged women to redecorate their houses every few years and introduced new colors and collections at a faster and faster pace. "Trade in now and get the latest styles," they shouted in their advertisements. Menswear companies retooled their cuts and fabrics twice a year to keep up with the cycles that were already standard in the world of women's fashion.

More controversial was corporations' new practice of building in shorter lives for the goods they sold, a process exposed by the social critic Vance Packard in his 1960 book *The Waste Makers.* He quotes a story in the magazine *Home Furnishings Daily,* explaining how companies were using cheaper materials and reducing the thickness of some of the plating in their products in order to cut costs and ensure that their goods would wear out faster. They designed washing machines, toasters, carpets, and television sets not for durability—the onetime ideal of craftsmen everywhere—but to fall apart after a predetermined number of years.

In factories and workrooms across the country, this development was hotly debated. The journal *Design News* printed letters from engineers and industrial designers who objected to the new trend. One reader wrote to say that "it is even a crime against the natural law of God in that we would waste that which He has given us."

But many business owners and professionals rationalized the trend in predictable ways. One executive wrote an article with the subtitle "If Merchandise Does Not Wear Out Faster, Factories Will Be Idle, People Unemployed." A leading designer named Brooke Stevens told the *Management Review* that obsolescence "isn't organized waste. It's a sound contribution to the American economy."

The marketing analyst Victor Lebow summed up the official ethos of the era when he wrote, in 1955, "Our enormously productive economy...demands that we make consumption our way of life, that we convert the buying and use of goods into rituals, that we seek our spiritual satisfaction, our ego satisfaction, in consumption. We need things consumed, burned up, worn out, replaced, and discarded at an ever-increasing rate."

FINALLY, HELPING THESE developments along was a revolution in consumer finance: the introduction of bank credit cards. While retailers had long offered credit and installment programs, Diners Club in 1950 launched the first charge card that could be used at multiple restaurants and retailers in place of cash. American Express and Bank of America's BankAmericard (later called Visa) followed in 1958, no doubt propelled by early studies indicating that Americans spent more money when paying with "plastic" than with cash. Bank of America attracted its first customers by simply mailing cards to sixty thousand residents of Fresno, California. It enticed them to join the program by offering a new kind of "revolving" credit that allowed them to maintain a balance and pay off purchases over time with minimum payments and high interest rates.

By the end of the 1960s, 29 million Americans had credit cards tucked into their wallets. Dichter's Institute for Motivational Research explained the appeal of the little plastic rectangles: "Credit cards are symbols of status. They are also magic, since they serve as money when one temporarily has no money. They thus become symbols of *power* and inexhaustible potency."

Still, it would be a mistake to assume that the public unquestioningly embraced postwar consumerism. At best, many individuals felt ambivalent about the pressure to spend, spend, spend. George Katona's surveys revealed that even as late as 1956, 33 percent of all Americans believed installment buying was "a bad idea." Of that group, about a third simply avoided all forms of debt, telling interviewers that "one should never borrow."

My mother's father belonged to this group. He refused to apply for a charge card in the 1950s until my grandmother insisted that they had to build up a credit profile for the house she one day hoped to buy in the suburbs. She got herself a Macy's account and charged a suite of living room furniture, much to her husband's dismay (he paid it off in full when the bill came). But the dream of owning a house never arrived. My grandfather wasn't willing to take on a mortgage, so they stayed until their deaths in the two-bedroom apartment they'd bought in Queens for $800 in cash in 1952.

Still, characters like my grandfather—the frugal, cautious men and women who were once a staple of didactic novels, advice books, and sermons—largely disappeared from popular culture. The stolid, thrifty heroes of the past, like Ben Franklin and Horatio Alger's Ragged Dick, were replaced by the comic figure of the penny-pincher. Disney's Scrooge McDuck, Donald's stingy Scottish uncle, made his debut in

1947. Jack Benny's radio and TV skinflint got some of the highest ratings (and longest laughs) of the era. Then there was the abstemious Fred Mertz, husband of Ethel and neighbor of Lucy and Desi Arnaz on the hit 1950s show *I Love Lucy*. Fred's complaints about Ethel's spending, and the arguments they had every time she asked him for money, were easy laugh lines in a period when opinion leaders and many Americans held up a free-spending, pleasure-seeking lifestyle as the ideal.

George Katona did find that Americans stubbornly held on to their belief in saving for emergencies, retirement, and their children's educations. But that didn't always translate into growing bank balances. In most surveys, more Americans said they would save money than actually accomplished that goal. Rising incomes—spread out more evenly than at any other time in the nation's history—allowed families at all class levels to disburse their dollars more freely than in the past and to join in the celebration of an easier, more leisurely future. A 1952 TV ad for Edison Electric showed a mother and daughter ironing their laundry in their suburban basement.

The daughter says, "Mother, wouldn't it be slick if we had an electric ironer, like Sally's mother has?"

"Of course it would," Mother responds. "And I'm looking forward to having an electric dryer. Just think—then we'd have a complete electric laundry."

"Wheee...good-bye old wash day!"

WHETHER AMERICANS CONSCIOUSLY responded to the message of patriotic consumption or whether they were simply happy to have more cash in their pockets and more credit to their names, one thing is clear: by and large, they joined the consumer society. Total household debt jumped from $9.8 billion at the close of 1946, the year after the war ended, to

$61.2 billion in 1960—an increase of 624 percent. Incomes also rose during that time, but only by 111 percent. More and more Americans were joining the comfortable middle class, but they were amassing debt at an even higher rate.

"Everybody was trying to achieve middle-class status," Grace Crawford, a housewife in suburban Washington State, remembered in the book *The Fifties: A Women's Oral History*. "Everybody had to have the same things everybody else had.... We went on the same kind of vacations, read the same books, we even had the same bubble hairdos."

As if to punctuate the postwar status quo, the forty-nine-year run of National Thrift Week came to an end in 1966. The National Thrift Committee, an offshoot of the YMCA and the organization behind the saving celebration, was closing down because of "lack of money and a decline in membership," according to the *Chicago Tribune*. The story continued: "The board of directors found that the program of promoting National Thrift Week, during the third week of October, had lost substantial support during the last few years because of new advertising and marketing concepts." Among the casualties was the group's annual essay contest.

Banks and schools also began to withdraw their longtime support of classroom thrift programs. In 1964, two Rhode Island banks announced that a yearlong study of school savings curricula "showed declining interest in the program and a failure in its objective of promoting thrift habits." One of the banks, the Providence Institution for Savings, found that "only 18,000 of 56,000 school savings accounts on its books showed a deposit within the last year." In high schools, as few as 3 percent of students made regular deposits in their accounts. As a result, the two banks were discontinuing the program. They weren't alone; by the end of the 1960s, the school savings movement had largely expired.

Mainstream advocacy of frugality was coming to an end.

Amid the bloom of postwar prosperity, thrift and self-restraint went underground. No doubt millions of Americans still lived cheaply, out of both necessity and choice. But for the most part they did so quietly. Thrift was no longer broadcast as an American ideal. Calls for this virtue could still be heard, but mostly as salvos issued from the edges of American society.

Dissent at the Margins and the Center

It's easy now to look back and see how our modern consumer culture crystallized during the three decades after World War II. We've come to think of the mid-1940s through the mid-1960s as a time of conformity. But even during those years of "the good life," dissenters recognized an underside to affluence and economic growth.

John Kenneth Galbraith published his mournful critique *The Affluent Society* in 1958, arguing that Americans had focused so much on private gratification that they had all but ignored public needs. Their schools were failing, their parks were overgrown, and their inner cities were desolate and dangerous. Other critics—such as Vance Packard (in *The Hidden Persuaders* and *The Waste Makers*) and Rachel Carson (whose book *Silent Spring* marked the beginning of the modern environmental movement)—were moderate voices who found a national audience as well.

On the fringes, a new breed of radicals offered not only critiques, but utopian visions as well. The iconoclast Paul Goodman—poet, urban planner, sociologist, activist—promoted the idea of "decent poverty" as a respectable alternative to mass consumption. He became influential to a rising generation of radicals, mostly young men who would form the backbone of the counterculture in the 1960s.

This period also saw the rise of a new brand of consumer activism. Ralph Nader and Martin Luther King, Jr., among others, suggested that despite the propaganda of big business and its boosters, corporations weren't always acting in consumers' or society's best interests. King used consumer boycotts (most famously, the Montgomery bus boycott) to point out the injustice of white-owned businesses relying on African American patronage while withholding jobs and equal treatment from those same customers. He also questioned the moral basis of a consumer society: "We must spend our money not merely for the adolescent and transitory things," he warned one audience, but for "this eternal, lasting something that we call freedom."

On a superficial level, these critics of consumption were echoing the themes of Thomas Eddy, Simon Straus, and other early apostles of thrift. But in many ways the modern critics struck a vastly different note. Straus and Eddy were firmly entrenched members of the establishment, and they aimed their disapproval largely at paupers and struggling workers, accusing them of throwing their money away on entertainments, lotteries, alcohol, and fancy clothing. The new opponents of consumption, by and large, reversed that prescription. They issued their critique from new countercultures and disenfranchised minority groups. And they aimed it squarely at the American mainstream—the middle class that had eagerly embraced the trappings of the consumer lifestyle. This reversal indicates just how much American values had flipped over the course of a hundred years. Restraint and antimaterialism were once mainstream values, foisted by elites onto the working poor; by the 1950s and 1960s, it was a message voiced mostly by cultural outsiders and aimed at the new American bourgeoisie.

As long as economic growth kept propelling Americans' standard of living higher and higher, these voices of dissent didn't find many allies in the political establishment. That began to change in the mid-1970s. The long boom was tapering off, and by 1973, the country was embroiled in sharp exchanges with the oil-producing countries of the Middle East. The river of oil, that critical ingredient of American manufacturing and American car culture, slowed to a trickle. Cars lined up at gas stations, inflation jumped, and corporations cut their payrolls.

President Jimmy Carter, an evangelical Christian, was sympathetic to the critics of consumption. He had made it clear from the moment of his inauguration that he would be no celebrant of American excess and triumphalism. After he took the oath of office in January 1977, he rejected the usual limousine ride and instead walked down Pennsylvania Avenue to the White House. He sold off the presidential yacht and did away with the hierarchical seating arrangements in the White House cafeteria. He was the man from Plains; to drive home the point, he spoke plainly and dressed plainly.

Yet despite the televised fireside chats he became known for, at which he advised Americans to wear warm sweaters instead of turning up their heat, the economy continued to tank. Carter and his aides passionately debated the stagflation of the period. Many of his advisers, including Vice President Walter Mondale, urged Carter to offer the public a program of action. But Carter's religious background—and his pollster, the young Patrick Caddell—guided him toward a broader view of the problem: a focus on the nation's soul.

On July 15, 1979, Carter delivered what became known as his "malaise" speech. He told Americans that they were stuck in a "crisis of confidence" that threatened American democracy. "We can see this crisis in the growing doubt about the meaning of our own lives and in the loss of a unity of purpose for our nation," he said.

Carter blamed this loss of purpose on, among other things, selfish materialism. "In a nation that was proud of hard work, strong families, close-knit communities, and our faith in God, too many of us now tend to worship self-indulgence and consumption. Human identity is no longer defined by what one does, but by what one owns. But we've discovered that owning things and consuming things does not satisfy our longing for meaning. We've learned that piling up material goods cannot fill the emptiness of lives which have no confidence or purpose." It was, as the historian Daniel Horowitz says, "the most sustained attack any American president had ever made on consumer culture."

But the speech, like the economy, tanked. The dollar fell, interest rates rose. Within days, pundits assailed the president for maligning the nation's character and for blaming Americans rather than inspiring and leading them. When Carter faced the California governor Ronald Reagan in the general election a year later, Americans made it clear that they weren't receptive to the message of soul-searching, restraint, and conservation that Carter was offering them. They preferred Reagan's assurances of continued American supremacy. There was no need to sacrifice and cut back, he promised voters; the United States could sustain—and even expand—its prosperity and power by believing in its own specialness and backing that up with tax cuts and a massive military buildup.

It was yet another striking reversal. During World Wars I and II, *sacrifice* and *thrift* were watchwords. Now, during another period of political and economic crisis, Americans heard just the opposite: don't deny yourself, the American economy is strong and you have the power to make it stronger.

This trend reached its apogee twenty years later, following the terrorist strikes of September 11, 2001. Within hours of the attacks, Rudy Giuliani, mayor of wounded New York City, told residents, "Go to restaurants. Go shopping. Show you're not afraid." President George W. Bush urged Americans to

"Get down to Disney World in Florida. Take your families and enjoy life, the way we want it to be enjoyed." The boosters even got a plug on *Sex and the City,* as Carrie Bradshaw and her gal pals hopped in a cab to "throw some much-needed money downtown."

Shopping would pull Americans out of the crisis. It was the triumph of a free-market, pro-business reinterpretation of American virtue. But that philosophy also helped set the stage for the housing and credit bubbles of the early 2000s, bubbles that nearly brought down the global economy and many of the real, hard-won gains of the postwar era.

Chapter 7

Spendthrift Nation

Do savings even matter anymore? The word itself sounds almost fossilized, like an old-fashioned bugaboo from a time before credit could be had as easily as water from a faucet. The old savings bank of myth featured Jimmy Stewart standing faithfully behind the desk, waiting for the good people of Bedford Falls to turn over their hard-earned dollars in exchange for a deposit book. That's an idea we still like to visit every year around Christmastime, but it holds less and less relevance in our era of global capitalism, where trillions of virtual dollars fly around the world every day, nothing more than figures on a computer screen, nesting for a moment before zipping out for the next transaction. For the last twenty or thirty years, in our ever more complex financial universe, it seemed that capital generally, almost magically, got where it needed to go: into a mortgage, paid out in a Social Security check, financing one company's takeover of another. Meanwhile, our government spent beyond its means (our national debt in mid-2009 was $11.4 trillion and growing), Americans ran up their credit card bills to the tune of $3.7 trillion, and massive investment banks like Bear Stearns leveraged themselves in drastic fashion, borrowing as much as $30 for every $1 they had on hand.

Then in 2007, the housing bubble burst, stranding millions of homeowners with variable-rate mortgages they could no longer afford. Bear Stearns and Lehman Brothers tottered and fell in 2008, nearly bringing down the rest of the banking system with them. Citigroup and Bank of America restructured and accepted federal bailout money. Unemployment rose to 9.4 percent in May 2009. In the background, we continued to hear the low hum of concern about long-term Social Security and Medicare obligations. For the millions of Americans who lost their homes or their jobs, and the millions more who worried whether they might be next in line for a pink slip, the recession that began in 2007 has forced a difficult reckoning. When times were good, Americans lived beyond their means, spent down their savings, and racked up debt. Now we're recognizing once again that savings matter, that we need to stash something away for those inevitable rainy days. What's at stake? Our families' financial security, the viability of a competitive U.S. economy, and, ultimately, a whole lot more.

Are Americans Saving Too Little?

Personal finance experts generally suggest that households keep enough savings on hand to cover three to six months of living expenses. That way, families have some cushion to soften the impact of unexpected crises: the loss of a job, taking unpaid time off from work to care for a sick relative, replacing a broken water heater in the dead of winter.

It's solid advice. But in 2004, just 41 percent of American families surveyed by the Federal Reserve said they save regularly, and only 56.1 percent estimated that they had put away money in the preceding year. Many Americans live every day with a dangerously high level of economic insecurity, leaving them vulnerable to bad luck, bad decisions, and financial meltdowns like the one we witnessed in 2008 when credit markets froze and the economy nearly stopped in its tracks. These low savings rates also suggest that millions are unprepared for retirement even as the Social Security and Medicare programs face crippling deficits in the near future.

According to the Department of Commerce, Americans saved 1.7 percent of their incomes in 2008—meaning that, for every $100 Joe Smith earned, he saved just $1.70. While this was an improvement over the third quarter of 2005, when our personal savings dipped into negative territory for the first time since the Great Depression, it was well below the double-digit savings rates of the early 1980s (when Mr. Smith banked $11 for every $100 he earned).

The chart that follows illustrates the decline in Americans' personal savings. It includes the two statistics the federal government uses to track savings rates. One line shows the Commerce Department's NIPA (National Income and Product Accounts) rate. This is the most widely cited measure; it takes total disposable income and simply subtracts total personal spending. But it's controversial because it doesn't count capital gains—increases in the value of stocks—as savings. As a result, many analysts believe the NIPA rate understates the value of Americans' nest eggs. To get a more complete picture, economists also consider the Flow of Funds Accounts, a measure put out by the Federal Reserve and shown here as well. This number indicates the change in households' total assets, so it counts capital gains and even durable goods—such as a new refrigerator or car—as savings (the Commerce Department categorizes those purchases as consumption, not savings). The FFA is more capricious, moving up and down with the stock market. In periods when the Dow is rising, the FFA shows a much higher savings rate than the NIPA number.

Comparison of Personal Saving in the National Income and
Product Accounts (NIPAs) with Personal Saving
in the Flow of Funds Accounts (FFAs)

The NIPA dots on this page were published on February 27, 2009.
Annual data shown.

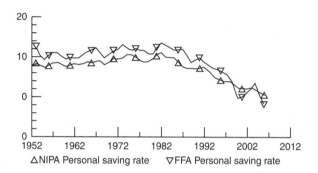

△NIPA Personal saving rate   ▽FFA Personal saving rate

The picture of Americans' savings at any one moment differs according to which measure you use. But the long-term
pattern is indisputable: we've been saving less and less money
over the past three decades.

Not only are we saving less money, but we've also entered
what the Harvard historian Niall Ferguson calls the "Age of
Leverage." Americans have taken on record amounts of personal debt over the last few decades, from home mortgages to
car payments to revolving credit card balances. The best way
to illustrate this is to look at the historical ratio of Americans'
total debt to our total disposable personal income (income
after taxes have been paid). After World War II, our debts
equaled approximately 25 percent of our collective annual
incomes; if our paychecks totaled $100 million, then we
owed $25 million for our homes, cars, and other possessions.
By 2007, that ratio had climbed to an astonishing 141 percent.
If we earned $100 million, we now owed $141 million. Much
of this gigantic leap can be accounted for by rising home
ownership rates, but the increase is also a function of the fact

that we're buying bigger and more expensive homes, we're charging more education and medical bills, we're buying more stuff, and we're socking away less money. Our wealth is now concentrated in illiquid investments like houses, computers, and home entertainment systems, things that can lose value fast and are tough to unload, rather than in safe financial instruments like savings accounts and government bonds.

At the end of 2008, for example, household mortgage debt totaled $10.5 trillion, up from $2.5 trillion in 1990. And according to the research company CardTrak.com, in 2008 average credit card debt for households with at least one piece of plastic reached $10,728—nearly twice the inflation-adjusted average of $5,652 in 1990.

These figures conceal a multilayered reality. As economic inequality mounts, the people at the top of the income scale are amassing large reserves of wealth. In general, they are saving plenty, in the form of home equity, stocks, cash, and other investments. In 2007, the wealthiest 10 percent of American families had an average net worth (assets minus debts) of $3.3 million; they owned approximately 70 percent of all the personal wealth in the country. That same year, upper-middle-class households were worth an average of $375,000. In addition, government incentives for saving—such as tax-advantaged programs like Individual Retirement Accounts—skew overwhelmingly to the wealthy, meaning Americans of all classes are subsidizing the retirements of already affluent people.

But the situation is serious and sometimes dire for Americans in the middle and working classes. According to a 2007 study by the Consumer Federation of America, more than 75 percent of Americans with incomes below $25,000 have no savings fund set up to protect them in case they face an emergency like job loss or an urgent root canal. Among middle-class Americans—those in the middle 60 percent of the income scale—only 29 percent had enough money salted away in 2004 to weather a spell of unemployment (down from 39 percent who were prepared for that disaster in 2001).

We are also spending a significant portion of our incomes to service our debts; in 2007, families carrying debt paid an average of 18.6 percent of their income just to cover interest and minimum payments on principal. The problem is especially severe for low-income and middle-class families. According to the Federal Reserve's Survey of Consumer Finances, 27 percent of debtors in the lowest income quintile are in what economists call "high debt"—the dangerous position of paying 40 percent or more of their income simply to pay off loans of various types. And 14.5 percent in the middle of the income scale are in the same boat. These high payments cut into family budgets for food, rent, and educational expenses and, of course, make it nearly impossible for them to save money for the future.

Americans' meager savings raises special concerns about retirement security. Economists across the political spectrum are worried that baby boomers and the generations coming up behind them are woefully unprepared for those so-called golden years and will face serious declines in their standard of living once their paychecks stop coming.

A constellation of factors are converging in the next few decades, all of them suggesting that we are heading toward a crisis point. In 1975, almost 40 percent of American workers could count on a steady income from their employers from the day they retired until they dropped dead. These "defined-benefit" (DB) plans, as they're called, were the traditional pensions many of our grandparents received.

Today's employee-retirement plans look very different. Approximately 63 percent of workers who participate in corporate-sponsored retirement programs are now enrolled only in "defined-contribution" (DC) plans—generally 401k accounts that allow participants to invest a portion of their pretax income in a limited number of assets, such as stock or bond mutual funds or company stock. Many firms match some part of the worker's contribution, though the number of employers who offer that benefit, and the amount they're willing to match, is shrinking.

The main result of the switch to 401ks is that they shift risk away from corporations and onto workers' shoulders. Back in the days of DB pensions, it didn't matter what was happening in the economy or the stock market; you got your check—for the same amount (or more, if your pension was adjusted for inflation)—every month. It was the company's problem to figure out where the money was coming from. Now, if you have a DC plan and the stock market tanks just as your colleagues are roasting you at your retirement party, that's your problem.

Classical economics tells us that Americans should save more money outside their pension plans to compensate for greater uncertainty in the plans. Instead, as we've seen, the opposite has happened.

Social Security isn't helping matters. The Social Security system as we know it is currently taking in more revenue—via our payroll taxes—than it pays out in benefits. But that equation will reverse in the next thirty-five years due to simple demographics. Right now the labor force is unusually large thanks to all the baby boomers who are working. But as that generation retires over the next couple of decades, fewer workers will be paying into the system and Social Security checks will be issued to more retirees. In 2017, according to government estimates, the system will start paying out more than it takes in, and by 2041, the Social Security Trust Fund, which holds the surpluses that are currently gathering, will be depleted. At that point, the government will be forced to reduce benefits or raise taxes to keep the system solvent. More likely, politicians will make some difficult but unavoidable decisions before that date, probably some combination of benefit cuts and tax increases.

The result is that Social Security benefits will probably shrink for those of us who are now in our forties, thirties, twenties, or younger.

Social Security was never meant to be a retiree's only source of income (though it is, for 21 percent of Americans over age sixty-five); it was designed to supplement personal savings and employer-provided pension plans. But a reduction in Social Security checks means Americans will have to make up the difference with other income or savings in order to avoid a drastic drop in their standard of living. And where will that money come from? Many Americans will end up working at full- or part-time jobs even in their so-called retirements. But assuming most of us won't be able to work until we die, we'll be relying on savings. That will be near impossible for the 43 percent of Americans who have little savings, or who will start saving too late and won't have enough money to offset the loss of a regular paycheck.

Medicare and late-life health care expenses represent perhaps the biggest wild card in the equation. Medical costs in the United States are rising four times faster than inflation. At that rate, according to projections from the Social Security Administration, Medicare is projected to consume around 57 percent of the federal budget in the year 2082 (up from 16 percent in 2007), crowding out spending on schools, roads, research, defense, and every other service the government provides. To address this monster, legislators will be forced to cut benefits, raise taxes, or both. Either way, a greater share of the burden for paying for health care will be transferred to individuals.

Hundreds of retirement-planning tools currently exist, such as online calculators that help determine how much you need to save to finance a decent post-working life. Yet for a host of reasons—financial illiteracy, low access to those tools, raw fear, denial—most Americans continue to avoid these questions and typically, in surveys, underestimate the amount of money they think they'll need to save. Given the rapid inflation in medical expenses, says Jonathan Skinner, an economist at Dartmouth University, even those tools are quickly becoming outdated. "The combination of eroding retiree health benefits and the risk of catastrophic future out-of-pocket health spending," he wrote in 2007, "suggests that even conventional retirement planning recommendations could be too low." In other words, the reasons to save are becoming more and more compelling. Yet large chunks of the population remain unprepared.

Big Spenders or Barely Scraping By?

As with any large-scale cultural phenomenon, there's no simple explanation for why Americans are saving so little. Scholars and observers have approached this question like the six blind men from the fable: after being asked to touch an elephant and describe it, one feels the trunk and says the animal is like a snake while another caresses a leg and says the elephant resembles a tree, and so on. We emerge with bits and pieces, but it's hard to get a complete picture.

Traditional economists scratch their heads about low savings rates, since they expect people to act like rational beings, carefully weighing current and future needs and striking some balance between immediate and deferred consumption. They suggest that stock market profits and rising home values in the last few decades created a "wealth effect": Americans who had invested in the securities or housing markets felt flush and confident, so they spent their paper gains. With characteristic American optimism, they expected that the Dow would keep going up; but even when it didn't, even when it tanked in the early 2000s, many people didn't adjust their expectations or their spending. In fact, consumer spending rose during the 2001–2002 recession, and this remains a puzzle for many economists. Surely, as people owned less wealth and felt poorer, they should have reined in their consumption, right?

One reason why it didn't happen then — and this is another explanation for our consistently low savings rates over the last decade — is that until the banking freeze that began in late 2008, credit has been so easy to come by. Banks and credit institutions lobbied hard for deregulation in the 1980s and 1990s, and were rewarded when legislation removed restrictions that had been in place since the Depression. New laws cleared the way for huge mergers in the financial services industry, resulting in banks with massive amounts of assets. At the same time, complex new financial instruments — credit-default swaps, derivatives, home mortgages bundled up into securities and sold like stocks — allowed lenders to sell or insure against the risky loans they were making. Since they were shouldering less risk, lenders became more reckless about extending credit. This explains why individuals with no steady income were able to buy $200,000 houses, and why banks kept stuffing our mailboxes with offers of new credit cards.

Deregulation also made it easy for banks to borrow from more and more sources. This fact, along with fairly steady global economic growth, meant there was a lot of money sloshing around the financial system. With a large supply of money, interest rates remained low, acting as another incentive for borrowing. Low interest rates discourage savings in other ways as well; for instance, when an individual can earn a real interest rate (the nominal rate minus inflation) of, say, only 1 percent in a savings account or on a certificate of deposit, the benefits of saving — of deferring consumption — are less attractive compared with the immediate benefits of buying an iPhone or renovating the bathroom.

But perhaps more to the core of the problem, evidence suggests that most Americans don't understand one of the most basic truths of saving. According to a long-standing rumor, Albert Einstein once called compound interest "the most powerful force in the universe." The attribution has never been proven, but the wisdom behind the quotation still shines. Compound interest is the interest that accrues on interest accumulated in previous periods. Sounds confusing, but here's the basic idea: When you save $100 at 5 percent annual interest, you end up with $105 at the end of year one. When year two comes to a close, your account statement shows a balance not of $110, but of $110.25, because you earned interest on $105 that year, not just on the original $100 investment. That extra 25 cents seems puny, but at the end of thirty years, your $100 has morphed into $432.19 (without compound interest, it would be just $250). What this means is that people who start saving early in life end up with dramatically higher rewards than those who start saving later. Research shows that individuals who don't grasp the benefits of compound interest are less likely to save.

PRESSING REAL-WORLD BURDENS have hurt Americans' ability to save, too. Over the last decade or so, the costs of housing, education, health care, and other essentials have been far outpacing the growth of real wages. From 2000 to 2005, the U.S. economy grew 14 percent, but workers' hourly wages were stagnant and median family income *fell* 2.9 percent. Meanwhile, mortgage payments, tuition and fees at a four-year college, and health insurance premiums all rose by more than 25 percent in the same period.

Elizabeth Warren, a bankruptcy expert at Harvard Law School and now chair of a congressional committee overseeing the government's Troubled Asset Relief Program, pioneered this line of research in the 1980s and 1990s, and her analysis remains trenchant. She rejects the idea that Americans are profligate spenders, arguing instead that economic changes like globalization and deregulation are forcing working- and middle-class Americans to divert more of their incomes—and pile up debt once they've exhausted their paychecks—to cover basic expenses like mortgage payments, insurance premiums, and interest on student loans. Add in some of the high prices we've seen over the last couple of years in energy and food prices (a gallon of gas cost $4.11 in July 2008, though it's back down to $2.31 as of May 2009), and it's easy to see why many Americans have been having a harder time making ends meet.

Warren's argument is convincing, but it still doesn't explain why so many Americans, even those in the middle and working classes, have closets full of clothes they seldom wear and garages so cluttered they no longer have room for a car. For instance, Americans in 2007 shelled out about 38 percent more money for both health care and housing than they did in 2000—but they also spent 45 percent more on entertainment, and 68 percent more on pets, toys, and hobbies, according to consumer expenditure figures from the Bureau of Labor Statistics. There are cultural dynamics—not just economic ones—at work in how we conduct ourselves as consumers.

This topic is a large one, so let me just briefly note that, as social creatures, we respond to the cues around us. This translates into, among other things, the cycle of competitive consumption that has Americans vying for status goods that match or trump their friends' and neighbors' stuff. If every house on your block boasts a swimming pool, it's not unreasonable to think you should have one, too. When I was covering the retail industry as a reporter for *Newsday,* I often asked shoppers about this subtle form of peer pressure. No one ever owned up to having these emulous tendencies. We human beings, whether teenage or adult, prefer to think of ourselves as unique, nonconformist, and impervious to status pressure. But the annual revenue of Louis Vuitton—which saw double-digit growth even in the gloomy days of 2008—suggests otherwise. And while it's true that housing costs have skyrocketed in recent years, part of the increase comes from the fact that Americans want bigger homes than ever before; the average new house built in 2003 was 38 percent larger than a house built in 1975, despite having fewer occupants.

ALL OF THESE factors—cultural pressures and aspirations, financial illiteracy, the escalating cost of providing the basics for ourselves and our families, the stagnation of real wages, and the deregulation of the financial sector—have contributed to the debt trap so many Americans now find themselves in.

There are modern-day Puritans among us who believe that Americans suffer from a self-control deficit, that we have simply jettisoned the restraint of earlier days. There's some truth to this. But the culture of spending is also a result of our years of plenty. The majority of Americans became so accustomed to abundance over the last few decades that we spent with the permanent expectation of even better times ahead. Since the end of World War II, and continuing with especial vim in the 1990s and 2000s, we've had unprecedented opportunities to consume and unprecedented access to easy, cheap money. Even the soberest Puritans could have fallen prey to this deadly combination.

The situation for families and individuals is so dire that personal thrift, while a crucial part of the equation, won't solve our broader problems alone. Individual retrenchment—a commitment to downscaling and low-cost living—must accompany across-the-board legislated change. A working insurance system, where the benefits of quality health care are equitably distributed along with the costs; grants and inexpensive loans for higher education; a rational energy policy; and regulation to abolish the sleaziest practices of financial institutions—these are all crucial reforms that will allow working Americans a decent shot at thriving in the twenty-first century. At the same time, though, we also need to take a hard look at our own consumption habits, or we might one day find ourselves too deep in the hole to climb out.

THE IMPLICATIONS OF our low savings rates go beyond the question of whether any particular family can afford a down payment on a house or a college education or retirement down the road. More broadly, a widespread lack of savings means there may not be enough money to fund the investments that lead to long-term economic growth. In plain English, savings finance investment. No savings, no investment.

Say I create the Helix Solar Panel Company and I want to expand—open a new research facility, renovate the headquarters, hire more workers, implement a software program to streamline our purchasing system. I would have to borrow money. As CEO, I'd go to my local bank and ask for a loan. The banker, aware that demand for solar panels is about to accelerate, would approve the loan and hand over a check. That loan comes out of a pool of money the bank is either holding or knows it will soon gather. That pool of money is other people's savings. Individuals, corporations, municipalities—all these economic entities park their money in the bank in exchange for some interest. The bank then lends the money at a higher interest rate, and Helix opens its new facility, hires its workers, and so forth. Banks need a pool of capital in order to lend money to companies, governments, or individuals who then invest the capital, and in classical economic theory, this is how the economic system grows: investments in new factories and jobs and equipment mean more money circulates through the economy, inducing additional spending by workers (some of whom are newly employed).

Over the last two decades, economic growth (as measured by the rise in gross domestic product, which is the value of all finished goods and services produced inside the United States) has averaged a decent 2.9 percent a year. How have we been able to maintain rising GDP while our net savings slip further and further down? Where's the money coming from to finance investment?

The simplest answer is that we're borrowing from other countries. Chinese and Japanese citizens, it turns out, are excellent savers. In 2007, the United States posted a trade deficit of $700 billion; we imported $2.3 trillion worth of electronics, toys, food, machines, and other stuff, and exported only $1.6 trillion in goods and services. The money we're sending to, say, China to pay for those items is going into the pockets of government coffers, local officials, factory owners, and Chinese laborers. Thanks to strong export-led economic growth in China, the country is amassing far more in dollars than it is spending for our exports. The surplus — the money that's not being consumed — is savings.

The People's Bank of China (the equivalent of our Federal Reserve Bank) then purchases those dollars from corporations, giving them local currency in return, and uses the dollars to buy U.S. Treasury securities. That's debt issued by our government. As of April 2009, the U.S. government had borrowed $764 billion from China, and another $686 billion from Japan. Foreign investors have also bought prodigious amounts of corporate bonds and bonds sold by government agencies (in total, China owns more than $1 trillion in U.S. assets). Taken together, all of these loans propped up not only the Bush administration's record budget deficits, but Americans' consumer spending as well. By keeping money circulating through the American economy and soaking up lots of government bonds, the foreign loans have helped the United States maintain low interest rates for the last decade. These low rates, in turn, have allowed Americans to keep spending—on newer, bigger homes; on vacations and cars paid for with refinance loans; and on credit card purchases backed by banks with easy access to more, and then even more, money. Until 1985, the United States was the world's creditor, lending money to other nations. Now, with obligations of over $10 trillion, we are the world's largest debtor nation.

So do savings still matter? Yes. It's just that we're now tapping into other countries' savings. The problem is, this status quo carries many risks and is probably not sustainable in the long run. If foreign banks decide to stop or slow their purchases of U.S. bonds—loaning us less money—our economic system would be in danger.

Countries like China and Japan buy American Treasury bonds because they've long been the safest investment in the world. Our strong, stable economy and our stable political system—little chance of military coups or Communist revolutions here—give our creditors confidence that we'll pay back whatever money we borrow.

But those lenders may not always be so sanguine about the U.S. economy. When the dollar's value is dropping relative to other currencies, for instance, the value of China's massive dollar reserves drops, too. Chinese officials have occasionally remarked on this and hinted that they would consider diversifying further into euros or yen. The subprime crisis was another warning sign to the Chinese and other foreign holders of U.S. corporate debt, according to Brad Setser, an economics fellow at the Council on Foreign Relations and an expert on international capital flows. "Until June of 2007, there was a great deal of demand for risky U.S. assets like mortgage-backed securities. But the subprime crisis exposed the risks in investing in U.S. paper."

Political crises, too, could play a role. For instance, if China and Taiwan clash diplomatically or militarily and the U.S. allies with Taiwan, China could punish us by selling dollar assets, or use its holdings to influence our foreign policy. "If you're a creditor, you have more freedom to act globally. But if you rely on China for financing, like any debtor, you're in a less favorable position," Setser said.

If foreign governments lose confidence in our economy and reduce their purchases of U.S. debt and U.S. dollars, chances are we'd see a very sharp adjustment in the U.S. economy. The dollar would plummet and interest rates at home would skyrocket as the government trolls for buyers of government securities (creditors will refuse to buy dollar-denominated investments unless they're offered a higher return).

Those high interest rates and a weak dollar would affect ordinary Americans in myriad ways. Mortgages, car loans, and consumer credit would all get more expensive. So would imports. All those computer parts from China, electronics from Japan, Brazilian-assembled shoes, German cars, and Italian wines would experience an inflationary jump since it'd cost more greenbacks to pay for them in their home currencies. That would raise the prices of almost everything we buy and put an enormous strain on low- and middle-income households. High interest rates would raise the cost of corporate borrowing, slowing investment and, in turn, job and wage growth. All these factors could set the stage for a long and painful recession on top of whatever else was going on in the economy.

It's unlikely that anything like this could happen quickly or suddenly, and in fact overseas governments have some very good reasons to keep buying our debt (it's still a safe asset, and China in particular wants to maintain American consumers' purchasing power, since we're that country's most reliable export market). But China, Japan, and our other creditors also have compelling reasons for diversifying away from dollar-denominated assets. In order to ensure that we maintain a sound economy if and when foreign banks move away from the greenback, Americans need to start saving so that individuals, companies, and governments (local, state, and federal) have domestic sources of capital to tap when they need it.

Here's one last reason for us to start saving as a nation: our chronic borrowing means that every year we pay higher costs to service the debt, in the form of interest. In 2007, the U.S. government paid $430 billion per year in interest payments alone—that's apart from the principal—on the loans it's taken out. That's $430 billion in taxpayer money that went largely to overseas governments rather than to schools, transportation networks, research programs, and other investments here at home. Like a compulsive shopping addict, the country has been charging up its credit cards with no plan for paying off the balances.

The Paradox of Thrift, Revisited

What about the Paradox of Thrift? you might be thinking. If everyone suddenly got the cheap religion, the economy would fall apart and then we'd all be worse off.

I frequently hear this objection, and it shows how much we've internalized the postwar creed that consumption amounts to a civic duty. At the same time, the appropriate role of consumer spending is a tricky question during times of economic contraction. Consumer spending began dropping in the middle of 2008, and, in the short run, this trend is likely to draw out the current recession. In the long run, however, consumers need to hunker down and pay off debt in order to clean up their balance sheets and get back to a place of economic well-being. We don't want to end up like Japan, which experienced what economists call a "Lost Decade" in the 1990s after a precipitous drop in consumer spending. But we do need to restore some sanity to our finances.

Personal spending now accounts for about 70 percent of GDP. That figure is one of the most revered numbers in the pantheon of economic indicators, circulated in story after story about how the American consumer is the key driver of the domestic and, increasingly, the global economy. When I was a retail reporter, I heard the same joke over and over again from shoppers: "I'm doing my part to help the economy," usually offered with a chuckle. Every Christmas season, economists and journalists "warn" that holiday spending might be weaker than the previous year; and then those same economists and journalists usually laud the "resilience" of American consumers after they rush to the mall in the week before December 25 and "rescue" the season for retailers and, by extension, the whole economy. Few of these stories mention the hangover that starts a couple of weeks after Christmas, when the credit card bills arrive and Americans face the long-term costs of their escalating debts. After 9/11, we heard the same message from President Bush and New York Mayor Rudy Giuliani—in essence that we could fight terrorists by pulling out our credit cards and charging another frock at Bloomingdale's. Even as the housing market blew up in 2006 and 2007 and millions of mortgage holders faced foreclosure, many analysts wrung their hands not over the implosion of so many people's American dreams but over their fears that Americans might begin to question the dogma of spending-as-patriotic-act. Their prescription was more of the same poison that made us sick in the first place—an uninterrupted spiral of consumption and debt. That's like telling an alcoholic suffering from withdrawal that a shot of whiskey will be just the thing to calm his nerves.

Relying on maxed-out individuals to rescue us from a systemic financial breakdown is shortsighted and dangerous, and it overstates the role of consumer spending as an engine of economic growth. Economists for centuries have debated what drives growth; J. B. Say, a nineteenth-century French economist, argued that supply (savings and business investment) is the key; Keynes said that demand (consumption) is primary. Keynes appeared to win that argument, but the classical view has made a comeback.

To show the evolution of economists' recent thinking on the Paradox of Thrift, one need only compare a few editions of Paul Samuelson's introductory economics textbook, the standard-bearer of mainstream economic thought. In a section about savings in the fifth edition of *Economics,* published in 1961, he wrote that "most of us were taught that thrift is always a good thing. Benjamin Franklin's 'Poor Richard's Almanac' never tired of preaching the doctrine of saving." But in a modern economic system, frugality only worsened the deflationary cycle of recessions. "Private prudence may be social folly," he wrote. Samuelson did note that thrift exerts a positive anti-inflationary influence at times of full employment, but he warned that the economy is rarely in that state.

Samuelson and his coauthor William Nordhaus repudiated their earlier advocacy of the Paradox when, in 1992, they removed it from the fourteenth edition of *Economics,* and gravitated instead to the classical theories of saving. "If people are willing to save—to abstain from present consumption and wait for future consumption—then society can devote resources to new capital goods....Forgoing current consumption in favor of investment adds to future production possibilities." In the sixteenth edition, published in 1998, they wrote that "over the long run, a nation's capital formation is determined by its national savings rate.... When a nation saves a great deal, its capital stock increases rapidly and it enjoys rapid growth in its potential output. When a nation's savings rate is low, its equipment and factories become obsolete and its infrastructure begins to rot away."

A more subtle understanding of how business cycles unfold supports this integrated theory of how saving and spending work together. For instance, some economists now say that savings and investment drive business recoveries, while consumer spending (which tends to stay relatively steady through all stages of the cycle) prevents slowdowns from getting too deep. As the economist Mark Skousen says, entrepreneurship, investment, and technology spending were all behind the economic boom of the mid- to late 1990s; when the stock market bubble burst in 2000, consumer spending helped minimize the pain of the downturn. Consumption is key to the equation, but—and this is the piece that gets lost in the media and in political debate about stimulus packages—so is savings.

Another key point that's frequently buried: consumer spending is just one component of total GDP. So even if millions of Americans cut back their consumption, whether by choice or circumstance, the economy will remain stable as long as government or business spending (the other two components of GDP) rise to make up the difference. This is not inconceivable. It was the principle behind FDR's New Deal (using government spending to compensate for anemic private spending), and Congress and the Obama administration in February 2009 passed an $800 billion stimulus plan that includes massive investments in infrastructure projects like energy-efficient public transportation networks, bridge and tunnel upgrades, green-technology research, job training curricula, and other programs that can increase our country's competitive position. The long-term benefits of such public investment—better-educated citizens, less dependence on foreign oil, less pollution and its related illnesses, shorter commutes—might produce even faster rates of growth than we had before the economic injection. Financing these projects is a thorny issue; it means adding to the deficits left behind by the Bush administration. But governments have many levers for handling debt, including interest rates and tax policy. Ultimately, deficits are a better option than asking consumers to load up their credit cards and take on more debt.

I asked Ron Wilcox, author of the book *Whatever Happened to Thrift?* and a professor at the University of Virginia's Darden School of Business, whether he would suspend his passionate advocacy of thrift in favor of Americans buying their way out of recessions like the one that began in 2007. A new emphasis on saving "will make the recession deeper and longer," he acknowledged. "But if people keep spending at very high rates, it'll just kick the problem down the road. I've come down to the view that it still makes sense for American families to save money."

SO WHAT IS the optimal savings rate in this country, a proportion that would provide financial security and fund domestic investment while at the same time driving steady growth? I asked several economists this question and received answers ranging from 5 percent to 20 percent. If we reached those levels, it is true that the economy would probably slow down for a while. But it would soon reach a new equilibrium, either making up the difference with new investment or maintaining a lower rate of growth while, on the upside, minimizing the significant long-term risks of inadequate savings. What we might end up with is a lower standard of living by traditional means—fewer restaurant meals and manicures, holding on to the old television set a couple years longer, and deciding to give up the second car in favor of riding a bike—but greater security and a higher quality of life.

Given our economy's complexity, there's no golden ratio, no fail-safe percentage. "Over the last decade, the low savings rate has not hurt business growth because we've been able to borrow cheap," says Ron Wilcox. "In the next decade, the exact same rate of U.S. savings might be completely inadequate." In other words, variable conditions require variable strategies, as Keynes rightly recognized decades ago. But if we simply muddle through, responding in a haphazard and disorderly way to the conditions of the moment—cutting back when times are tough, spending freely when the cash is flowing—we've lazily followed exactly the wrong approach. Our consumer schizophrenia amplifies the fluctuations of the business cycle, leading to more pain during recessions and then exuberance and bubbles during the upswings.

Can we try to do things differently? Can we opt for lives of greater moderation and balance? As this book went to press, savings rates were climbing to their highest levels since early 1999. That's a good sign, but if we don't make this a permanent shift, the American dream could easily turn into a nightmare. Even worse, we might put at risk a whole lot more than just our bank accounts.

Chapter 8

Eco-Cheap

If you climbed into a hot-air balloon and floated a few miles above the earth, then traced a path around the entire planet and looked down on its expanses of water and land, what would you see?

You'd see landfills piled high with the detritus of the American dream. You might happen upon the infamous "trash island" in the Pacific Ocean, a floating archipelago of plastic bags, fast-food containers, and other flotsam. You'd see toxic wastes belching out of trucks, container ships, and factories. We drill, mine, and log to feed our material longings and needs, and in the process we're releasing greenhouse gases and air pollution, discarding packaging and excess, and disrupting vital ecosystems with our consumer lifestyle.

So after all that talk of interest rates and Medicare shortfalls and credit card debt, the truth is that ultimately, some of the best reasons to consume less have nothing to do with financial security. Reducing our consumption may be the only way we can halt and even reverse some of the ecological damage we've wrought over the last few centuries of industrial culture.

Just as Americans imagined until recently that we inhabited

a world of unlimited credit, so we have also been enjoying a sense of entitlement and false confidence about the natural resources that support and sustain us. The United Nations recognized this a while back; its 1992 report "Agenda 21" cautioned that "the major cause of the continued deterioration of the global environment is the unsustainable pattern of consumption and production, particularly in industrialized countries." That's why cheapness—buying less, blocking out the message that spending equals happiness or patriotism—can help us solve not just the economic insecurity of our time, but the environmental insecurity as well.

Americans consume the world's raw materials far out of proportion to our numbers. This point is well understood now, so I'll just offer a few facts about the resources required to sustain our much-celebrated standard of living.

All those catalogs stuffed into our mailboxes? They chew up 14 million trees a year. And the typical cubicle worker throws out one to two hundred pounds of paper per year. Altogether, Americans consume about 30 percent of the world's paper, even though we account for just 5 percent of the global population.

As it's being produced, every laptop computer (including the one on which I'm typing right now) generates four thousand times its weight in industrial waste.

In *National Geographic*'s recent global "Greendex" survey, Americans were the least likely of any nation to use public transportation, and the most likely to drive alone on a regular basis. We use about 25 percent of the world's oil and 27 percent of its aluminum.

And whether we're air-conditioning our houses, eating a Big Mac, or buying a pair of flip-flops produced at a factory on the other side of the world and then shipped to our nearest Target or Amazon.com warehouse, most of our consumption requires the burning of massive amounts of fossil fuels, which releases carbon dioxide and other greenhouse gases into the atmosphere and contributes to global warming. The typical resident of Houston or Peoria is responsible for the release of 19.7 tons of carbon dioxide emissions per year—twice as much as a person in Berlin and eighteen times as much as someone in Mumbai or Delhi.

Now consider what happens as China, India, Brazil, and other developing countries continue their rapid industrialization, pushing billions of people out of subsistence agriculture and into the ranks of urban wage earners. These social transformations are alleviating a great deal of poverty—a wonderful goal by any measure—but they're also unleashing new waves of demand for cars, cell phones, bottled water, computers, nail polish, processed foods, meat, and video games, with all the natural resources, packaging waste, and then disposal that these goods entail. The newly affluent (and even the newly solvent) are joining a worldwide consumer society that already numbers 1.7 billion people. It's a global community that is fundamentally based not on philosophies of political freedom or human rights, but on promises of prosperity. The result is consumption (some of it as conspicuous, in Veblen's sense, as in the West) writ larger than ever.

Says Lester Brown, a statistician and the founder of the Washington, DC–based Earth Policy Institute: "The Western economic model, the fossil-fuel-based, auto-centered, throwaway economy, is not going to work for China. And if it does not work for China, it will not work for India, which has an economy growing at 7 percent a year and a population projected to surpass China's by 2030. Nor will it work for the other 3 billion people in the developing world who are also dreaming the American dream." By some estimates, we would need four more Earths—four planets just like ours—if the rest of our global neighbors consumed at the same level as Americans do now. Unfortunately, we don't yet have the technology to clone our forests, oceans, billion-year-old rock formations, and molten core and shoot the whole mess off into space.

DURING THE POSTWAR boom, the occasional Cassandra emerged from the margins to sound a warning about the high costs of Americans' ever-rising living standard. The prescient John Kenneth Galbraith cautioned in his 1958 article "How Much Should a Country Consume?" that Americans' almost religious devotion to economic growth came at a high environmental price. And in 1973, a German-born economist named E. F. Schumacher started a minor revolution with his book *Small Is Beautiful,* which argued that societies had to scale down their material needs in order to live in balance with the natural environment, other human beings, and their own souls. In the decades that followed, college students organized recycling clubs, "eco-villages" sprouted around the country, and some hardy individuals went off the grid, choosing to live without the modern conveniences most of us take for granted. Despite these scattered efforts, resource use has continued to climb.

But thanks to a confluence of factors—growing alarm about climate change, the proselytizing of thinkers like Al Gore, the growth of recycling programs, celebrities' advocacy of green living—more and more people today are seeing a society built on consumer gratification as wasteful, resource-intensive, and irreparably harmful to the earth. A growing eco-consciousness has led to rapid increases in cultivation and sales of organic foods, the development of low-electricity washing machines and lightbulbs, the rise of energy-efficient architecture, more interest in solar and wind power, and other strategies for low-impact living.

Unfortunately, the environmental movement of today has to some extent been hijacked by fashion. Canny marketers know a good opportunity when they see one, and they understand that Americans these days aren't especially interested in sacrifice. We want our organic spelt cake *and* we want to eat it. So we're exhorted to buy nontoxic toilet bowl cleaners and four-hundred-thread-count sheets made out of bamboo, as if that were the solution to our problem. The journalist Elizabeth Royte wrote in her 2005 book *Garbage Land,* "I resist the green buying message because I hate to think our strength is based in consumption, not in moral clarity." Similarly, I avoid Whole Foods because it is too seductive; no other retailer, not even the UNICEF Christmas catalog, has married shopping with a sense of virtue quite so skillfully.

I prefer what Royte calls "the third choice: not buying at all." Indeed, cheap people get little credit for this, but, knowingly or not, they've been quietly at the forefront of conservation efforts for decades. There's a natural synthesis between saving money and saving resources. As the environmental activist Ivy Main has written, "The absolute cheapest way to save the planet is to stop buying stuff. Even organic cotton T-shirts take energy to produce and ship. If you live in a teeny-tiny house with old vinyl flooring and Formica counters, you are much more eco-friendly than the guy down the street who tears down a house like yours and builds a 6,000-square-foot mansion, even if he does put solar panels on top." The less we buy, the fewer materials and industrial products we consume. Cheap is the new green.

There are exceptions to this equation; for instance, a hybrid car requires a big up-front investment that may or may not break even over time, depending partly on the price of gas. But in more cases than not, thoughtful, low-cost living equals low-impact living, in the kinds of daily choices we make about how we get to work (walk? bike? subway? car?), the temperature in our homes, where and how often we shop, what we eat, the clothes we wear. Each of these choices involves considerations about the stuff of life—water, fuel, metals, wood, plastic—and about our wallets. It's what I call the eco-cheap economy, an economy based on two of the three Rs of the green movement, reducing and reusing. Adhering to the old World War II cry of "Use it up, Wear it out, Make it do, or Do without," frugals reduce both their expenses and their footprint on the environment.

Take the example of a person who commutes to work on a bicycle instead of in a car. It's far cheaper and less resource-intensive to produce bikes than to build cars. Once you own a bike, maintenance costs are close to zero (just the occasional tire patch kit and new inner tube). There's no insurance expense or gasoline costs. No parking tickets, either. On the green side, bicycles emit no pollution and need no fuel besides the calories we eat. According to the advocacy group Bikes Belong, a ten-mile round-trip commute by bicycle instead of by car spares the air ten pounds of carbon dioxide emissions per day.

THE ENVIRONMENTAL SENSIBILITY and the thrifty sensibility share an abhorrence of one thing: waste. It comes down to a fundamental respect for the value of objects. This is a trait that's hard to come by in our throwaway society, perhaps because we're so disconnected from the origins of our possessions and the people who labored to make them. A kitchen table becomes something more when our own hands sanded it down; a wool sweater knitted by a friend has greater value than one that was made on a machine loom in Vietnam and picked up for a low price at Macy's.

Jesus recognized the hubris of waste; even though he could turn five loaves of bread into food for thousands, he told his disciples, "Gather up the fragments that remain, that nothing be lost." You don't have to be religious to appreciate the wisdom of Jesus's command: this bounty isn't ours to squander, and we take it for granted at our own peril.

But unlike Sarah Tabitha Reid, the nineteenth-century New Jersey farmwife who found a use for every scrap of food or fabric, we have a lower threshold for "using up" our possessions today. We discard things when they show signs of wear or merely because we get tired of them. We enjoy the luxury of disposability—and the ease of trash pickup and removal from sight and mind. In the days of scarcity, food grease was saved for soap making, table scraps went out the window to feed the pigs and chickens, and machinery and household goods were glued, soldered, or tied back together when they cracked or broke. You couldn't count on the municipal garbage trucks to come by every Monday and Friday to haul away the unsightly detritus of our busy lives.

In our modern world of plenty, most of the stuff we buy winds up in the trash. Vegetable peels go into the garbage can under the sink. Purchases come wrapped in disposable plastic and foam packaging that's discarded as soon as we get home from the store (according to some estimates, Americans throw away 100 billion plastic bags each year). And very few people today possess the skills or tools to fix the complicated appliances we need to keep our lives functioning. The DVD player and computer are now largely made out of plastic anyway, a cheaper and less durable material than the metals that once brought our technologies to life. So when that computer breaks, it generally ends up on the curb and we buy a replacement. The planned obsolescence that Vance Packard warned about in 1960 has become the status quo.

In 2007, according to the Environmental Protection

Agency, Americans generated 254 million tons of trash a year from residential use (in other words, not including industrial or construction waste). That amounts to an average of 4.6 pounds of garbage per person, per day. Of the total, 54 percent, or 137 million tons, ended up in landfills. Before the Fresh Kills landfill on New York's Staten Island stopped accepting municipal trash in 2001, it was one of the biggest "man-made" structures on earth, visible from the moon and larger in volume than China's Great Wall.

For rats, a bag of garbage is like a shopping mall's food court. But human beings aren't quite so thrilled with our waste. Garbage is unsightly and often stinks. So American cities locate their dumps in industrial or rural locations far from downtowns, or export their waste on trucks and barges to other states. Landfills are unsafe places, packed with sharp objects, broken glass, and unstable piles, but these are not the only dangers or difficulties they pose. Organic waste — rotting vegetables, paper, yard waste — makes up a significant percentage of the contents in landfills. When these materials decompose, they release methane, one of the greenhouse gases that contribute to global warming (methane is twenty-one times more potent than carbon dioxide). According to the Environmental Protection Agency, U.S. landfills emit 30 million metric tons of carbon equivalent (MMTCE) per year, the equivalent of emissions from approximately 20 million cars.

How do we cut down on all of this waste in a meaningful way? Recycling helps, of course, but we have to do more. The terrible truth is that we don't even see most of the trash we generate; it's created farther "upstream" in the production process, when raw materials are pulled from the earth and transformed into the T-shirts, microwaves, cars, hamburgers and, yes, books, we consume. For every bag of trash we set out by the curb on garbage day, there are seventy more bags of waste thrown out during extraction and production of those finished goods. "When you avoid buying new goods," writes Elizabeth Royte, "you help avoid all that other waste upstream."

At the heart of the eco-cheap economy is the thriving world of secondhand commerce and exchange. Thrift stores, clothing swaps, and the "Really Really Free Markets" that are springing up around the country are essential resources for low-cost living. They're also forums for reuse and recycling, extending the lives of dresses, television sets, sinks, and many more goods that would otherwise be added to those mountainous landfills, along with the industrial waste created by the act of producing all of that stuff for the new, or "primary," market. The secondhand market rings up more than $17 billion in sales every year in the United States, with almost 20 percent of Americans shopping at thrift stores and consignment stores and untold numbers more bidding on eBay or foraging for dishes and winter coats at Saturday-morning garage sales.

The online network Freecycle, on which people give away and claim everything from never-used digital cameras to leftover paint from a renovation project, boasts 6.2 million members worldwide and a mission of "reuse and keeping good stuff out of landfills." And Really Really Free Markets—swap gatherings at which everything is, naturally, free for the taking—emerged in the past decade among radical groups as an alternative to capitalism. These innovative responses to consumption-gone-wild take the ethics of sharing, reuse, and low-cost living to their logical end point, where any item one gets tired of or no longer needs might still be valuable to someone else. At one market I attended, a pink birth-control diaphragm sat on a table, waiting for a taker. It didn't come home with me, but I did walk away with a Diane von Furstenberg shirt that had only a few small, easily mendable tears.

MANY PEOPLE HAVE told me that the environmental movement has given them cover for their cheapskate ways. Rik Treiber, a foundation executive who lives in Brooklyn, says he uses his window blinds, along with "self-images of hardiness," to minimize the use of air-conditioning in the summer and heat in the wintertime. "Luckily," he added, "I now have the popularity of environmentalism to lean on as well."

Looking back now on how I used to make fun of my father for obsessively turning off lights and carping about my showers, I see he was on to something, though he didn't know it at the time. He just wanted to cut our electricity bills, but in his own accidental way, he was also a green pioneer. And all his complaints about "dippy-shit trips" to the store or to drop me off at my friend's house half a mile away? At the time these seemed like petty concerns, but now I see what happened as a result of his visceral indignation about waste. He may have been watching his wallet, but he also maintained a low carbon footprint before that became popular.

My mother taught me in her quieter way to appreciate the usefulness of things that others might discard. Every morning after she'd left for work, I'd find my vitamins and half an orange sitting next to a torn old envelope, on the back of which she'd scribbled one of her notes. "Please take in the laundry after school. Have a good day. Love, Mom." Or "Your dentist appointment is at 3 PM. I'll pick you up afterward. Love, Mom." She also used these old envelopes for her grocery lists (her coupons were tucked inside) and phone messages. Old envelopes were the only scrap paper we ever used.

Erik Kriss, a spokesman for New York State's Correctional

Services Department in Albany, says he uses his clothes dryer only sparingly. Even when it's too cold to use the clothesline outside, he first takes the laundry out of the washer and hangs everything up inside the house, then uses the dryer at the very end. "Why run the dryer and use up the electricity? That's one cheap habit I have. But there's always a secondary [environmental] benefit there. I don't know if that's a rationalization or not." He adds, "I live a mile and change from the supermarket and it's almost unheard of for me to get in my car and go to the supermarket to go shopping. If I'm home and I need stuff I'll either walk or ski or ride my bike no matter the weather. I generally stop at the supermarket in the car only if it's on my way home from somewhere else."

In a world of $1-a-gallon gasoline, these habits seemed eccentric. But when fuel prices tripled in 2005 and went even higher in 2008, they seemed perfectly sensible, even wise. And by reducing their use of fuel and other raw materials, cheap people are minimizing total demand on resources, which keeps prices lower (infinitesimally lower, perhaps) for the rest of the population. (Cheap commodities, however, act as a *dis*incentive for people to cut back. In the United States, per capita consumption of gas and diesel is almost *six times* higher than in Europe, where taxes raise the cost of gas to around $6 per gallon.)

As with our economy, there is room here for public policy responses on top of these modest, private actions. More than seven thousand communities in the United States have adopted "pay-as-you-throw" garbage disposal programs. Unlike traditional programs, which are financed through property taxes or a fixed fee no matter how much trash residents generate, the PAYT initiatives generally charge homeowners a flat rate for each trash can they put out or each bag they bring to the dump. In the hamlet of South Kingstown, Rhode Island, residents cut their solid waste by more than two thirds after the town started requiring $1 tags on each bag of trash brought to the local dump (and opened a sorting center to handle the higher flow of aluminum, glass, and paper recyclables). The average family of four also went from paying $92 per year for garbage disposal to paying $52. These programs work for larger cities as well. In 1993, San Jose, California, abandoned its flat-rate billing program and began offering residents the choice of paying lower fees for putting less garbage out every week. Within months, the typical household had reduced its solid waste from three 32-gallon containers every week to just one.

What about the opposite end of the mass-consumption stream, the factories where all of our stuff is made? Currently, manufacturers don't pay in any systematic way for the industrial waste, pollution, and greenhouse gases they generate, and so those costs also aren't priced into the amount we consumers pay at the cash register. As this book went to press, Barack Obama was fighting for a cap-and-trade system to reduce carbon emissions. But there are other ideas out there as well. Herman Daly, the pioneering "ecological economist" at the University of Maryland, has suggested overhauling our corporate tax system to reflect the realities of a limited-resource planet. He proposes that governments impose taxes on corporations and manufacturers based on their natural resource use and pollution emissions rather than on payroll and profits, as they currently do. The traditional taxes make sense, he says, when labor and money are expensive and raw materials are cheap. But in a world where the trend lines run in the opposite direction—where resources are getting scarcer and their prices are rising—it's labor and capital that become cheap relative to fuel, timber, copper, and other materials. Taxing our disappearing natural resources gives companies incentives to develop efficient technologies (and removing some payroll taxes may encourage firms to hire more workers). It's an alternative to outright regulation, the kind of market-based response to scarcity that everyone from environmentalists to financial conservatives can understand. While not necessarily the best solution to our long-term resource problems, Daly's idea underscores the need to think creatively about how we can transition away from a culture of careless, ceaseless waste.

THE FARMER-POET Wendell Berry has written that we ought to be a *more* materialistic society. Materialistic people, he says, would care about their things, not just use them up and blithely discard them. "The great fault of the selective bookkeeping we call 'the economy' is that it does not lead to thrift; day by day, we are acting out the plot of a murderous paradox: an 'economy' that leads to extravagance. Our great fault as a people is that we do not take care of things."

An ever-flowing river of toys, T-shirts, microchips, and fiber-optic cable streams toward us from the factories of Asia, the mines of Africa, and the fields of South America. Until our recent economic troubles began, bringing up the specter of scarcity or limits was decidedly unfashionable. But limits are what we face, and they can have some positive consequences. Confronting the prospect of limits—limited oil and gas resources, temperature thresholds at which ice caps will melt with devastating consequences, toxic air and water—may encourage a reckoning with the downsides of our individualistic, growth-obsessed culture.

We may begin to take care of our things. We may adopt the prescription suggested by the poet Gary Snyder, who in 1970 penned a farsighted disquisition on the perils facing the earth.

"Learn to break the habit of unnecessary possessions—a monkey on everybody's back," he wrote, "but avoid a self-abnegating, anti-joyous self-righteousness. Simplicity is light, carefree, neat, and loving—not a self-punishing ascetic trip." We may start asking, "How much is enough?" Even better, we may discover that we've already got everything we need.

Chapter 9

Living Cheap in the Age of Mass Consumption

W hen I started working on this book, I believed that thrift was a dying virtue. That's the conventional wisdom, after all. But every time I mentioned the subject to someone new, the invariable reaction was "You should talk to my brother." Or grandmother. Or boss. Or husband. Some said, "You should interview me." Thrift—or cheapness, frugality, underconsumption, whatever you want to call it—is everywhere. That's become even more true in the last few years, as a combination of hard times and heightened awareness about the environment has spurred Americans into cutting back and questioning the imperatives of our debt-driven economy.

People all over this unlikely country of ours are practicing and thinking about low-cost living. Until recently we rarely heard about them. The story that's told about the United States, both at home and abroad, is that we're a nation of spendthrifts, a debtor nation, a credit card nation. In the aggregate, that's absolutely true, and the statistics bear it out. But look a little closer and you find a different story. On the margins, often quiet and invisible, are pockets of Americans who are questioning and, to varying and sometimes astonishing degrees, opting out of consumer culture.

Sure, there are fringier radicals who view consumption through an explicitly anticapitalist, anarchist, vegan, animal rights, or human rights lens. But I'm also talking about ordinary people here. There's no single motivation or demographic that describes individuals who consciously reject the get-and-spend ethos of our era. I've spoken to artists, investment bankers, activists, engineers, environmentalists, teachers, and people with extremely fluid jobs and careers, all of whom fall into this category of underconsumers. Erik Kriss skis to the grocery store during Albany winters in order to save on gas and step more lightly on the planet. My friend Eve Abrams, a part-time teacher in New Orleans, lives cheaply so she can devote more time to writing and making radio documentaries, her real (and often uncompensated) passions. Adam Dowis, an artist and electrician in New York City, just doesn't feel as if he's a part of this consumption-driven society. He does most of his work for trade rather than cash; he'll rewire a restaurant in exchange for a few months' worth of meals. "I hate spending money, but I also hate anyone else spending money," he says with a laugh. What unites all of these individuals is a willingness to think against the grain of consumer culture, to resist the seduction of the retail-industrial complex: the idea that buying things can make us happy and can help us define who we are. They're rebelling against an age of mass consumption.

For the most part, these rebels operate in their own atomized spheres, mending their appliances, parboiling and then freezing the surplus spinach from their gardens, or forgoing new clothes quietly and privately (exposed only, perhaps, to some ridicule from friends and family). Now and then, they organize into a group, or realize their frugal ways connect them to a larger circle. When reporters started writing articles about the Compact, a band of San Franciscans who in 2006 decided not to buy anything new for a year besides food and medicines, thousands of people signed on to the group's Yahoo! message board. "There was a lot of 'Oh, I had no idea there were other people living this way,'" says Shawn Rosenmoss, one of the Compact's original members.

But there are. There are lots of people living on the cheap and, in small personal acts and grand political gestures, undermining the consumerization of daily life in America. In doing so, they're expressing not just their own preferences and politics, but also what I've come to believe is a broader discomfort with the consumer society America has evolved into.

Of course, millions of people live cheaply through no choice of their own. I'm talking about poor people, those who struggle to get by as a fact of life. Many of the under-consumers in this chapter live well below what the Bureau of Labor Statistics would call the poverty line. But they're lucky—most of them come from middle-class backgrounds and have college educations. They're "poor" (economically speaking) by choice. Those who are poor—really poor, with far fewer possibilities for upward mobility and financial security—have a much harder road than the cheapskates I highlight here.

SHAWN ROSENMOSS WATCHED in shock from her home in San Francisco as Hurricane Katrina swept through the Gulf Coast in August 2005. She was born and raised in southern Louisiana; the uprooted trees, smashed-up towns, and flooded streets she saw on television represented the landscapes of her childhood, now suddenly flattened. "Katrina was a huge, huge horrible wake-up, like, 'Okay, this is global warming. This is happening,'" she said.

So with a sense of righteous purpose, a couple of months

after the storm, she joined her friend John Perry for an experiment in low-impact living. In the fall of 2005, Perry invited Shawn and a handful of other friends to ante up for a challenge: a yearlong embargo on buying new stuff. No new clothes, no new gadgets, no new books, and so on. They could buy anything they wanted secondhand, and they could still buy food, medicine, safety-related items, and services like concert and train tickets. The main idea was to reduce their consumption of stuff, all those tangible things that clutter the house, consume raw materials, and eventually take up residence in landfills.

Several years later, Shawn still adheres to the guidelines of the Compact, the name the group gave itself in homage to the social contract signed by the *Mayflower* Pilgrims in 1620.

For Shawn, who's in her forties and now manages grants for San Francisco's Department of the Environment, the commitment wasn't much of a change. She'd already been living an essentially low-impact life. From the time she was a child, she made her own clothes and combed thrift stores for cheap ensembles. She'd held a string of low-paying jobs that matched her left-of-center politics: working for nonprofit organizations, starting a school in a low-income neighborhood, and even performing as a trapeze artist. After she and her husband divorced, Shawn and her two daughters lived in a small apartment in the city's Bernal Heights neighborhood. The Compact was not a radical shift for her; it was an extension, a slightly more challenging version, of the life she'd carved out over the previous twenty-five or so years. "We were taking a stand, in a way, but really it just meant putting a name to the way most of us had been living all along," she said.

Still, there were adjustments. Whereas before the Compact, she might have unthinkingly bought a new dish rack, or a hook for her bathroom door, that was no longer an option.

At one point, she wanted red velvet curtains and found some energy-efficient ones at an outlet store, which led to an extensive inner dialogue: "Do I buy these new? Do I try to make them at home? Is the trade-off of energy-efficiency worth violating Compact guidelines?" With two preteen daughters at home, Shawn wondered how much she could impose her choices on them. Even though many of the families in their community share similar values, it's still tough for a twelve-year-old to bring a thrift-store or handmade gift to a birthday party where the other girls are giving cell phone accessories and gift cards to trendy clothing stores. Shawn's compromise was to let her kids spend their allowances however they wished.

Shawn is quick to point out that the Compact was never explicitly about saving money. Its origins speak more to environmental stewardship than to personal finances. But in wider practice the commitment inevitably leads to questions like, Do I really need a new blender/shirt/laptop/handbag/coffee table? Can I go another season with the winter coat I have? How can I improvise or make a Halloween costume for my kid? Where can I borrow an electric drill or a carpet-cleaning machine? The lower consumption fostered by the Compact manifests in savings of resources and money. Activities like drinking tap water out of a refillable bottle or fixing the DVD player rather than replacing it follow the same logic: fewer natural resources consumed, less money to make and maintain.

AS SHAWN AND I parsed her experience with the Compact over the last couple of years, we talked about how consciously lowering consumption is part of a broader reevaluation of how we define a meaningful life. Growing up in the South, she inhabited a world where families shared meals, neighbors

stopped by, a friend might sit down at the piano after dinner and get everyone singing and dancing. But that kind of
community life exists in fewer and fewer places in today's
America. Instead, people isolate themselves in ever-larger
houses, and spend more of their leisure time alone, in front
of computer screens. Our cultural roots disintegrate as we
lose the interdependence of earlier eras. Loneliness, depression, and anxiety, the indicators of some vast existential emptiness, are all on the rise. Into this void, mall culture inserts
itself, promising relief of the most ephemeral kind. Shopping
isn't only patriotic—it's now entertainment; it's what we do
when we're bored or blue, when we've got a little extra time
on our hands. It has replaced, to some extent, the intangible
things that once bound us together—eating, music, storytell-
ing, relying on one another in fundamental ways. It's hard not
to get caught up in this culture of acquisition. As Shawn said,
"I sometimes think if I find the perfect black boots, I'll be
fine. So I end up with twelve pairs of black boots, and none of
them are exactly right." The problems those boots were supposed to fix stick around; maybe the boots weren't the answer
after all. I've shopped under those same delusions.

Shawn says that with the money she saves by buying less,
she gives more donations to community groups and attends
more concerts with her daughters. She now borrows tools
from her neighbors and pitches in when friends need some
child care or a dog walker. In a sense, she's rediscovered
the kind of community fabric—interdependence, mutual
aid, bonding over activities that exist outside the realm of
commerce—that characterized her childhood.

That quest for a sense of meaning beyond material abundance has been present in America since our beginnings. It's
often lain dormant and obscure, but it breaks through again
and again in our history, in philosophies like Quakerism
and the Transcendentalism of Emerson and Thoreau. More

recently, these ideas were taken up by the voluntary simplicity movement that surfaced in the 1980s. In cities like Seattle and Madison, Wisconsin, small clusters of people began to question the greed-is-good ethos of the Reagan years and decided to downshift their own lives. Some moved into smaller homes, some biked to work rather than drove, some changed jobs so they'd have more time for family and leisure. "Simple livers" began to find one another and create networks; a few philosophers emerged to articulate their new creed. One of these, Duane Elgin, wrote that the objective of simple living "is not dogmatically to live with less, but is a more demanding intention of living with balance in order to find a life of greater purpose, fulfillment, and satisfaction." Seekers coalesced around "financial integrity" workshops led by Joe Dominguez and Vicki Robin, which asked participants to evaluate whether their financial lives — how they earned and spent money — aligned with their personal values, and then offered a nine-step plan for creating that alignment. Vicki and Joe eventually put their ideas on paper, in the 1992 book *Your Money or Your Life*. It combined Vicki's impassioned environmental politics and Joe's conviction that too many Americans sought spiritual succor in their possessions. The book took off, selling more than 600,000 copies in ten languages.

The nascent movement gained shape. Newsletters, conferences, and websites sprang up to connect and motivate people who were transforming their relationship to money and consumption. It makes sense that this would happen. Rozie Hughes used to run the New Road Map Foundation, one of the public voices of the voluntary simplicity movement. "You have to be willing to be independent-minded to live this way, because this is not the way the culture teaches you to act," she says. "But that's also why community is so important. If you're bucking the dominant paradigm, you have to have other people telling you you're not insane. It's the dominant paradigm that's insane."

Something similar happened with the Compact. Soon after the original Compacters made their pledge, a friend of the group's, a reporter at the *San Francisco Chronicle,* wrote an article describing their experiment. That story touched off a minor media storm; over the last few years, dozens of news outlets, from as far away as China and Poland, have written or broadcast features about the Compact. The coverage ranged from incredulous to skeptical to unabashedly supportive. For people who were already questioning the consumption dynamic in their own lives, the stories about the Compact helped connect them to a web of like-minded souls. After that first *Chronicle* article, the Compacters were overwhelmed with requests from people who wanted to "join" the project. There was nothing to join at that point, but the Compacters put together a Yahoo! message board and were astonished when more than ten thousand people signed up. The board spawned local offshoots in other cities and regions. Groups organized monthly potlucks and clothing swaps and shared tips online—how to sew reusable toilet wipes (to replace toilet paper) and clear up sinus infections with cayenne pepper. Thanks to the media's fascination with the Compact story, people who were experimenting with low-cost and low-impact living on their own sought one another out.

But why did a small group of friends who decided not to buy anything new for a year elicit so much interest? "It was kind of fascinating and a little appalling to me that this was news," Shawn said. To the reporters and editors who seized on the story, and to many of their readers as well, the project touched a nerve, disrupting some of our most cherished ideas. In the United States, convenience and instant gratification have become two of the gospels by which we live. We've raised disposability to a high art, with our throwaway contact lenses and cardboard cameras. We take for granted the knowledge that anything we want is at our fingertips any time of the day or night, whether at the big-box store down the road or at the twenty-four-hour emporia of the Internet.

The Compact rejects those values. It also rejects the notion that one's standard of living can be measured by one's belongings. And it suggests the possibility of an alternative. Why did the story gather such momentum? I think it's because many Americans, explicitly or not, feel uneasy about the spiritual vacuity and hyperconsumptive dynamics of modern life in the United States. As the essayist Richard Todd wrote recently, "We have mixed feelings about our things."

ADAM WEISSMAN SPENDS most of his waking hours in an unventilated basement deep in the heart of postindustrial Brooklyn. The musty room serves as the headquarters of Freegan.info, a website and organization that promotes unraveling ourselves from the "money economy," an economy that requires people to sell their labor in order to earn enough cash for basic needs like food and housing. That work-and-spend cycle, say "freegans," dehumanizes individuals, exploits animals and people, frays our connections to self-sufficiency and community life, and is rapidly poisoning the environment. In order to liberate themselves from this alienated existence, freegans practice an extreme version of low-cost living. A freegan (the term is a play on *vegan*) might Dumpster-dive for her food, squat in an unoccupied building rather than pay rent, bike or walk instead of drive, give away and obtain clothes at Really Really Free Markets, grow an urban garden, and share skills like computer repair and wild-food foraging.

Though he won't be pleased with this description, Adam is the unofficial chief of New York City's freegan underground (the group runs on anarchist principles and so operates without formal leaders). He's intense and utterly earnest, a bit stocky, with long black hair and a full beard—a pro-agrarian, pacifist, animal-liberation Communist revolutionary living approximately four miles from Wall Street, the nexus of American capitalism. Despite his small stature and thick features, Adam is undeniably compelling.

Adam's father is a pediatrician and his mother teaches in a gifted-and-talented program, but Adam never identified with his upper-middle-class New Jersey upbringing. "I always had a fundamental lack of trust that society was inherently just, maybe related to the fact that my great-grandmother was a Holocaust victim," he says when I interview him one afternoon on the rooftop of the building that houses Freegan.info. He considers that for a moment. "I don't know, that's a lot of rationalization. It was just always obvious to me that you don't kill and you don't exploit. For me, it wasn't just an obsession with consumption, it was an overall politics." He stopped eating meat at the age of eight and turned vegan a few years later. When he was around thirteen, Adam went door-to-door in his neighborhood campaigning against electric bug-zappers on the grounds that they're unnecessarily cruel and destroy insect species. After high school, he passed on college and instead worked full-time for an environmental organization in upstate New York.

Since then, his politics have evolved into a broad critique of what others would call the progress of the last few centuries, progress that has given most Americans lives of physical ease and material comfort. In his view, human beings need to return to a more localized, cooperative, preindustrial existence, one based on small-scale production and a symbiosis with, rather than a plundering of, the natural environment. If we don't adapt in these ways, he says, industrial civilization will destroy itself. "I kind of feel that the world would be better off without us, but it's not coming from a perspective of wanting people to suffer. It's just that I'm not sure we're good for the planet. So I'd like to try to arrange some kind of détente of either downscaling our role here or saying a quiet good-bye."

I crossed paths with Adam when I went on my first "trash tour" in March 2008. Trash tours are freegans' main outreach activity; once or twice a week, members lead bands of newcomers—some just curious, others intent on cutting down their food bills or experimenting with freegan living—on a circuit of one neighborhood's supermarkets and bagel shops to pick through garbage bags in search of salvageable food to bring home and eat. It's Dumpster diving, New York–style. In a city with almost no outdoor parking lots and thus very few Dumpsters, retailers put their trash out on the sidewalk, making it fair game for freegans and other foragers.

At that first tour, Janet Kalish gave an opening speech seeded with practical advice: feel the bags first to get an idea of what's in them; bruised fruit and vegetables can almost always be rescued; don't rip the bags (instead, untie and retie them); and never leave a mess (it's rude and it raises the ire of store owners and sanitation workers). She assured us that no matter how many people were in our motley group—I was one of about thirty novices that night—there was always enough good food for everyone to go home with one or two full bags.

She was right. I had understood that we live in a profligate society, but nothing had prepared me for the sight of such extravagant waste. In front of a bakery near Columbia University, the scents of garlic and onion filled the air as our crew converged on two giant sacks of warm bagels, all perfectly pristine. At a nearby supermarket, I plunged my hands into a bag filled with tomatoes and heads of lettuce. The tomatoes had seen better days, and some of the lettuce had turned slimy, but the veterans quickly worked their way through the hodgepodge and separated out what was salvageable. I regretted not having brought latex gloves; on the other hand, it's crucial to be able to identify foods by touch, and to do so quickly, when it's ten thirty at night and you're rooting through black trash bags while a wary supermarket manager stands close by. (Delving into other people's trash is legal, as the U.S. Supreme Court determined in the 1988 case *California v. Greenwood,* but store owners sometimes try to harass and intimidate foragers).

About halfway through the tour, Adam stood in the middle of our crowd and delivered a speech. Eloquent and wide-ranging, his ten-minute talk condemned the industrial food system's paradigm of overproduction and waste, a paradigm that continues even as food prices rise and millions around the world go hungry. He quoted statistics and figures. He connected agribusiness practices to the exploitation of farmworkers, the abuse of animals and land, and the pollution of rivers, oceans, and air. He decried our culture's cavalier attitude toward waste.

By the time I peeled off from the tour that night, I was carrying a whole wheat baguette, half a dozen bagels, a lime, a tub of hummus, a container of chicken fried rice made that day, a sealed bag of Parmesan-garlic pita chips, and a liter of chicken-and-rice soup that had reached its sell-by date. There was plenty more we left behind. On the subway, I contemplated my haul, torn between my delight about all the free food I'd scored and my horror at the volume of groceries casually jettisoned every day in a city where 400,000 people can't afford to feed themselves. The most common question freegans get is, "Why isn't this food donated to soup kitchens or food pantries?" There are a few explanations. Legally, grocers can't donate food that's at or past its sell-by date. Even when that's not an issue, stores still worry about liability in case a recipient of the food gets sick (there's little need to worry, as it turns out; there's a federal "Good Samaritan" law that protects donors of food and other goods from being sued for reasons related to their donations). But often, as in the case of the bagel shops, it's just laziness—the owner or manager can't be bothered to deliver the food to a charity or to arrange a pickup from the many organizations that serve New York's hungry.

In 1997, the Department of Agriculture said that American households, supermarkets, and restaurants throw out more than 96 billion pounds of food a year, a figure they acknowledged was a conservative estimate. That adds up to 122 pounds a month for a family of four (24 pounds of fruit and vegetables, 22 pounds of milk, 18.5 pounds of bread and other grains, and so on). Recovering just 5 percent of that total would feed 4 million Americans, the DoA said; recovering 25 percent would put food on the table for 25 million. As this book went to press, the DoA was updating its figures, but in the meantime we have a rough update from Jonathan Bloom, founder of the blog Wastedfood.com, who says that the total is now up to at least 150 billion pounds a year (again, a conservative estimate, and it doesn't include food lost on farms or by wholesalers and processors). At a time when the bellies of 963 million people around the world growl from hunger, many of us in the developed world discard mushy bananas and limp carrots, pour milk down the drain once it's hit its sell-by date, and celebrate the oversize portions at restaurants only to leave much of that chicken fettuccine on the plate at the end of the night.

"All this waste is like a nightmare," said Quinn Hecht-kopf, a thoughtful freegan I interviewed a few weeks later. "And we don't want to contribute to the overproduction so we consume the waste. And we feel good about it because we're doing something positive with the trash and we find food that tastes good and things we want. But then we forget that it's a nightmare. We're trying to do the right thing, but we're so far from being in a system where we *can* do the right thing. It's all distorted."

ALMOST AS SOON as Adam and three comrades fired up the freegan website in 2004 and began holding regular trash tours, media requests poured in. As with the Compact, this statement of anticonsumerism elicited intense fascination. People who were not poor or homeless (in the traditional sense of those words) were voluntarily eating food trash? The story was irresistible. Since then, the group has been featured in hundreds of news articles and television reports around the world. They were even invited onto *Oprah;* the correspondent Lisa Ling joined a trash tour for the program. That segment, in 2008, was unusually respectful. Most of the media stories come swathed in voyeurism and judgment, the subtext being, *Isn't this strange?* or *isn't this gross?* And the stories focus without exception on Dumpster diving, the most easily sensationalized aspect of freeganism.

In fact, as Adam and many others made clear to me through words and actions, feeding themselves off the discards of the industrial food system is just one small element of their daily freegan lives. When we talked on the roof of his building, Adam said, "It's sort of unfortunate in a way that Dumpster diving has become the signature piece of freeganism, in the mind of the media. It really paints a distorted picture of what freeganism is. I mean, to us, turning this rooftop into a garden is as much of a freegan practice, even more so if it's an abandoned lot.... Fundamentally, freeganism is a commitment to nonparticipation in capitalism, to living without money, to living without employment, to doing everything that one can to facilitate ethically avoiding participation in that system."

Freegans are very much of their time—their main organizing tool is a website, and like all websites it relies on a vast
and modern production and technology infrastructure—but
their work has many spiritual antecedents. The Diggers, an
artist-anarchist-hippie collective that sprouted in San Francisco in 1966, wanted to create a world free from all buying
and selling (they took their name from a seventeenth-century
British group that fought for the abolition of private land
ownership). The Diggers hosted a Death of Money parade,
opened up free stores (which were just that—people taking and leaving things, without a dime changing hands),
and passed out free grub, like whole wheat bread baked
in coffee cans and a vegetarian Digger Stew cooked in a
thirty-two-quart pot. One of their manifestos began, "Money
is an unnecessary evil. It is addicting," and ended by asking
"all responsible citizens" to "turn in their money. No questions will be asked."

A decade and a half later, a group called Food Not Bombs
coalesced in Cambridge, Massachusetts, around antinuclear
activism. Dedicated to nonviolence and the belief that "our
society needs things that give life, not things that give death,"
FNB chapters around the country still make and distribute
free vegan food to anyone who needs a meal, usually after
scavenging the ingredients via supermarkets donations and,
when necessary, Dumpster diving. Many freegans sharpened
their understanding of the connections between capitalism
and violence—a system that prioritizes profit above all else has
little room for compassion and justice, they believe—through
involvement in FNB. According to Adam Weissman, the
word *freegan* emerged from a Food Not Bombs impasse over
a hunk of cheese. One day a bunch of FNB volunteers salvaged some cheese and no one was quite sure what to do with
it. It wasn't vegan, but some argued that the group shouldn't
toss it, as that would mean consigning it to the waste stream.

"Someone said, 'It's not vegan, but it's 'freegan,' so that's kind of how the term got started," Adam said.

Among the dozen or so freegans I met, there's a broad range of fidelity to the vision of a moneyless, anticapitalist society. Adam is among the most rigorous; he estimated that his total living expenses from December 2007 to May 2008 were around $400, mostly for subways and phone cards. But then there are freegans like Janet Kalish, a forty-six-year-old public school teacher who owns her house in Queens. She kept the car she inherited from her father and, thanks to the money she saves by scavenging nearly all of her food and clothes, recently bought a second home in upstate New York, which she hopes to use as a personal oasis and freegan retreat. Quinn Hechtkopf graduated from Wesleyan University a few years ago; now he lives in a semi-freegan apartment in Brooklyn with ten other people. He does odd jobs—electrical work, moving, carpentry, demolition—to cover his $300 rent, but he spends most of his time running a free bike-repair workshop, tutoring kids from the housing projects near his home, and choreographing modern dances. Christian Gutierrez, a former-model-turned-investment banker-turned-freegan, lived such a stripped-down life that his only regular expense for a long time was a cell phone. He recently started working again, as a dominatrix, and rents an apartment in the East Village.

At the first trash tour I attended, a beginner asked if freeganism was a political movement. One of the core members replied that every freegan would probably have a different answer to that question. For some, like Adam, being a freegan is the only way to align his daily life with his critique of industrial capitalism; it's a deeply political act and he's all about turning it into a movement of like-minded souls. That's not the case with everyone in the group. Janet told me that she's had a visceral aversion to waste since she was a small child, whether it was money needlessly spent or a tea bag thrown away after a single use. As a teacher, she writes all of her lesson plans on the back of junk mail. She's delighted by the elegant efficiency of eating found food and reading found books, the way freeganism captures use-value that would otherwise be lost (not just lost, but sent to landfills and converted into greenhouse gases and toxic sludge). While the political critique of consumerism is important to her, she views freeganism more as a personal choice, a way of living an ethically rewarding life.

Quinn and Christian sought something different from freeganism. It offered them self-determination and freedom — freedom from soul-killing jobs, freedom to devote their time to art and activism. Christian was engineering reverse mergers for an investment-banking firm a few years ago, but he hankered to make movies. The job gave him the money — he was making $300,000 a year — but not the time for his creative work. So he quit the job and spent down his savings and gradually found himself without any cash. It was the dilemma known to almost every artist. "I had the money at first and I didn't have the art, and then I worked on the art and I didn't have much money," he said. "And then I met freegans and all of a sudden it was like I was rich again. So it was like my dream. How can you have a wealthy life and still have free time to make art, you know? I found what I wanted."

BEING A FREEGAN necessarily means living resourcefully and cheaply. It's a part of the ethic — to respect the value of goods — and it's also a requirement for anyone with no steady income. If something breaks down, like a bike or a radio, you don't throw it away or pay someone else to repair it. You fix it yourself or find someone who can, for free or for barter. To facilitate this way of life, tangible skills — carpentry, plumbing, electrical, cooking, computer repair—are highly valued and actively cultivated among freegans. So are communal exchange and mutual support, since a tight-knit community means more intensive use of resources. One vacuum cleaner suffices instead of five; tools and books circulate among the group. In Quinn's household, one resident contributed her $50 knife to the apartment's kitchen. "Out of eleven people, nine of us cook," said Quinn. "So that's a great use of that knife. That's resource sharing." In many ways, it's not so different from the neighborhood sufficiency of the colonial era, when Americans got along only by sharing goods and assisting one another with big tasks like harvesting the fields and constructing homes and barns. But freegans live this way by choice, and they do so surrounded by the whiz and bang of the most highly developed consumer culture in history.

"You can't be a freegan alone," Quinn added. "With Dumpster diving, everything you find is by accident. Some things are consistent, like food, but most things aren't. It's much easier if you have a group of people looking out for one another. There's a one hundred percent probability that you'll go to the hardware store and they'll have nails. If you open a black trash bag, there's maybe a 2 percent probability of finding nails. So it's much easier with a group where everyone is looking out for usable trash." When Quinn and I went Dumpster diving together during move-out time at the Pratt Institute dormitories, for instance, he collected dozens of mirrored tiles that he knew his roommate Terry needed for an art project. In fact, he took nearly every salvageable item he could find—half-filled shampoo bottles, wigs, clothing, mops, mustard, four unopened jars of pasta sauce, toilet bowl cleaner, and more—with the expectation that someone, a fellow freegan or some down-and-out stranger, would eventually claim it.

I was especially struck by freegans' ethic of radical generosity.

Though they scrounge for just about everything they have, this leads not to a sense of deprivation but to inspiring acts of magnanimity. They operate from a conviction that hoarding is unnecessary when there's so much that's free for the taking. At Pratt, I watched Quinn interact with the other scavengers who came by. When one inquired about our growing pile of goodies, Quinn told him that if he saw something he wanted, he should just ask about it. He also passed down some odds and ends to a ragged-looking man who was collecting scrap metal. When a couple of cigarette-smoking art students came by and said they'd noticed us "spelunking" in the Dumpsters, we gave them the brand-new drawing pads we'd just fished out. "These would cost twenty dollars each in the store," one said gratefully. I saw this happen over and over again. Part of it is an unspoken fellowship with other scroungers, and a faith that there's more salvageable trash around the corner, more than enough to go around. And though freegans have a greater degree of respect for the value of objects than most people I know, they also live with a sense of "easy come, easy go," an ease with the ephemeral nature of the stuff in our lives.

NONE OF THE strategies freegans use is new, as Adam is quick to say. Hoboes, loosely organized groups of anarchists, homeless people, and artists have all provided models for the kind of cheap living that sustains freegans. Whether it's squatting or hopping trains or picking through trash, these are tried-and-true methods for getting by on less. What's new, really, is Freegan.info's effort to turn these shadow cultures and marginal activities into something that might be considered a full-fledged political movement, an organized response to mainstream society.

"We need mass change at a much faster rate than we could get by hoping that people will join off-center subcultures,"

Adam said. "We've tried to frame what we're doing not as the creation of a subculture, but as the development and sharing of strategies that can help people in their everyday lives." That's why Freegan.info welcomes news crews and reporters, even when the coverage ends up being tawdry or hostile. It's kind of working; the website at one point had six thousand subscribers, and trash tours regularly attract twenty to forty newcomers on top of a rotating group of a dozen or so regulars.

But the freegans' work is seriously limited by internal divisions, especially over questions about ethical purity versus expediency and accessibility to outsiders. For instance, they've had requests to start up chapters in other cities. But Freegan.info's core members want to have some quality control, mainly by ensuring that any satellite groups adhere to a statement of principles. The problem is, they've been held up by disagreement over a "live animal policy"—what to do with live animals like raw clams or the occasional mouse that freegans find in trash bags. Some volunteers insist that, for instance, shellfish be returned to their natural habitat. Other members think such rigid policies just alienate potential converts. If freegans can't agree on how to deal with a mollusk, it won't be easy to create the broader movement that will bring down industrial capitalism, or even hasten the collapse that Adam sees as inevitable.

While freegans continue to argue about ideology, though, they're still bringing in new crowds to every trash tour. One evening I met two middle-aged women from suburban New Jersey, both of them on their second freegan outing. "We saw it on *Oprah,*" one said. "I made dinner the other night for my family and almost all of it came out of trash bags. They couldn't believe it," said the other one. Then, with gusto, they plunged their arms into a garbage bag filled with doughnuts.

★　★　★

FOR EVERY PERSON who identifies with a political or communal form of anticonsumerism, there are dozens more who
are solo operators. A common thread runs through the stories of these underspenders. They are people who, in the
time-versus-money equation into which so much modern life
can be distilled, choose time. Helena Shoe dropped out of a
well-remunerated career in San Francisco in the mid-1990s.
Her work as a software analyst was making her sick; she was
skinny and depressed, beset by headaches. She arranged to
take a sabbatical and travel around Europe. When her three
months were up, she stopped by her parents' house in Connecticut, sat them down, and said, "I don't want to alarm you,
but I'm never going to have a career again."

Helena landed in New Orleans, a good place for marginal
living. "I liked being here, where people talk about everything
except shopping and what they do for a living," she said. "And
I got the general knowledge that there was a large population
of people living on the cheap." From them, and from trial and
error, she learned how to get by on less and less. She found a
job taking tickets at a movie theater, and, late at night, wove
through the city's streets with a garbage bag full of leftover
popcorn balanced on her handlebars. That was dinner some
nights. Later on, she moved into an old school bus that sat in
a friend's backyard in the Lower Ninth Ward. She slept there
for a year, paying about $60 a month and sharing the bath-
room, kitchen, and living room in the main house. She made
her own food, listened to music at bars with no cover charge,
and splurged on a beer when she wanted to. Now she lives
in a row of five houses whose occupants have an informal
cooperative-living arrangement. It's called the Truck Farm;
they share an enormous backyard, where many of them raise
food, and there's a communal washing machine and dryer to
which they all contribute money.

"There is an art to this, a set of skills," Helena said of cheap living. We don't often think of it that way. We're more apt to view choices like the ones Helena's made as quirks or eccentricities. But she's right: it takes planning, thoughtfulness, and working knowledge to live cheaply. We learn a lot of those skills from the people around us. Helena picked up some of her values when she decamped for France after high school and lived with a single woman and her three children. The woman worked in a grocery store and brought home all of the shop's bruised vegetables, from which she concocted "amazing meals." From her, Helena saw the possibilities for converting refuse into gold and gleaned the value of a freezer. Now she freezes the excess butter and milk she buys when they're on sale, and makes stocks and pasta sauces in bulk when the ingredients are cheap.

All of these activities take time. It's what economists call "household production"—the idea that we can spend time (our own labor) rather than money (the compensation we receive for our labor at other activities) to meet our needs. Thrifty people are inclined to prefer the former when they can. And in exchange for her labor and her assiduous attention to resources, someone like Helena has more autonomy in her life than most people. She now works a couple of days a week at a store in the French Quarter, sometimes fills in at an art gallery, and does some gardening work for her landlord. But aside from those paying gigs, her time is her own. "I wanted to not be a prisoner of my own existence," she said. "I realized pretty early on that any day I was out in the street in the daytime and not in a job was a reason to be joyous."

In the end, what do all of these disparate experiments add up to? They don't represent a unified challenge to our consumer-driven society. They won't topple capitalism or, perhaps, even make a dent in global warming.

What they suggest, though, are "new possibilities of collective sustenance and autonomy," in the words of Jeff Ferrell, a sociologist who wrote a book about his own yearlong experiment in trash picking and low-cost living. Freegans, Compacters, and independent devotees of cheap survival are all thinking deeply about issues like community, sustainability, self-determination, and the contours of a meaningful life. They are creating alternatives to a culture that thrives on store-bought pleasures and disposable dreams, and building worlds based on imagination and durability.

Can anyone adopt these models of cheap living? I'd like to think so; I'd like to think we all have available to us such ingenuity and resourcefulness. But it's probably easier for some people than for others. You see, some cheapskates are made; many others are born.

Chapter 10

Cheapskate Psychology

Several years ago I asked my Great-Aunt Esther, a psycho-therapist, why my father—her nephew—is cheap.

"Freud would say it has something to do with unresolved potty-training issues," she said.

I laughed. My father wasn't potty-trained correctly?

"Well," she said, "it's all about what you hold on to and what you let go of."

Something clicked when I heard that phrase. I thought about how my father's features froze in a glower every time some irritating expense—a parking ticket, a lost schoolbook that had to be replaced—came up. I thought about my own anxieties around money, the silent and tortured negotiations I sometimes hold with myself when I consider buying some-thing as innocuous as a sandwich. I've fantasized about spend-ing with abandon, burning through money, surrendering to every urge and desire. *What would it mean to let go like that?* Would that feel like liberation?

And yet, there is something terribly simplistic about this formulation. Is my, or my father's, approach to spend-ing all about withholding? That doesn't sound right to me. It speaks of meanness, rigidity, abstinence, and deprivation.

It overlooks the satisfactions and psychic rewards of cheapness, and the extreme generosity I see in my father and plenty of other parsimonious individuals I know. Like any theory, especially one meant to describe something as intricate and ineffable as human behavior, it felt woefully inadequate.

As I TRIED to untangle the psychodynamics of cheapness — why we cheapskates are the way we are, how we think, how we make decisions — I thought I would find some guidance in the academic literature from a few different fields. Consumer researchers, it seems, have studied every facet of why people buy, but have hardly looked at why people *don't* buy, thus leaving out a significant area of potential interest. Perhaps cheapness is simply invisible on some level; after all, spenders leave behind tangible evidence of their desires and decisions, in the form of cash register receipts and the physical substance of their purchases. Underconsumers leave nothing but a ghost trail of purchases weighed but not consummated, or never even considered at all. In the ebb and flow of commerce, we're a spectral presence, difficult to trace.

The dearth of research is a striking oversight, especially since every American could probably name at least a handful of relatives and acquaintances who fall under the cheap umbrella. In fact, one of the only academic studies that investigate cheapness as a psychological trait found some evidence that as much as one quarter of the general population are tightwads, and that tightwads outnumber overspenders. In 2006, three researchers at Carnegie Mellon University — George Loewenstein, Scott Rick, and Cynthia Cryder — developed a Tightwad-Spendthrift Scale and administered it to over thirteen thousand subjects, mostly readers of the *New York Times.* They asked the participants whether they found it difficult to spend money or to limit their spending, and then scored them on a scale of 4 to 26 points. Those who scored from 4 to 11 were labeled tightwads, those who scored from 19 to 26 were labeled spendthrifts, and those in the middle were "unconflicted" consumers, meaning they felt their spending reflected their needs and desires. (I scored a 6; you can take the survey at www.behavioraldecisionresearch.com.) The results surprised even the researchers: 24.4 percent of the subjects scored in the tightwad range, while only 15.4 percent appeared to be spendthrifts. (Context matters, though; when the same survey was conducted at a shopping mall, overspenders had a much higher showing.)

THE TIGHTWAD-SPENDTHRIFT SCALE helped me get a read on the prevalence of cheapness, but it doesn't offer much detail about the source or dynamics of the trait. Which brought me back to Sigmund Freud, one of the few thinkers to investigate, if only briefly, the origins and experience of frugality. In 1908, he published a short essay called "Character and Anal Erotism." In it, he elaborated on his well-known theory that children pass through three stages of psychosexual development—oral, anal, and genital—on their way to becoming functional adults. During the anal phase, he posited, children develop a fascination with the process of holding in and releasing their bowel movements, and also with the feces itself. For babies and toddlers, he said, defecating is a source of pleasure and autonomy. It's one of the few aspects of their lives they can control at a young age, and it becomes a means for pleasing or defying their parents. Children who never fully emerge from this stage develop what Freud called an "anal personality."

In particular, he noticed a trio of properties in the patients who fell into this category. "The people I am about to describe," he wrote in the essay, "are noteworthy for a regular combination of the three following characters. They are especially *orderly, parsimonious,* and *obstinate.*"

Orderliness expressed itself, he said, in a preoccupation with physical cleanliness or in conscientious attention to small tasks (its opposites were "untidy" or "neglectful"), while obstinacy sometimes appeared as defiance, rage, and vengefulness. In its extreme form, parsimony tipped over into avarice.

According to Freud, the childhood fixation on controlling defecation often expressed itself, in adulthood, as an anxious fixation on controlling money. He wrote that patients who came to him with chronic constipation couldn't clear up their malady until they had uncovered their "money complexes." It's worth noting (though Freud himself does not) that another favorite English euphemism for feces is *waste,* a word that also suggests squandered materials and is anathema to any frugal zealot.

Following up on Freud's theory, analysts have suggested that people who are anal-retentive develop rigid personalities in order to manage or compensate for unresolved conflict. They say that as children grow up and internalize the subtleties of social behavior, they repress their anal fascination and start to regard their "anal wishes" as disgusting and shameful. Children who fail to resolve this conflict between pleasure and disgust become obsessed with regulating their shameful urges and grow up to be rigid, tightly wound, and controlling. Dr. Leon Hoffman, a psychoanalyst and director of the Pacella Parent-Child Center in New York City, says excessive cheapness relates to "the whole idea of control and losing control. These people have a fear of being overwhelmed, a fear of being annihilated. They're terrified that if they spend all their money, it's all going to go down the drain and they won't be able to take care of themselves."

Freud's belief that major personality traits can be traced to toilet training and early psychosexual dramas has been largely discredited. But his ideas bequeathed a language for understanding the ways that unconscious forces drive human behavior, revolutionizing the study of psychology forever. And the personality types he identified have stood up over years of scrutiny and testing. For instance, the "anal triad" of orderliness, parsimony, and obstinacy reappears in modern form in the diagnosis of obsessive-compulsive personality disorder. The fourth edition of the *Diagnostic and Statistical Manual,* the bible of psychiatric diagnosis, describes the essential features of OCPD as "a preoccupation with orderliness, perfectionism, and mental and interpersonal control, at the expense of flexibility, openness, and efficiency."

The *DSM* goes on to say that individuals with OCPD "may be miserly and stingy and maintain a standard of living far below what they can afford, believing that spending must be tightly controlled to provide for future catastrophes." They are also likely to be rigid, stubborn, and unwilling or unable to change course once they've made decisions.

The existence of a formal diagnosis that includes cheapness as one of its diagnostic criteria raises the question: when does frugality indicate prudence and a commitment to plain living, and when does it indicate true pathology, a mental illness?

There's no definitive answer. Any behavior, taken to extremes, can be harmful or impair one's ability to function in the world. Take the case of Homer and Langley Collyer, the brothers who barricaded themselves in their Harlem brownstone in the 1930s and 1940s. The Collyer brothers were hoarders, a form of OCPD and a condition closely related to miserliness (hoarders collect stuff—usually what others would call junk—rather than money). They turned their home into a reliquary for old magazines, broken pianos, bicycle wheels, abandoned chandeliers, and any other bits of treasure and trash they found in their nocturnal wanderings along New York City's streets. They even kept the rusted chassis of an old Model T Ford in their basement. The Collyers are the most famous hoarders in American history. When they died in 1947 (Langley was crushed when some piles collapsed on him; Homer, an invalid who relied on Langley to feed and care for him, passed away from neglect a few days later), New York firefighters hauled 136 tons of debris out of the house.

Hoarders can't let go. They don't necessarily acquire more than the average person (though some do, buying cases of shampoo or multiple jars of olives), but they cannot discard anything. Every item—a piece of junk mail, a newspaper, a paper clip, a broken blender, worn-out sneakers—holds some potential value. A compulsive hoarder thinks, I may need this someday, or This is too valuable to throw away. They hold on to things, just in case.

Just in case of what? Hoarding, at its root, is a means for controlling the anxiety of the unknown, the future catastrophes that might lurk around the corner. Compulsive hoarders are tormented by uncertainty and have a related tendency to overestimate threats. They see disorder and danger all over. The world is an unpredictable place, they believe. Best to be prepared.

Hoarding, especially when taken to the level of the Collyer brothers, is a serious pathology. But there's a tremendous gray area between personality quirk and mental illness, and that's where most cheapskates fall.

Many thrifty people, for instance, are prone to the same kind of catastrophic thinking that plagues compulsive hoarders. Jill Slater, a frugal thirty-nine-year-old food activist in New York City, told me that she used to watch personal-finance shows on TV, the ones where the host gives "money makeovers" to guests and exhorts audience members to save money and pay off their credit card debt. "The financial adviser would always ask, 'What are you saving for?'" Jill said. "And I hated that question. I would be, like, You save because you never know what's going to happen! What kind of a question is that? You save because that's what you do."

FOR CHEAP PEOPLE, spending money can cause tremendous anxiety. George Loewenstein, from Carnegie Mellon, and Drazen Prelec, a professor at the Massachusetts Institute of Technology, have done pioneering work in the field of behavioral economics, which combines insights from psychology with the quantitative methods and research agenda of mainstream economics. For more than ten years, they've been studying a concept they call "pain of paying."

Traditional economists think about spending in terms of immediate pleasure versus delayed pleasure. Spend now and enjoy, say, a chocolate milk shake, or spend later and enjoy, perhaps, a new iPod or an early retirement with the savings accumulated from all the forgone milk shakes. But according to Loewenstein and Prelec, and generations of consumer researchers who study actual shopping behavior, buying decisions are almost never that simple. They're infused with conflict in an immediate, sometimes visceral sense. *Should I buy a new television set? Maybe I'd be better off saving my money. Will I still have a job in six months? Okay, if I buy a new TV, which one should I get? Do I splurge and buy a flat-screen, wall-mounted plasma model? I might regret that later. I could stick with the old box and put the extra cash into my retirement fund. Or maybe I should buy a midpriced TV and then take my mother out for dinner with the rest.* Even minor purchases can elicit these internal dialogues. *I need to buy a bottle of wine to bring to a party. Should I get the $10 bottle or the $20 bottle? How's my wallet feeling today? I shouldn't have bought those three CDs earlier, especially since my 401k lost $6,000 last quarter. I should probably get the $10 bottle. But will my friends know I skimped?*

The traditional economic formula—pleasure now or

pleasure later?—fails to account for the stress that consumers experience when they're considering a purchase, say Loewenstein and Prelec. The way they see it, the real choice is not between immediate pleasure and future pleasure but between immediate pleasure and immediate pain—the pleasure of consuming versus the pain of paying.

"Because humans are inherently myopic, we train ourselves, or are trained (via parenting, schooling, etc.), to experience immediate negative emotions such as guilt or fear when we succumb to various types of temptations," Loewenstein wrote in a 2006 article coauthored with the Cornell economist Ted O'Donoghue. "These immediate negative emotions serve the function of bringing the negative consequences of current indulgence into the present, thereby counteracting what would otherwise be a natural tendency to discount them.... The use of negative emotions is a crude method of self-control." These feelings operate like electric-fence dog collars; they zap us when we get too close to indulging some urge to spend. In 2006, Loewenstein, Prelec, and a few other researchers confirmed their hypothesis about the pain of paying when they sent some volunteers into MRI machines and scanned their brains while flashing images of DVDs, gadgets, and other consumer goods onto screens. When the price was displayed against a product the volunteers could buy, Prelec told me, parts of the brain that are associated with pain and discomfort lit up.

These emotions operate independently of a person's financial circumstances. The Tightwad-Spendthrift scale found little correlation between subjects' scores and their incomes. A school bus driver is just as likely to be a tightwad as a corporate lawyer because each is responding primarily to deeply ingrained anxieties and convictions, not to their bank account balances. "The whole question of whether you can afford something is difficult," Prelec says. "Anything you have funds for, you can afford. Of course I can afford a twenty-five-dollar bottle of olive oil. But it makes me nervous. It's a question of, is this an extravagance, a lapse in judgment? Part of the pain of paying is associated with these quasi-moral concerns about whether we should do something or not."

On the Tightwad-Spendthrift scale, spendthrifts are people who report that they "have trouble limiting [their] spending"; in other words, they don't experience *enough* pain of paying. Tightwads, on the other hand, experience *too much* pain; they have trouble spending money even when they'd like to. When faced with purchasing, say, tickets to a Bruce Springsteen concert or even a new coat whose price has been slashed by 60 percent, tightwads feel acute pain, in the form of anxiety or guilt, which acts as a deterrent to spending. Ultimately, the cheapskate often decides, the pain of paying outweighs the pleasure of the purchase, and the credit card remains tucked in his wallet.

ANXIETY, FEAR, GUILT, pain. According to the few psychological or economic theories of thrift that researchers have suggested, it's emotional distress that triggers cheap behavior. Some aspects of frugality surely do spring from anxiety and neurotic self-regulation. But cheapness is far more complicated than that. For both the proud and the conflicted cheapskates I interviewed, it's a jumble of positive and negative emotions. Occasional feelings of deprivation or anxiety blend with pride, a general sense of life satisfaction, a healthy distrust of consumerism, and a confident belief that products — *things* — offer only the most ephemeral kinds of happiness.

The psychoanalytic and psycho-economic explanations don't do justice to the pleasures and satisfactions of thrift, the psychic rewards of cheapness. In fact, the qualities of the frugal personality—cautious spending, self-control, independent thinking, discipline—are all ingredients for a successful life. Even the *DSM* points out that "obsessive-compulsive personality traits in moderation may be especially adaptive, particularly in situations that reward high performance."

And spending money *shouldn't* always feel good, or we might all develop shopping addictions and run up thousands of dollars in credit card charges we couldn't afford. We'd be like Woody Allen in the movie *Sleeper,* endlessly rubbing the pleasure orb for its intoxicating high.

The historian Avner Offer wrote in his book *The Challenge of Affluence: Self-Control and Well-Being in the United States and Britain since 1950* that overconsumption is a type of self-control problem that society has largely approved of, unlike, say, overeating or road rage. As we've seen, overconsumption serves economic purposes and, for some people, social and emotional ones, helping them win respect and envy from their peers.

But discipline and self-control, in spending as in other areas, are critical to success and even survival. John Calvin and Cotton Mather understood this, though they served up their message in a heavy sauce of moralism and sanctimony. We admire self-control in modern icons, people like Tiger Woods and Warren Buffett. Would Woods have set the sports world on fire if he hadn't spent untold hours on the golf course, practicing drives and perfecting his swing? Would Buffett have amassed his billions if he'd gotten caught up in every Wall Street fad rather than exercising the most disciplined judgment and restraint?

In a famous experiment from the late 1960s, the Stanford University psychologist Walter Mischel assembled a group of four-year-olds and gave them each a marshmallow. He told them that they could have a second marshmallow if they waited twenty minutes before eating the first. Naturally, some children dug in immediately. Others held off and received their reward. Mischel and his team then followed the children through adolescence and discovered that the kids who had waited were better adjusted and more dependable. They had also scored an average of 210 points higher on the Scholastic Aptitude Test. Mischel concluded that the ability to delay gratification was an early predictor of later success and satisfaction. His findings confirmed what ordinary people and philosophers like Aristotle have known for millennia: that self-control—when it comes to eating, drinking, taking drugs, spending money, or any number of other behaviors—is a crucial human quality. It helps us function in daily life and, by steering us away from addictions and excesses, it makes us happier people, too.

It's difficult to master, though, as evidenced by the high levels of alcoholism, drug addiction, and uncontrolled spending we see in the United States (according to one study, 5.8 percent of the American population are compulsive shoppers). We're always faced with temptations, and our human brains aren't generally very good at understanding the future costs of giving in to temptation right now. It's simple to resolve that we'll save more money next year or we'll have just one last cigarette and then quit. "Things seem easy to do as long as they are to be done in the future," says the psychologist Howard Rachlin in his book *The Science of Self-Control*. "We cannot seem to avoid the fact that the future keeps converting itself into the present."

In psychologists' parlance, self-control is a combination of qualities and habits. It shows up most often in individuals who have clear goals, monitor their behavior closely, and avoid exposing themselves to too many temptations. So people who go to the grocery store with a shopping list and make beelines for the items on the list generally don't arrive home and find they've bought a tub of ice cream, some chips, an overpriced pineapple, and a load of other items they neither wanted nor needed when they set out. "We have to limit our desire in order to survive as human beings," says Ron Faber, a professor of mass communications at the University of Minnesota, who studies compulsive shopping. "Most people go to a store and see things and think, Oh, that would be nice to have. But most people don't buy them. Similarly, we don't have four helpings of dessert. All of these are limits on our desires. It's not a puritanical thing or a bad thing. It's just that we have to make choices."

In 1995, State University of New York professors Jane Romal and Barbara Kaplan gave a thirty-six-page survey to members of an upstate New York credit union and discovered that the people who had stashed the most money in their savings accounts also, according to their survey answers, demonstrated a greater capacity for self-control in other areas of their lives.

How do we humans regulate our own behavior? How do we stick with our resolutions and goals? As the behavioral economists Richard Thaler and H. M. Shefrin wrote in a seminal 1981 article titled "An Economic Theory of Self-Control," one of the strategies we use is to create incentives and rules for ourselves. Incentives are rewards for good behavior, while rules provide a sense of structure and certainty, an almost totemic, if illusory, feeling of security. Rules around spending may include a personal ban on borrowing, or self-permission for borrowing only on major, durable items, such as a house or a car.

And cheapskates love rules. *I'll go out for dinner only once a week. Even if I'm thirsty, I won't buy bottled water. If I'm going fewer than twenty blocks, I'll walk rather than take the bus. I won't spend more than $60 on a new coat. I won't use more than the four-hundred daytime minutes my cell phone plan includes. I won't turn the heat above sixty degrees this winter.*

Thaler and Shefrin wrote that "rules of thumb are likely to

become habit." But they can also choke off spontaneity and the occasional indulgence, for better and for worse. Jill Slater, the food activist from New York, went to Italy not long ago (she makes enough money subletting her Manhattan apartment to cover most of her travels) and she and a friend fell in love with necklaces they saw in a shop there. "We went and visited the necklaces every day," she said. "And we thought, What does it mean to spend a ridiculous amount of money on a piece of jewelry? Are we allowed to do this? If you spent that thousand dollars, would you miss it later? Would you be wondering every day, where did that money go? Or would I just love the necklace? It was an existential crisis." Jill tried to rationalize buying the necklace, but she couldn't. Ultimately, she fell back on her rules. "Who spends a thousand dollars on a necklace? Not me."

EVEN ABSTINENCE AND self-denial have their ecstasies. Early Christians understood this; they exalted poverty and believed that extreme austerity brought one closer to the sufferings of Jesus and the kingdom of God. Ascetics and mendicants fasted, gave away their possessions, moved to desert caves, and renounced all worldly pleasures. In the fifth century, a hermit named Hero consumed food once every three months; Macarius of Alexandria once went through a forty-day Lent period eating nothing but a few cabbage leaves every Sunday; and some travelers, walking through the "Egyptian desert" around AD 450, once heard moaning coming from a cave along their path. They went in, only to discover a "holy virgin." She said, "Behold, I have passed eight and thirty years in this cave and I have satisfied my wants with grass, for I labor with Christ," and promptly died. These ascetics established an indivisible connection between self-denial and beatification, deprivation, and sanctification.

This connection can go too far. Anorexics, for instance, take a morbid pride in their ability to abstain from eating. Jim Mitchell, an expert on the disorder at the Neuropsychiatric Research Institute in Fargo, North Dakota, told me that anorexics like to test their willpower. It's not unusual for them to collect cookbooks and prepare elaborate meals for other people, but they won't eat the food they've so carefully planned and cooked.

But one needn't be quite so extreme to enjoy the experience of self-mastery. My father can go into a restaurant with other people and not order a thing. Instead, he happily drinks water.

I asked Ken Clark, a psychologist and financial planner in Little Rock, Arkansas, about this. Among his clients and in workshops he leads about the psychology of money, he often sees this dynamic at work. "Frugality becomes a quasi hobby, a quest or a little stand against the world," he said. "It also becomes a badge of honor. There's pride in beating the system or in not being a chump when it comes to the pressure to buy from advertisers or peers. There's a sense of pride in one's discipline or exceptionality."

IN A SMALL town in the Adirondacks not long ago, I accompanied some friends to the local dump. The town supervisors had installed a small shed there where townspeople could drop off their unwanted but still usable goods. The locals called it "Little Wal-Mart." It was stuffed with old clothes, mugs, popcorn makers, and exercise videos. Skis leaned against the walls, along with wooden doors and glass windowpanes. I sifted through the clothes and came across a pillow-soft black V-neck T-shirt. It was an expensive brand, and probably would have cost $60 or more at Bloomingdale's. Why would someone throw out this treasure? I figured it out a few days later: there was a gaping hole under one arm. I took out my sewing box and patched it up.

It was a small effort, but it gave me an inordinate amount of pleasure. In a culture where goods are increasingly disposable, where one tear or stain has become cause to discard an otherwise valuable item, there is great satisfaction in using things well. I felt an almost childlike pride: not quite "I made this," but "I saved this." I saw some value in a thing that someone else had given up on, and I resuscitated it.

We don't have many opportunities to feel resourceful and productive (productive in a fundamental sense, of making the things we use ourselves) anymore. We don't grow our own food but buy it at the grocery store; the beds we sleep in and the tables we eat on were made in factories far away from us, by people we'll never meet. But to sew that hole, or glue our sandals back together, or unclog the drain in the bathtub ourselves, connects us in some small but meaningful way to a sense of independence and self-sufficiency that is mostly missing in our modern lives.

An aversion to spending money—and a faith that contentment comes in forms not always bearing a price tag—also fosters pleasure in simple habits and modest needs. I'll never forget the day I was driving down a country road with my father and, out of the blue, he said, "Nothing makes me happier than a good, crunchy apple." He meant it. By the yardstick of his own profession of economics, which measures "standard of living" purely on the basis of one's annual spending, my father should be deeply unhappy. He consumes little, so his standard of living is, technically, low. But his quality of life is one of the highest of anyone I know. I've frequently wished my own needs were as simple as his. Give him a stretch of water to walk along, a newspaper to read, and an apple to eat, and he's happy for hours.

My friend Adam told me that his late uncle, Ezra Kaplan,

"was the cheapest person in the world." Ezra lived near Columbia University in the upper reaches of Manhattan. But every day, he walked to his office on the southern tip of the borough, where he worked as one of the first computer programmers for a giant security firm. The walk probably took three hours each way, and he did it so he wouldn't have to pay subway or bus fare. Most days, said Adam, Ezra ate peanuts for his lunch, straight out of a bag, shells and all. His apartment was sparse, just a mattress on the floor. He got most of his clothes from the food pantry where he volunteered, and probably ate his meals there, too. Was he a miser, freeloading off services meant for the truly poor and destitute? It turns out not. After Ezra died, naming Adam the executor of his will, Adam discovered that his uncle had been giving away more than a million dollars a year for as far back as there were records. In his will, he left $23 million more to charities, including the food bank. He spent his last years living in a shack in Florida behind Adam's sister's horse farm, where he fulfilled his longtime dream of owning a goat.

The rest of the family worried that Ezra wasn't taking care of himself, or that he was crazy or too eccentric. Was he unhappy in his asceticism? I asked Adam. Did he feel deprived? "He was happy, more than most," Adam said. "He had a lifestyle he enjoyed and believed in."

The same is true for my father and for Erik Kriss, the upstate New Yorker who rarely uses his clothes dryer. For both of them, and many other cheapskates, frugality is not just about saving money. Fundamentally, it has something to do with waste, with inefficient use of resources. For years, my father yelled whenever we held the refrigerator door open a moment too long. Yet it was my mother who paid all the bills; Dad didn't even know the price of a kilowatt-hour of electricity. He wasn't making a cost-benefit analysis of his efforts. Of course, he knew that using less electricity saved money.

But he had no idea if we'd save 5 cents or $50 by keeping the fridge door shut. Something else was at work. What I eventually realized is that he is deeply, profoundly offended by waste. Waste of anything—money, heat, water, food (he eats anything we leave on our plates), resources of any kind.

When I asked him recently what cheapness was about to him, my father replied, "Cheapness means, where I see waste, I want to avoid it. It just seems like common sense. You have to pay to put the heat on, whereas you don't have to use as much heat if you put a sweater on." (Freudian analysts have their own interpretation of this aversion. "That was the whole issue in terms of toilet training," Dr. Leon Hoffman, the psychoanalyst, told me. "This is a valuable product which you're presenting to your mother. The idea of value relates to pleasing Mother. So if you waste something that's valuable, there's guilt and shame about that." My father rejected this explanation, but then again, that's why we call it the "unconscious.")

Erik Kriss also eschews any kind of waste or poor use of resources. I met Erik when we worked together as journalists in Albany, the capital of New York. He was the butt of friendly jokes around the Capitol press room for his frugal ways. Other reporters often repeated the story of how he'd refused to split a bill equally when a bunch of them had gone to a steak house while covering an out-of-town political convention. Their newspapers would be reimbursing the expenses, but Erik argued that he'd eaten only a salad; why should his employer pay for part of the other reporters' steaks? That money could go toward raises for reporters or to expand the paper's coverage, he told me.

In the mornings when Erik runs water for his shower, he places a pitcher under the faucet to collect the water as it turns from cold to hot. Once the stream is warm enough to immerse himself, he removes the pitcher and uses it later to water his plants and fill his dog's dish. He uses the leftover milk in his kids' cereal bowls to sweeten and lighten his coffee. His life is a patchwork of these strategies. "It's not because I worry about bankruptcy or financial collapse," he said. "I think the whole idea that I'm not wasting things and I'm conserving is a matter of principle and pride."

ERIK ISN'T TOO troubled by the fact that his friends lampoon his penny-pinching. Nor did it hurt my father's feelings when his Aunt Bebe used to joke that he was a "cheap bastard." Their lack of concern is a signal trait of frugal folks, it turns out. In 1999, an Arizona State University marketing professor conducted in-depth interviews with six self-professed frugal consumers and concluded that thrifty people tend to be independent-minded and relatively impervious to social pressure. One interviewee told the author, John Lastovicka, that she had little interest in going shopping with her friends while she was in college: "They'd say, 'You don't have to spend money. Let's just go window-shopping.' I'd say, 'I don't want to go look at things I can't afford to buy.' That's when I noticed I was different."

Ken Clark, the psychologist and financial planner, said he had a college professor who bought his clothes at estate sales. "He would wear dress shirts with other people's monograms, which we thought was hilarious," Clark said. "There's a social risk there, a risk to saying, These yellow shoes are hideous, but they're only one dollar."

Frugal people are nonconformists. They don't worry too much about those social risks—impressing other people or fitting in. So they save money on the kinds of status objects—the right clothes, the right cars, the right vacations—that spenders like to have. My father has no reservations about wearing the polyester pants he's owned for decades or old clothes that someone else would have donated to Goodwill long ago. My mother told me she sometimes feels embarrassed when he goes to the library "in pants that are torn and a sweatshirt with holes. He looks like the Unabomber." He also drove our rusty old Plymouth Duster for fifteen years, and would have driven it longer had it not fallen apart. As a teenager, I was mortified whenever he picked me up from field hockey practice in that car. But now I appreciate that he lives life on his terms, not those prescribed by Madison Avenue or the neighbors down the street.

I THINK TOO about the law of diminishing returns, the economic principle that tells us that the more of something we have, the less pleasure we derive from each additional unit of it. That first bowl of strawberry ice cream is heavenly; we revel in the richness of the cream and sugar and the slight tartness of the fruit. By the second bowl, we're feeling a little overwhelmed, not tasting each ingredient quite so distinctly. By the fifth bowl, we're just sick. So if you own three pairs of expensive jeans, how special is the fourth pair? If you dine at gourmet restaurants every week, how much will you savor and remember each individual meal?

This is what I worry about, for myself and for the future of a pleasure-seeking culture like ours: that too much indulgence dulls our appreciation for those treats, those luxuries that punctuate the routines and boredoms of ordinary life. My sister, a college professor, tells me that she sometimes rewards herself for accomplishing a task—writing the syllabus for a class, reading a student's thesis—by buying herself a cookie. Not just any cookie. She considers which bakery she'll go to, whether she'll buy the ginger shortbread or the dark chocolate macaroon. She imagines what it will taste like. It pushes her onward in her task. It's Pavlovian, but it works.

If she bought a cookie every day, would it taste as good? She and I both believe it wouldn't.

"There's a desensitization when you have too much material stuff," says Clark. "By being frugal, people maximize psychic enjoyment when they do treat themselves. That's the mission of the frugal person. It creates perspective."

CAN PEOPLE LEARN to be frugal, or is it a trait that's imprinted on the psyche early in life by overzealous potty-training parents or traumatic experiences like the Depression?

I often wonder if there's just something different about the way cheapskates think. I have friends who fret about money but don't seem to connect their $10-a-day lunch habit to their listing bank account. It's an orientation; you've got it or you don't. Scott Rick, one of the authors of the Tightwad-Spendthrift study, agrees. "My unverified instinct is that it's largely something you're stuck with. It's genes, parenting, schooling, a combination of influences," he said.

But as frugality rolls back into fashion, a lot of books promise that it's trainable. In recent years, we've seen an efflorescence of how-to manuals for saving money and cultivating one's inner cheapskate. *The Cheap Book, The Ultimate Cheapskate's Road Map to True Riches, America's Cheapest Family Gets You Right on the Money, The Frugal Duchess*—these are but a few of the products you can buy to help you learn to buy less. They offer a route to cheapness that bypasses neurosis and pathology. If it works, that's wonderful; the more cheap people, the better. But I will always have a soft spot for the eccentrics, the compulsives, the neurotics. They are my people.

Conclusion

I thought I'd always lived pretty close to the bone. But over the two years it took me to write this book, I subjected my spending to a whole new level of scrutiny. This was partly just practical, because my income shrank to the size of the advance I'd received from my publisher, supplemented by a couple of freelance paychecks and occasional withdrawals from my savings. Just as important was the fact that, as I discovered, you can't pen a book about the virtues of being cheap without questioning each and every one of your spending habits. Driven by this combination of necessity and Maoist-style self-criticism, I found all kinds of new ways to shave my expenses.

I made my own laundry detergent, a blend of borax and washing soda. I replenished my wardrobe at Really Really Free Markets and clothing swaps. I became scrupulous about packing my lunch when I spent the day at the library. I gave up my car and relied on public transportation and my bike. I lived on lentils and beans, but swore off *canned* beans (79 cents for four servings) for dried beans ($1.49 for twelve servings). I mostly gave up haircuts, but now when I reach my wits' end with long hair, I go to salons that offer $15 cuts with "apprentice" stylists.

When friends suggest we go out for dinner, I sometimes propose a lunchtime picnic instead, and then offer to bring homemade food for both of us. While I was hanging out with freegans, I Dumpster-dived about 20 percent of my food. I still fill up bags with bread from my favorite organic bakery after the employees put out the trash at eight p.m. As I made these changes, one by one, I was able to cut my monthly expenses by around 40 percent.

WE CHEAPSKATES TAKE great pride in our frugality, and harnessing all those skills, especially in the midst of a consumer culture as omnipresent as ours, can make us a little smug. One day when I was feeling particularly satisfied with myself, I opened my closet and realized that I own about twenty long-sleeved T-shirts *alone*. I have eighteen pairs of shoes and four winter coats. Two hundred years ago, farmers and pioneers typically owned two sets of clothing at any one time—a set of work clothes for Monday through Saturday, and a nicer frock or suit for Sunday. Although I sometimes talk as though I'm a master tightwad, I still buy too many things I can't claim to truly need.

The truth is that I don't want to return to the deprivation and austerity of those early days. Let's face it: as much as we exalt early American "thrift," it wasn't fun to be frugal back then. Thrift often meant only the difference between dignified survival and destitution (and even dignified survival was an arduous and miserable undertaking). No matter how little cash I live on or how many things I move from the "essentials" to the "luxuries" column of my budget, I can't deny that I'm still a consumer, and often grateful to be one. Surely

I do identify with that role, since I love nothing more than calling my sister to brag about the agnès b. sweater I found at the Goodwill store for $6. I may be critical of aspects of our consumer society, but I can't claim to be anticonsumption.

So then I ask myself, what kind of a consumer do I want to be?

This is where things get murkier. We don't consume in a vacuum, as more and more Americans recognize. The money we spend on a computer gets recycled into, among other things, wages for the workers who assembled it and payments for the raw materials that were used to build and transport it. When we buy anything, we face choices. Do I buy the inexpensive made-in-China toy that may contain lead, or do I pay a higher price for a handcrafted wooden toy made in the United States, Japan, or Germany, countries with stricter oversight of the production process? Do I shop at a thrift store, and thereby bypass the production process entirely?

The *Wall Street Journal*'s fashion reporter, Christina Binkley, explored these questions in 2007, in a modern-day version of Cornell University's old home-economics experiments. Binkley bought two black cashmere turtlenecks, a $99.50 Lands' End sweater and a $950 version by the Italian luxury brand Brunello Cucinelli. She compared the sweaters' quality, styling, and the labor conditions under which they were made. The Lands' End turtleneck came from a Chinese factory, though the company refused to tell her where the facility was, or provide any specifics about working conditions or wages. The Cucinelli sweater, as the brand's spokesman proudly explained, was knit in a seventeenth-century castle in Italy where employees work eight hours a day and eat a multicourse lunch prepared by three local women who shop every morning for fresh ingredients. It's probably safe to say that the Cucinelli cashmere trumps the other one in terms of labor conditions and social responsibility. But whether that's worth paying ten times the price, Binkley says, "is a matter for you and your wallet."

Consumption has always been a complicated activity, vexed by political and social considerations during, for instance, the nonimportation movements of the 1760s, the shortages of World War I, and the postwar boom of the 1940s. But in a globalized world like ours, I think it might be more complicated today than it's ever been before.

A person whose primary goal is to save money—and who won't or can't buy everything at secondhand stores—will probably find himself doing a lot of shopping at Wal-Mart or Target. These companies tout their "everyday low prices," and more often than not, anything from milk to laptops to mountain bikes can be had there for less than you'd pay at an independent shop or a smaller chain store. Such is the global economy we live in. Thanks to factory workers in China, Bangladesh, and Lesotho, it's now cheaper to buy a new sweater than to make one yourself. And forget about bringing your broken DVD player to the repairman in town. It'll probably cost less to junk the old one and replace it with a new model made in Vietnam.

If we all cared only about getting the best deal, we would be living in a world where every company races to the bottom—in terms of wages and quality—in order to provide shoppers with ever-lower prices. In the short term, sure, we'd save money, but in the long run, we'd pay a different kind of price, in the environmental damage caused by the endless production of junk and in the low-paid jobs that our consumption supports. Multinational, publicly traded corporations have one mission that trumps all others: to deliver profits to their shareholders. This imperative leads to all kinds of abuses in the name of increasing revenues and earnings, from illegally dumping industrial waste into rivers to trampling on workers' rights. Wal-Mart, for instance, has been named in dozens of lawsuits alleging that its managers forced employees to work overtime without paying them for it. That kind of corner cutting means lower prices for shoppers, but at what cost?

As my frugal friend Danica says, "The ethic of cheapness does not stand alone. It needs a counterbalance, or else you just end up in Crapville."

How do we live low-cost lives while also recognizing that how we spend money has an impact far beyond our wallets? How do we consume conscientiously, without supporting poor labor conditions or the deterioration of the environment? These are questions that vex me as I try to align my actions as a frugal consumer with the other values I hold dear, like fairness, equity, responsible distribution of income and resources, environmental stewardship, and sustainability.

Most cheapskates who are also concerned with their impact on the world around them don't have a simple answer to these questions. Instead, most of us (even non-cheapskates, who deal with the same issues) muddle through, trying to find a balance between competing values as we decide what to buy, where to buy it, and for how much. I try to adhere to what I call "ethical cheapness," which is the term I give to my own ambiguous, constantly changing calculus of consumption.

When making spending decisions, we can't pay attention only to the single variable of price. The idea of ethical cheapness acts as a helpful reminder, pointing me to a philosophy of mindful consumption: considering each purchase, embracing a stricter set of guidelines for winnowing down what I buy (what I actually *need* versus what I *want*), thinking about the values that are most important to me, and spending or saving accordingly. The practice of ethical cheapness might lead me to buy locally grown vegetables at the farmers' market, even if the price is higher than the conventional produce at the supermarket, or shop at local small businesses rather than the cheaper national discount chains, even as I'm busy making my own birthday cards, reusing tea bags, and doing my own hemming.

In the end, I hope that shopping less means that we can make conscious, ethical choices when we *do* spend money. Here's a more precise example of what I mean. Although I generally try to keep my food costs to a minimum, I've chosen in recent years to buy a share in a local CSA. A CSA—it stands for Community-Supported Agriculture—brings organic produce to city dwellers by allowing them to buy a stake in a nearby organic farm. CSA members pay a few hundred dollars up front, usually in the early spring. These funds give the farmer the money he needs to plant his fields and run his operations. Then, when harvests come in, the farmer trucks boxes of fruits and vegetables to the city once a week, and members pick up their "shares" at a local community center. You never know what you're going to get in a particular week. Any given box might contain, for example, lettuce, beets, squash, burdock root, and purslane. If the region experienced a drought or monsoon rains that season, the boxes will probably be on the small side. If there was a bumper crop of heirloom tomatoes, you get armloads of them for a few weeks running. As a shareholder, you join the farmer in both the risks and the rewards.

A CSA is the perfect way for a cheapskate like me to buy organic, local vegetables. When I go to the grocery store and see conventionally grown spinach for 99 cents a bunch and organic spinach for $2.99 a bunch, my internal compass begins to go a little haywire. After a few moments of internal debate, I almost always go for the pesticide-sprayed bunch. But with my CSA, I pick up my vegetables without having to think about how much each item cost per pound, or its price relative to the conventional produce at the supermarket down the street. Sure, that $400 check at the beginning of the season is a big chunk of change, but I see it more as an investment—in

good health, fresh food, better working conditions for growers, and better long-term environmental management—than
as the cost of a few dozen bags of groceries.

This mind-set is consistent with the findings of Drazen
Prelec and George Loewenstein, the behavioral economists
who study "pain of paying" and have also looked at the effects
of different payment arrangements. Thinking of my CSA as
an investment, along with the fact that I don't have to obsess
about the per-unit cost of my veggies when I pick them up,
reduces my pain of paying, making the CSA an excellent
arrangement for me.

My CSA solves one part of the puzzle of ethical cheapness.
But it's a big puzzle, and one that I know I'll keep struggling
with for the rest of my life.

THESE ISSUES SEEM especially salient in the circumstances
we're living in now. As I write this in May 2009, I read every
day about mass layoffs, destitute families, homes foreclosed
on by banks, stock market losses, and college endowments
drastically reduced by the twin shocks of the recession and
Bernard Madoff's con artistry. Citizens all over the world are
suffering from the aftershocks of a decade and more of careless spending, indulgence, and greed.

In this context, frugality is experiencing a renaissance of
sorts. Newspapers tout the "return of thrift" and write about a
new austerity that's sweeping through corporate boardrooms
and Paris couture shows. Blogs celebrate "cheap pride." President Barack Obama talks about a fresh era of responsibility
and sacrifice. Whether out of desperation, fear, fashion, or a
new spirit of patriotism, cheapness is "in" these days.

Indeed, whenever times are tough, Americans develop a
speedy interest in simple living and thrift. History shows that
during extreme crises and dislocations—wartime, the Great

Depression, immigration to a new country—individuals muster the resourcefulness and shrewdness required for low-cost living.

It's not clear yet how our story will end. If there's anything my research has taught me, it's that these adjustments in favor of frugality are often temporary. Americans are deeply attached to their belief in prosperity and an ever-rising standard of living, as measured not by levels of emotional well-being (the United States scored sixteenth out of ninety-seven countries in one of the most widely cited surveys of national happiness) but by the size of the houses we live in and the brand of car we drive.

The one factor that's different today from past revivals of thrift is a widespread consciousness about global warming and environmental degradation. This awareness just might change the game. More and more Americans are adapting to the idea that our natural resources are limited, and that we have to do a better job of stewarding them for future generations—proof that you can get to cheapness from almost any direction.

So put a pot of lentils on the stove. Ride your bike to work. Ski to the grocery store. Scrape the last bit of jam out of the jar. Take good care of your shoes. And don't be afraid to turn down the thermostat. If your kids complain, tell them they can put on another sweater. Someday they'll understand. And maybe, just maybe, they'll thank you for it.

TALK IS CHEAP:
A PRIMER ON FRUGAL LIVING

If I had to offer some advice about how to live cheaply, I'd boil it down to two sentences: "Don't buy stuff. Don't spend money." (My three exceptions are physical health, mental health, and winter boots.)

But for those who want to study the art of cheapness, or who want a little practical guidance on low-cost living, I've compiled a brief list of resources. This list is subjective, incomplete, and very much a work in progress. It includes some classics and some obscure monographs and websites, mostly sources I used to write this book or, in a case of life imitating nonfiction, for getting by on a writer's income.

SKIP *The Way to Wealth,* the compendium of Ben Franklin's precious and overly familiar proverbs on industry and frugality, and instead go to a less-worn version of the great man. His "Plan for Saving One Hundred Thousand Pounds," from the 1756 edition of *Poor Richard's Almanack,* is perhaps the first really practical how-to essay on frugal living. "When you incline to have new clothes," he instructs his readers, "look first well over the old ones, and see if you cannot shift with them another year, either by scouring, mending, or even patching if necessary. Remember a patch on your coat, and money in your pocket, is better and more creditable, than a writ on your back, and no money to take it off." Franklin's letters and essays, collected in various sources, contain more of this kind of honest, stripped-down wisdom.

The American Frugal Housewife, by Lydia Maria Child. Want to get a sense of what life was like for the vast majority of Americans in the nineteenth century as they scraped together a living and made do on meager incomes? Child's no-nonsense book overflows with household hints for the thrifty and poor. It's a cabinet of curiosities for us modern-day softies, with our store-bought cough syrups and processed foods.

Walden, by Henry David Thoreau. "I am convinced, both by faith and experience, that to maintain one's self on this earth is not a hardship but a pastime, if we will live simply and wisely," Thoreau wrote in his memoir of the two years he spent living in the Massachusetts woods. The young philosopher wasn't above boasting about his thrifty chops; the budget for his DIY shack came to only $28.13, or $641.75 in today's dollars. The book didn't get much traction when it was published in 1854, but it went on to inspire untold numbers of people searching for an "authentic" life of inner riches and outer simplicity.

Household Engineering, by Christine Frederick. This advice book for women was written at the height of the "efficiency" mania of the early twentieth century. Forget about "leftovers." In Frederick's world, there are only "planned-overs." Tucked in among the didactic and outdated disquisitions on a woman's role in the home are some ingenious tips for saving time and money.

The Simple Life, by David Shi. This is an academic survey of all the major American experiments in "plain living and high thinking," from Puritan asceticism to Transcendentalist communities like Brook Farm and Fruitlands in Massachusetts to Ralph Borsodi's School for Living, a farm outside of New York City that was designed to transform urbanites into rural homesteaders. In vibrant language, Shi illustrates the deathless appeal of the simple-living philosophy.

The Gleaners and I, by Agnès Varda. This film by the adventurous French auteur explores the European tradition of gleaning, in which people go through fields after harvests and salvage whatever fruits or vegetables the farmer left behind. Varda meets and follows all kinds of modern-day gleaners—a teacher who eats only the "trash" left over in Paris's daily food markets; an artist who assembles tableaux of found objects on the shelves of discarded refrigerators; an old man whose front yard houses old bikes, mattresses, shovels, and other so-called junk.

The Tightwad Gazette, by Amy Dacyczyn. The bible of cheapskates everywhere. In the seven years she published her newsletter of the same title, Dacyczyn was not only an unapologetic tightwad, but a spokeswoman and catalyst for an uncelebrated movement of frugal living. The newsletters have been compiled into a single volume filled with ingenious and sometimes insane tips for saving money. Dacyczyn's unique voice and wit jump off of every page. She is my hero.

The Ultimate Cheapskate's Guide to True Riches, by Jeff Yeager. Most of the how-to books on cheap living rehash the same material over and over, offering very little in the way of new insight or ideas. Yeager's is a step above these. My favorite suggestion? He recommends that aspiring cheapskates go on a "fiscal fast," not spending a dime for a week or so. As a former nonprofit exec and unrepentant liberal, he also keeps his progressive politics front and center, with an emphasis on community, charity, and the connection between green living and cheap living.

Your Money or Your Life, by Vicki Robin and Joe Dominguez. A classic of the voluntary simplicity movement. It's all about finding ways to drop out of the rat race and align your financial life with your personal values. This book offers a step-by-step program for finding "financial integrity." It's changed many, many lives.

Nowtopia, by Chris Carlsson. A smart, thought-provoking manifesto for a postcapitalist world. Carlsson, the brainy subversive who helped start the Burning Man festival and the Critical Mass bike rides that take place in cities around the country every month, explores grass-roots models for living outside the constraints of our free-market, hyperindividualist American culture.

Empire of Scrounge, by Jeff Ferrell. My sister gave me this odd and wonderful book for my birthday in 2007. Combining first-person experience with the keen insights of a sociologist, the renegade professor Ferrell explores the subculture of "scrounging" in this unorthodox meditation on waste and overconsumption. In 2001, Ferrell quit his tenured academic job and moved to Fort Worth, Texas, determined to use his professional interests (he had studied borderline-illegal activities like graffiti art and Dumpster diving) as a script for his real life. For eight months, he rifled through curbside trash piles, scoured riverbeds for resellable golf balls, and lived off the discards of others. Ferrell uses anecdotes and lists of his scavenged discoveries to catalog the astonishing level of usable stuff we throw away.

The poet Gary Snyder's 1969 essay "Four Changes" in the Pulitzer Prize–winning book *Turtle Island*. Snyder wrote this short essay, as he says, "in response to an evident need for a few practical and visionary suggestions." Indeed, the four changes he calls for (and the actions that follow from them) straddle the line between pragmatic and utopian, mainly having to do with saving the environment from a rapacious and "plutonium-based" economy. It was printed and distributed for free after he wrote it, and remains quick, dirty, and inspiring.

There are dozens of websites devoted to low-cost living. Here are just a few of my favorites:

www.swaporamarama.org—a listing of clothing swaps around the country

www.homegrownevolution.com—a blog for urban gardeners and homesteaders

www.fallenfruit.org—a project to map public fruit trees in the Los Angeles area

www.thedailygreen.com—billed as "the consumer's guide to the green revolution"

www.lifehacker.com—a compilation of helpful tips for doing just about anything smarter and more efficiently. Check out the "Frugality" and "Saving Money" categories.

www.freenyc.net—a daily digest of free events in New York City

www.freegan.info—the home of the freegan movement

ACKNOWLEDGMENTS

I usually avoid debt of any kind. But by the time I finished writing this book, I had amassed enormous debts of friendship, love, and gratitude. Fortunately, those are the very best kinds of IOUs and I look forward to repaying them.

This book wouldn't exist if I hadn't grown up with a maniacally cheap father. David Weber is the living, breathing spirit behind every page of *In Cheap We Trust.* Each time I forgot why I was writing a book defending frugality as a way of life, I thought of my father and remembered once again why cheapness is a virtue. My mother, Corinne Weber, is a moderating influence on my father's parsimony. She made sure that no matter how stripped-down our lives were in a material sense, we were never, ever deprived of profligate love. My parents' encouragement and confidence in me have been limitless; everything I do is a testament to them. Mom and Dad, this book is for you.

I hit the jackpot, too, with the dream team that helped see this book through from start to finish. John Parsley, my editor at Little, Brown, applied intelligence and insight to my writing. His gentle prodding and smart suggestions had a way of breaking down my stubbornness, and the book is much the better for it. My agent, Rob McQuilkin, has been fiercely in my corner from the moment we began working together. He is a combination of advocate, straight talker, cheerleader, pit bull, and friend. Many thanks to him and everyone else at Lippincott Massie McQuilkin.

Also at Little, Brown, my publicist Carolyn O'Keefe took on this project with enthusiasm and creativity. Jayne Yaffe Kemp copyedited the manuscript with awe-inspiring skill. Cara Eisenpress helped make sure nothing fell through the cracks. And long before I joined the L,B family, Geoff Shandler provided crucial encouragement and guidance.

Several friends merit special mention. Paul Erickson and Rachel Weber read large chunks of the manuscript and offered detailed comments and corrections. In particular, Paul saved me from committing many sins against the historical record. Rachel pushed back against me in ways that only a big sister can, forcing me to sharpen my arguments. Darcy Frey shared his insights about the writing life and passed along a line in which I took great comfort: "All first drafts are written in an atmosphere of self-contempt." Daniel Weiss stepped in at critical moments with excellent editing, feedback, and support. John Kearney read chapters on short notice, edited them lovingly, sent me articles to read, talked me through ideas and quandaries, and adopted my book as though it were his own.

Other friends read early drafts of chapters and gave me valuable suggestions, including Erin Healy, Donald Weber, Jody Rosen Knower, Danica Bornstein, Barbara Spindel, Patty Kao, Ray Fisman, and Dan Charnas. A big thank-you to Eve Abrams, Suzanne Snider, Ben Weber, Isabelle Barker, Cara Palladino, Amy Halloran, Josh Mills, Elyssa East, John Slocum, Doni Gewirtzman, Suzanne Wise, Jake Slichter, and Claire Weinraub for cheering the book along. Errol Cockfield and Roman Bachli made sure I occasionally ate something other than lentils. My longtime friend Eugene Kuo designed my website. Many thanks also to Reshma Kapadia Gardner, Katie Rosman, Steve McGuirl, Tami Luhby, Steve Zeldes, and everyone else who shared with me articles, books, reports, and events that touched on the topic of frugality.

I also want to thank Gianna Chachere, who suggested that I go on a date with Adam Dowis. Too wary to ask him for a date, I asked him for an interview instead. He turned out to be cheap in all the best ways and full of stories about leading a scavenged and improvised life. I'm grateful to Adam for his loving embrace of me and this book.

Several institutions also supported the book. I spent two wonderful months at artist residencies, one at Yaddo and one at Blue Mountain Center; it's a miracle that these places exist. The Knight-Bagehot Fellowship provided me with a year of study at Columbia University's Graduate School of Business. I'm grateful to Terri Thompson, who directs the fellowship, and to my fellow Badgers, who put up with me asking every Tuesday dinner guest about the risks of Americans' low savings rates.

While at Columbia, I was lucky enough to take Sam Freedman's book-writing seminar at the Journalism School. My thanks go out to Sam and my classmates for their thoughtful critiques in the early stages of this project.

In response to a couple of e-mailed questions, Gonçalo Fonseca, proprietor of the "History of Economic Thought" website, sent me a three-thousand-word explication of Keynes's Paradox of Thrift and then disappeared into the ether. Why would he help a stranger and not accept even a cup of coffee in return? I don't know, but in the course of my research, many individuals similarly went out of their way to answer questions, share sources, and dig up obscure information, at no benefit to themselves. Among them are John Tofanelli at Columbia University's Butler Library, Patricia Maus at the Northeast Minnesota Historical Center, Seth Rockman and

Deborah Cohen at Brown University, and Thomas Carey at the San Francisco History Center.

I owe my gratitude to the entire staff at the American Antiquarian Society in Worcester, Massachusetts, where I spent three weeks in the winter of 2008. In particular, I'd like to thank Paul Erickson (again), Tom Knoles, Gigi Barnhill, Laura Wasowicz, and the research fellows whose time there overlapped with mine, especially Steve Marini.

I interviewed a lot of people in the course of writing this book, including experts in economics, psychology, and the art of low-cost living. I've listed them by name in my Source Notes; my thanks go out to all of them for sharing their time, expertise, and tales with me.

SOURCE NOTES

Several books were especially helpful to me, including the very first two I read when I began my research in 2006: David Tucker's *The Decline of Thrift in America* and Lendol Calder's *Financing the American Dream.* I also relied a great deal on *The Simple Life,* a history of American simplicity movements, by David Shi.

INTRODUCTION: CHEAP THRILLS
ON THE ORIGINS OF THE WORD *CHEAP*

Ayto, John. *Word Origins.* London: A & C Black, 2005.

Cassidy, Frederic, ed. *Dictionary of American Regional English.* Cambridge, MA: Belknap Press of Harvard University Press, 1985.

Chantrell, Glynnis, ed. *The Oxford Dictionary of Word Histories.* Oxford: Oxford University Press, 2002.

OTHER SOURCES

Calder, Lendol. *Financing the American Dream.* Princeton, NJ: Princeton University Press, 1999.

Dacyczyn, Amy. *The Tightwad Gazette, vols. 1–3.* New York: Villard, 1992–1995.

Deutsch, Claudia. "Trying to Connect the Dinner Plate to Climate Change." *New York Times.* August 29, 2007.

Lynd, Robert S., and Helen Merrell Lynd. *Middletown: A Study in Contemporary American Culture.* New York: Harcourt, Brace, 1929.

Mann, Bruce H. *Republic of Debtors.* Cambridge, MA: Harvard University Press, 2002.

Todd, Richard. *The Thing Itself.* New York: Riverhead Books, 2008.

CHAPTER 1: "THE CROWD APPROVED THE DOCTRINE, AND IMMEDIATELY PRACTICED THE CONTRARY"

For this chapter, I'm indebted to the librarians and staff at the American Antiquarian Society in Worcester, Massachusetts. They cheerfully steered me to databases, manuscripts, ephemera, and other resources I might have otherwise missed. The Society maintains several invaluable digital collections, including the *Archive of Americana* and *America's Historical Newspapers,* which I used prodigiously.

ON JESUS CHRIST AND JOHN CALVIN

Arbuthnot, C. C. "Jesus and Christian Socialism." *The Biblical World,* vol. 41, no. 3, March 1913, pp. 147–61.

Aristotle. *The Nicomachean Ethics,* trans. by H. Rackman. Cambridge, MA: Harvard University Press, 1947.

Blomberg, Craig. *Neither Poverty nor Riches: A Biblical Theology of Material Possessions.* Grand Rapids: William Eerdmans, 1999.

Calvin, John. *The Institutes of Christian Religion.* London: Thomas Tegg, 1844.

Countryman, L. William. *The Rich Christian in the Church of the Early Empire: Contradictions and Accommodations.* New York: Edwin Mellen, 1980.

Crocker, David, and Toby Linden, eds. *Ethics of Consumption: The Good Life, Justice and Global Stewardship.* Lanham, MD: Rowan and Littlefield, 1998.

Hoppe, Leslie. *There Shall Be No Poor Among You: Poverty in the Bible.* Nashville: Abingdon, 2004.

Lattimore, Richmond, trans. *The Four Gospels and the Revelation.* New York: Farrar, Straus and Giroux, 1979.

Tawney, R. H. *Religion and the Rise of Capitalism.* New York: Harcourt, Brace, 1926.

Weber, Max. *The Protestant Ethic and the Spirit of Capitalism.* New York and London: Penguin Books, 2002 (1905).

ON COLONIAL AND POST-REVOLUTIONARY AMERICA

Bushman, Richard. *The Refinement of America.* New York: Knopf, 1992.

Dorfman, Joseph. *The Economic Mind in American Civilization, 1606–1865.* New York: Viking, 1946.

North, Gary. "The Puritan Experiment in Sumptuary Legislation." *The Freeman,* vol. 24, 1974.

O'Toole, Patricia. *Money and Morals in America: A History.* New York: Clarkson Potter, 1998.

Robertson, James Oliver, and Janet C. Robertson. *All Our Yesterdays: A Century of Family Life in an American Small Town.* New York: Harper-Collins, 1993.

Shammas, Carole. "Consumer Behavior in Colonial America." *Social Science History*, vol. 6, no. 1 (Winter 1982), pp. 67–86.

———. "How Self-Sufficient Was Early America?" *Journal of Interdisciplinary History*, vol. 13, no. 2 (Autumn 1982), pp. 247–72.

Smith, Billy. *The "Lower Sort": Philadelphia's Laboring People, 1759–1800.* Ithaca, NY: Cornell University Press, 1990.

———. ed. *Down and Out in Early America.* University Park: Pennsylvania State University Press, 2004.

Taylor, Dale. *The Writer's Guide to Everyday Life in Colonial America.* Cincinnati: Writer's Digest Books, 1997.

Volo, Dorothy Denneen, and James M. Volo. *Daily Life During the American Revolution.* Westport, CT: Greenwood, 2003.

Wechsler, Louis K. *The Common People of Colonial America, as Glimpsed through the Dusty Windows of the Old Almanacks, chiefly of New-York.* New York: Vantage, 1978.

Wildes, Harry Emerson. *William Penn.* New York: MacMillan, 1974.

ON THE BOYCOTTS OF BRITISH GOODS

Ames, Nathaniel. *An astronomical diary; or, almanack, for the year of our Lord Christ 1768.* Newport, RI: Samuel Hall, 1767.

Andrews, Charles. "Boston Merchants and the Non-Importation Movement." *Publications of the Colonial Society of Massachusetts,* vol. 19, 1916–1917, pp. 159–258.

Breen, T. H. " 'Baubles of Britain': The American and Consumer Revolutions of the Eighteenth Century." *Past and Present,* no. 119 (May 1988), pp. 73–104.

———. *The Marketplace of Revolution.* New York: Oxford University Press, 2004.

Witkowski, Terrence. "Colonial Consumers in Revolt." *Journal of Consumer Research,* vol. 16, no. 2 (September 1989), pp. 216–26.

ON REPUBLICAN VIRTUE

Kierner, Cynthia. *The Contrast: Manners, Morals, and Authority in the Early American Republic.* New York: New York University Press, 2007.

Koch, Adrienne, and William Peden, eds. *The Life and Selected Writings of Thomas Jefferson.* New York: Random House, 1944.

McCoy, Drew. *The Elusive Republic: Political Economy in Jeffersonian America.* Chapel Hill: University of North Carolina Press, 1980.

———. "Benjamin Franklin's Vision of Republican Political Economy for America." *William and Mary Quarterly,* third series, vol. 35, no. 4, (1978), pp. 605–28.

Shi, David. *The Simple Life.* New York: Oxford University Press, 1985.

Trenchard, John. *Essays on Important Subjects.* London: A. Millar, 1755.

Tucker, David M. *The Decline of Thrift in America: Our Cultural Shift from Saving to Spending.* New York: Praeger, 1991.

Withington, Ann Fairfax. *Toward a More Perfect Union: Virtue and the Formation of American Republics.* New York: Oxford University Press, 1991.

Wood, Gordon. *The Creation of the American Republic, 1776–1787.* Chapel Hill: University of North Carolina Press, 1969.

ON BENJAMIN FRANKLIN

Carlton, Mabel Mason. *Benjamin Franklin: Apostle of Thrift.* Boston: John Hancock Mutual Life Insurance Company, 1921.

Franklin, Benjamin. *The Autobiography of Benjamin Franklin.* New York and London: Penguin Books, 1986.

———. "Advice to a Young Tradesman," in *The Papers of Benjamin Franklin,* vol. 3. Ed. Leonard Labaree. New Haven: Yale University Press, 1959.

———. *The Franklin Miscellany.* Dover, NH: Samuel C. Stevens, 1827.

———. *Profile of Genius: Poor Richard Pamphlets.* Philadelphia: Franklin Institute, 1938.

Huang, Nian-Sheng. *Benjamin Franklin in American Thought and Culture, 1790–1990.* Philadelphia: American Philosophical Society, 1994.

Isaacson, Walter. *Benjamin Franklin: An American Life.* New York: Simon and Schuster, 2003.

Lemay, J. A. Leo. *The Life of Benjamin Franklin.* Philadelphia: University of Pennsylvania Press, 2006.

Lepore, Jill. "The Creed: What Poor Richard Cost Benjamin Franklin." *The New Yorker.* January 28, 2008.

Lopez, Claude-Anne, and Eugenia Herbert. *The Private Franklin: The Man and His Family.* New York: Norton, 1975.

Wood, Gordon. *The Americanization of Benjamin Franklin.* New York: Penguin Press, 2004.

Zall, P. M., ed. *Ben Franklin Laughing: Anecdotes from Original Sources by and about Benjamin Franklin.* Berkeley: University of California Press, 1980.

CHAPTER 2: A NATION OF SAVERS

Again, for this chapter I'm deeply indebted to the librarians and staff at the American Antiquarian Society.

ON HETTY GREEN

Slack, Charles. *Hetty: The Genius and Madness of America's First Female Tycoon.* New York: Ecco, 2004.

Sparkes, Boyden, and Samuel Taylor Moore. *The Witch of Wall Street, Hetty Green.* Garden City, NY: Doubleday, Doran, 1935.

SOURCE NOTES

ON SAVINGS BANKS

Alter, George, Claudia Goldin, and Elyce Rotella. "The Savings of Ordinary Americans: The Philadelphia Saving Fund Society in the Mid-Nineteenth Century." Cambridge, MA: National Bureau of Economic Research Working Papers Series, July 1992.

Articles of Association of the (Phila.) Saving Fund Society. Philadelphia: W. Fry, Printer, 1817.

Centenary 1825–1925: New Bedford Institution for Savings: A Register of Industry and Thrift. New Bedford, MA: The Institution, 1925.

Hamilton, James Henry. *Savings and Savings Institutions.* New York: Mac-Millan, 1902.

Knowles, Charles. *History of the Bank for Savings in the City of New York 1819–1929.* New York: Bank for Savings, 1929.

Miller, Elliott C. *The Society for Savings: A Heritage of Integrity, Frugality and Prudence.* New York: Newcomen Society of the United States, 1987.

Tucker, David M. *The Decline of Thrift in America: Our Cultural Shift from Saving to Spending.* New York: Praeger, 1991.

ON POVERTY AND CHARITY

"Constitution of the Society in Lynn for the Promotion of Industry, Frugality and Temperance," Lynn, MA, 1826.

Rockman, Seth. *Welfare Reform in the Early Republic: A Brief History with Documents.* Boston: Bedford/St. Martin's, 2003.

Smith, Billy, ed. *Down and Out in Early America.* University Park: Pennsylvania State University Press, 2004.

ON THE MARKET REVOLUTION AND SOCIAL MOBILITY

Bernstein, Peter. *Wedding of the Waters: The Erie Canal and the Making of a Great Nation.* New York: W. W. Norton, 2005.

Carnegie, Andrew. *The Empire of Business.* New York: Doubleday, Page, 1902.

Cayton, Mary Kupiec, Elliott J. Gorn, and Peter W. Williams, eds. *Encyclopedia of American Social History.* New York: Scribner, Maxwell Macmillan International, 1993.

Craig, Adam. *Room at the Top: Or, How to Reach Success, Happiness, Fame and Fortune.* Augusta, ME: True and Company, 1884.

A Father's Gift to His Son, On His Becoming an Apprentice, to Which is Added Dr. Franklin's Way to Wealth. New York: Samuel Wood and Sons, 1821.

Fletcher, Edward H. *The Temptations of City Life; A Voice to Young Men Seeking a Home and Fortune in Large Towns and Cities.* New York: Edward H. Fletcher, 1849.

Freedley, Edwin T. *A Practical Treatise on Business, or How to get, save, spend, give, lend and bequeath money.* Philadelphia: Lippincott, 1852.

Frost, John. *The Young Merchant*. Boston: George Light, 1841.

Hunt, Freeman. *Worth and Wealth: Maxims for Merchants and Men of Business*. New York: Stringer and Townsend, 1857.

Kierner, Cynthia. *The Contrast: Manners, Morals, and Authority in the Early American Republic*. New York: New York University Press, 2007.

Newton, Sarah. *Learning to Behave: A Guide to American Conduct Books Before 1900*. Westport, CT: Greenwood, 1994.

The Pleasant Art of Money-Catching. Philadelphia: Lindsay and Blakiston, 1848.

Stephens, J. W. *How to Get Rich; or the Money Maker's Manual*. New York: Stephens, 1867.

Stickney, Robert. "An Address Delivered Before the Equitable Union, Union College, July 9th, 1839." Schenectady: Isaac Riggs, 1839.

Turnbull, J. *Advice to Young Tradesmen, On the Formation of Business Habits*. Steubenville, OH: James Wilson, 1835.

Wyllie, Irvin. *The Self-Made Man in America: The Myth of Rags to Riches*. New Brunswick, NJ: Rutgers University Press, 1954.

On Booker T. Washington

Fleming, Walter. *The Freedmen's Savings Bank: A Chapter in the Economic History of the Negro Race*. Chapel Hill: University of North Carolina Press, 1927.

Foner, Eric. *A Short History of Reconstruction, 1863–1877*. New York: Harper and Row, 1990.

Harlan, Louis. *Booker T. Washington: The Making of a Black Leader, 1856–1901*. New York: Oxford University Press, 1972.

———. *Booker T. Washington, The Wizard of Tuskegee, 1901–1915*. New York: Oxford University Press, 1983.

Washington, Booker T. *Up From Slavery*, William M. Andrews, ed. New York: W. W. Norton, 1996 (1901).

———. *Character Building*. New York: Doubleday, 1902.

On Transcendentalism

Bartol, C. A. "Extravagance: A Sermon for the Times," a sermon preached in West Church, April 7, 1864. Boston: Walker, Wise, 1864

Emerson, Ralph Waldo. *Complete Works*. Boston: Houghton Mifflin, 1903–1922.

Miller, Lillian. "Paintings, Sculpture, and the National Character, 1815–1860." *The Journal of American History*, vol. 53, no. 4 (March 1967), pp. 696–707.

Shi, David. *The Simple Life*. New York: Oxford University Press, 1985.

Thoreau, Henry David. *Walden*. Princeton: Princeton University Press, 1971 (1854).

On the Gilded Age and Progressive Era

Buenker, John, and Edward Kantowicz, eds. *Historical Dictionary of the Progressive Era, 1890–1920.* New York: Greenwood, 1988.

Hall, Bolton. *Thrift.* New York: B. W. Huebsch, 1916.

Kaplan, Justin. *When the Astors Owned New York.* New York: Plume, 2007.

Martin, Frederick Townsend. *The Passing of the Idle Rich.* New York: Doubleday, Page, 1911.

On School Savings Banks and the Thrift Movement

"Clean-Up Week and Thrift Campaign Soon Will Be Here." *San Francisco Chronicle,* April 3, 1917.

"Gov. Hiram Johnson Proclaims Aug. 12 as 'Thrift Day' in California." *San Francisco Chronicle,* August 3, 1915.

Grogan, Lulu. *Gateway to Independence.* Duluth, MN: Duluth Thrift Committee, 1923.

Malone, Dumas, ed. *Dictionary of American Biography.* New York: Charles Scribner's Sons, 1936.

Papers of Sara Louisa Oberholtzer, at the Historical Society of Pennsylvania, Philadelphia. (These papers include many of John Thiry's personal archives.)

Proceedings of the Conference on Thrift Education in Philadelphia, June 29, 1926. New York: American Society for Thrift, 1926.

Roe, Alfred. "Bankers and Thrift in the Age of Affluence." *American Quarterly,* vol. 17, no. 4 (Winter 1965), pp. 619–33.

"S. W. Straus Dead; Banker Long Ill." *New York Times,* September 8, 1930.

Straus, Simon W. *History of the Thrift Movement in America.* Philadelphia: J. B. Lippincott, 1920.

Thrift: A Short Text Book for Elementary Schools of Philadelphia. Philadelphia: Educational Committee of the Chamber of Commerce, 1917.

Todd, Frank Morton. *The Story of the Exposition.* New York: Putnam, 1921.

Tucker, David M. *The Decline of Thrift in America: Our Cultural Shift from Saving to Spending.* New York: Praeger, 1991.

CHAPTER 3: "WHAT USE CAN A WOMAN HAVE FOR ARITHMETIC?"

On Daily Life for Rural and Urban Women

Cott, Nancy. *The Bonds of Womanhood: "Woman's Sphere" in New England, 1780–1835.* New Haven: Yale University Press, 1977.

Dodyk, Delight, ed. *The Diary of Sarah Tabitha Reid, 1868–1873.* Freehold, NJ: Monmouth County Historical Association, 2001.

Freeman, Ruth. *The Frugal Housewife.* Watkins Glen, NY: Century House, 1957.

Nylander, Jane. *Our Own Snug Fireside: Images of the New England Home, 1760–1860.* New Haven: Yale University Press, 1993.

Osterud, Nancy Grey. *Bonds of Community: The Lives of Farm Women in Nineteenth-Century New York.* Ithaca, NY: Cornell University Press, 1991.

Strasser, Susan. *Waste and Want: A Social History of Trash.* New York: Metropolitan Books, 1999.

Winterer, Caroline. *The Mirror of Antiquity: American Women and the Classical Tradition, 1750–1900.* Ithaca, NY: Cornell University Press, 2007.

ON LYDIA MARIA CHILD

Child, Lydia Maria. *The American Frugal Housewife, Dedicated to Those Who are Not Ashamed of Economy.* Mineola, NY: Dover Publications, 1999 (1829).

Clifford, Deborah Pickman. *Crusader for Freedom: A Life of Lydia Maria Child.* Boston: Beacon Press, 1992.

Hoeller, Hildegard. "A Quilt for Life: Lydia Maria Child's *The American Frugal Housewife.*" *American Transcendental Quarterly,* vol. 13, no. 2 (June 1999), pp. 89–104.

Karcher, Caroline. *The First Woman in the Republic: A Cultural Biography of Lydia Maria Child.* Durham, NC: Duke University Press, 1994.

"Literary Notices." *Ladies' Magazine and Literary Gazette.* January 1830, p. 42.

———. *Ladies' Magazine and Literary Gazette.* April 1830, p. 189.

ON SARAH JOSEPHA HALE

Hale, Sarah Josepha. *The Good Housekeeper, or the way to live well and to be well while we live, containing directions for choosing and preparing food, in regard to health, economy and taste.* Boston: Weeks, Jordan, 1839.

Tucker, David M. *The Decline of Thrift in America: Our Cultural Shift from Saving to Spending.* New York: Praeger, 1991.

ON HOME ECONOMICS AND OTHER ADVICE TO WOMEN

Beecher, Catharine, and Harriet Beecher Stowe. *The American Woman's Home, or Domestic Science.* New York: J. B. Ford, 1869.

Beeton, Isabella. *Beeton's Book of Household Management.* London: Beeton 18 Boueverie St., 1861.

Frederick, Christine. *Household Engineering: Scientific Management in the Home.* Chicago: American School of Home Economics, 1920.

Freeling, Arthur. *The Young Bride's Book.* New York: Wilson, 1849.

Leavitt, Sarah. *From Catharine Beecher to Martha Stewart: A Cultural History of Domestic Advice.* Chapel Hill: University of North Carolina Press, 2002.

McKeever, William. "Teaching the Girl to Save." *Home-Training Bulletin,* no. 7. Manhattan: Kansas State Agricultural College, 1904.

Newton, Sarah. *Learning to Behave: A Guide to American Conduct Books Before 1900.* Westport, CT: Greenwood, 1994.

Six Hundred Dollars a Year. A Wife's Effort at Low Living, Under High Prices. Boston: Ticknor and Fields, 1867.

Smiles, Samuel. *Thrift.* New York: Harper, 1876.

Sprague, William. *Letters on Practical Subjects, to a Daughter,* 2nd ed. New York: John P. Haven, 1831.

Strasser, Susan. *Never Done: A History of American Housework.* New York: Pantheon, 1982.

Thayer, William Makepeace. *The Poor Girl and True Woman.* Boston: Gould and Lincoln, 1859.

The Young Lady's Mentor, By a Lady. Philadelphia: H.C. Peck and Theo. Bliss, 1851.

CHAPTER 4: CHEAP JEWS AND THRIFTY CHINESE
ON CHEAP JEWS

"American Views of the Jew at the Opening of the Twentieth Century." New York and Newton, MA: Publications of the American Jewish Historical Society, no. XL, June 1951, pt. 4, pp. 322–44.

Anti-Semitism in America, 1878–1939. New York: Arno Press, 1977.

Baldwin, Neil. *Henry Ford and the Jews.* New York: Public Affairs, 2001.

Beard, Miriam. "Anti-Semitism—Product of Economic Myths," in *Jews in a Gentile World: The Problem of Anti-Semitism,* ed. by Isacque Graeber and Steuart Henderson Britt. New York: MacMillan, 1942.

Chazan, Robert. *Medieval Stereotypes and Modern Anti-Semitism.* Berkeley: University of California Press, 1997.

Denning, Michael. *Mechanic Accents: Dime Novels and Working-Class Culture in America.* New York: Verso, 1998.

Eaton, Herbert, ed. *An Hour with the American Hebrew.* New York: Jesse Haney, 1879.

Felsenstein, Frank. *Anti-Semitic Stereotypes.* Baltimore: Johns Hopkins University Press, 1995.

Gilman, Sander. *Multiculturalism and the Jews.* New York: Routledge, 2006.

Glanz, Rudolf. *The Jew in the Old American Folklore.* New York: Waldon, 1961.

———. *Studies in Judaica Americana.* New York: Ktav, 1970.

Goldstein, Eric. "Different Blood Flows in Our Veins: Race and Jewish Self-Definition in Late Nineteenth Century America." *American Jewish History,* vol. 85, no. 1 (1997), pp. 29–51.

Heinze, Andrew. *Adapting to Abundance: Jewish Immigrants, Mass*

Consumption, and the Search for American Identity. New York: Columbia University Press, 1990.

Higham, John. *Strangers in the Land,* 2nd ed. New Brunswick, NJ: Rutgers University Press, 1988.

Kammen, Michael. *People of Paradox: An Inquiry Concerning the Origins of American Civilization.* New York: Knopf, 1972.

Kohn, Abraham. "A Jewish Peddler's Diary," in *Memoirs of American Jews, 1775–1865,* ed. by Jacob Marcus, vol. 2, pp. 1–20. New York: Ktav, 1974.

Krefetz, Gerald. *Jews and Money.* New Haven: Ticknor and Fields, 1982.

Markens, Isaac. *Abraham Lincoln and the Jews.* New York: Self-published by Isaac Markens, 1909.

Mayo, Louise. *The Ambivalent Image: Nineteenth Century America's Perception of the Jew.* Rutherford, NJ: Fairleigh Dickinson University Press, 1988.

Merwin, Ted. *In Their Own Image: New York Jews in Jazz Age Popular Culture.* New Brunswick, NJ: Rutgers University Press, 2006.

Riis, Jacob. *How the Other Half Lives.* New York: Charles Scribner's Sons, 1902.

Rosenstock, Morton. "The Jews: From the Ghettos of Europe to the Suburbs of the United States," in *The Immigrant Experience in America,* ed. by Frank Coppa and Thomas Curran. Boston: Twayne, 1976.

Spiegelman, Art. *Maus: A Survivor's Tale.* New York: Pantheon Books, 1986.

Steinberg, Abraham. "Jewish Characters in Fugitive American Novels of the Nineteenth Century." *YIVO Annual of Jewish Social Science,* vol. 11 (1956–1957), pp. 105–21.

Tawney, R. H. *Religion and the Rise of Capitalism.* New York: Harcourt, Brace, 1926.

Vance, Zebulon. *The Scattered Nation.* New York: J. J. Little, 1904.

On Thrifty Chinese

Barth, Gunther. *Bitter Strength: A History of the Chinese in the United States, 1850–1870.* Cambridge: Harvard University Press, 1964.

Ching, Frank. "The Asian Experience in the United States," in *The Immigrant Experience in America,* ed. by Frank Coppa and Thomas Curran, Boston: Twayne, 1976.

Choice Dialects and Vaudeville Stage Jokes. Chicago: Frederick Drake, 1902.

DeLeon, Arnoldo. *Racial Frontiers: Africans, Chinese, and Mexicans in Western America, 1848–1890.* Albuquerque: University of New Mexico Press, 2002.

Giles, Herbert Allen, trans. *Quips from a Chinese Jest-Book.* Shanghai: Kelly and Walsh, 1925.

Lee, Calvin. *Chinatown USA.* Garden City, NY: Doubleday, 1965.

Lee, Erika. *At America's Gate: Chinese Immigration During the Exclusion Era, 1882–1943.* Chapel Hill: University of North Carolina Press, 2003.

Loh, Sandra Tsing. *Aliens in America.* New York: Riverhead, 1997.

McClellan, Robert. *The Heathen Chinee: A Study of American Attitudes Toward China, 1890–1905.* Columbus: Ohio State University Press, 1971.

McCunn, Ruthanne Lum. *Chinese American Portraits: Personal Histories 1828–1988.* San Francisco: Chronicle Books, 1988.

Miller, Stuart Creighton. *The Unwelcome Immigrant: The American Image of the Chinese, 1785–1882.* Berkeley: University of California Press, 1969.

Pan, Lynn. *Sons of the Yellow Emperor: A History of the Chinese Diaspora.* Boston: Little, Brown, 1990.

Parsons, William Barclay. *An American Engineer in China.* New York: McClure, Phillips, 1900.

"Report of the Joint Special Committee to Investigate Chinese Immigration," 44th Congress, United States Senate. Washington, DC: Government Printing Office, 1877.

Ripley, George, and Charles Dana, eds. *The New American Cyclopaedia: A Popular Dictionary of General Knowledge.* New York: D. Appleton, 1858–1963.

Ross, Edward. *The Changing Chinese.* New York: Century, 1911.

Smith, Arthur. *Chinese Characteristics.* New York: Fleming H. Revell, 1894.

"The Sojourners." *Time,* December 21, 1959.

"Some Reasons for Chinese Exclusion, Meat vs. Rice, American Manhood Against Asiatic Coolieism. Which Shall Survive?" Washington, DC: American Federation of Labor, 1902.

Tucker, David M. *The Decline of Thrift in America: Our Cultural Shift from Saving to Spending.* New York: Praeger, 1991.

Vella, Walter. *Chaiyo! King Vajiravud and the Development of Thai Nationalism.* Honolulu: University of Hawaii Press, 1978.

Voskressenski, Alexei, ed. *Cranks, Knaves and Jokers of the Celestial: Chinese Parables and Funny Stories.* Commack, NY: Nova Science, 1997.

Wu, William. *The Yellow Peril: Chinese Americans in American Fiction, 1850–1940.* Hamden, CT: Archon Books, 1982.

Yin, Xiao-Huang. *Chinese-American Literature Since the 1850s.* Urbana: University of Illinois Press, 2000.

CHAPTER 5: "USE IT UP, WEAR IT OUT, MAKE IT DO, OR DO WITHOUT"

ON WORLD WAR I

Baruch, Bernard. *American Industry in the War: A Report of the War Industries Board.* New York: Prentice Hall, 1941.

Bogart, Ernest. *Direct and Indirect Costs of the Great World War.* New York: Oxford University Press, 1919.

Bradley, Alice. *Wheatless and Meatless Menus and Recipes from Miss Farmer's School of Cookery.* Boston, 1918.

Carver, Thomas Nixon. *War Thrift.* New York: Oxford University Press, 1919.

Churchill, Allen. *Over Here! An Informal Recreation of the Home Front in World War I.* New York: Dodd, Mead, 1968.

Clark, John Maurice. *The Costs of the World War to the American People.* New York: A. M. Kelley, 1970.

Cooper, John Milton. *Pivotal Decades: The United States, 1900–1920.* New York: Norton, 1990.

"Edison Sees Luxury War-Winning Force." *New York Times,* June 8, 1918.

Gale, Oliver Marble, ed. *Americanism: Woodrow Wilson's Speeches on the War—Why He Made Them—and—What They Have Done.* Chicago: Baldwin Syndicate, 1918.

Greenough, William Sidney. *The War Purse of Indiana: The Five Liberty Loans and War Savings and Thrift Campaigns in Indiana During the World War.* Indianapolis: Indiana Historical Commission, 1922.

Harries, Meirion and Susie. *The Last Days of Innocence: America at War, 1917–1918.* New York: Random House, 1997.

Kennedy, David. *Over Here: The First World War and American Society.* New York: Oxford University Press, 1980.

Koistinen, Paul. *Mobilizing for Modern War: The Political Economy of American Warfare, 1865–1919.* Lawrence: University Press of Kansas, 1997.

Litman, Simon. *Prices and Price Control in Great Britain and the Untied States During the World War.* New York: Oxford University Press, 1920.

O'Brien, Francis William. *The Hoover-Wilson Wartime Correspondence.* Ames: Iowa State University Press, 1974.

"Officials Explain War Savings Plan." *New York Times,* November 16, 1917.

Patriotic Food Show Official Recipe Book, from the Patriot Food Show, February 2–10, 1918 in St. Louis, put on by the Women's Central Committee on Food Conservation.

"Profiteers' Accomplices." *New York Times,* August 17, 1919.

Tobin, Harold, and Percy Bidwell. *Mobilizing Civilian America.* New York: Council on Foreign Relations, 1940.

Traxel, David. *Crusader Nation: The United States in Peace and the Great War, 1898–1920.* New York: Knopf, 2006.

Vaughn, Stephen. *Holding Fast the Inner Lines: Democracy, Nationalism, and the Committee on Public Information.* Chapel Hill: University of North Carolina Press, 1980.

Wanamaker, John, ed. *War-Time Recipes: A Cookery Book to Help Make the World Free for Democracy.* New York and Philadelphia (no publisher or date cited).

On the 1920s and the Depression

Andrews, Benjamin. "Thrift as a Family and Individual Problem: Some Standard Budgets." *Annals of the Academy of Political and Social Science,* vol. 87, "The New American Thrift" (January 1920), pp. 11–20.

Calder, Lendol. *Financing the American Dream.* Princeton, NJ: Princeton University Press, 1999.

Hastings, Robert. *A Nickel's Worth of Skim Milk: A Boy's View of the Great Depression.* Carbondale: Southern Illinois University Press, 1986.

————. *A Penny's Worth of Minced Ham.* Carbondale: Southern Illinois University Press, 1986.

Kyvig, David. *Daily Life in the United States, 1920–1940.* Chicago: Ivan Dee, 2002.

Leuchtenburg, William. *The Perils of Prosperity, 1914–1932.* Chicago: University of Chicago Press, 1956.

Lynd, Robert and Helen Merrell Lynd. *Middletown: A Study in Contemporary American Culture.* New York: Harcourt, Brace, 1929.

Olson, James. *Historical Dictionary of the 1920s.* New York: Greenwood, 1988.

President's Research Committee on Social Trends. *Recent Social Trends in the United States; Report of the President's Research Committee on Social Trends.* New York: McGraw-Hill, 1933.

Roe, Alfred. "Bankers and Thrift in the Age of Affluence." *American Quarterly,* vol. 17, no. 4 (Winter 1965), pp. 619–33.

Terkel, Studs. *Hard Times: An Oral History of the Great Depression.* New York: Pantheon, 1970.

Watkins, T. H. *The Hungry Years: A Narrative History of the Great Depression in America.* New York: Henry Holt, 2000.

On John Maynard Keynes

Davis, Kenneth. *FDR, the New Deal Years, 1933–1937: A History.* New York: Random House, 1986.

Harris, Seymour. *John Maynard Keynes: Economist and Policy Maker.* New York: Charles Scribner's Sons, 1955.

Keynes, John Maynard. *Essays in Persuasion, Vol. IX of The Collected Writings of John Maynard Keynes.* London: St. Martin's Press for the Royal Economic Society, 1972.

————. *The General Theory of Employment, Interest, and Money.* New York: Harcourt, Brace, 1936.

Rosenof, Theodore. *Economics in the Long Run: New Deal Theorists and Their*

Legacies, 1933–1993. Chapel Hill: University of North Carolina Press, 1997.

Skidelsky, Robert. *John Maynard Keynes 1883–1946: Economist, Philosopher, Statesman.* London: MacMillan, 2003.

ON WORLD WAR II

Cohen, Lizabeth. *A Consumers' Republic.* New York: Vintage, 2003.

Flamm, Bradley. "Putting the Brakes on Non-Essential Travel: 1940s War-time Mobility, Prosperity and the U.S. Office of Defense." *Journal of Transport History,* March 2006.

Horowitz, Daniel. *The Anxieties of Affluence: Critiques of American Consumer Culture, 1939–1979.* Amherst: University of Massachusetts Press, 2004.

Lingeman, Richard. *Don't You Know There's a War On? The American Home Front 1941–1945.* New York: Putnam, 1970.

McCullough, David. *Truman.* New York: Simon and Schuster, 1992.

Nathan, Robert. *Mobilizing for Abundance.* New York: McGraw-Hill, 1944.

Pastor, Ethel. *How to Live on a Reduced War Budget: Manage Your Home Economically and Well for Gracious and Useful Wartime Living.* Chicago: Consolidated Book Publishers, 1942.

Raushenbush, Winifred. *How to Dress in Wartime.* New York: Coward-McCann, 1942.

Ward, Barbara McLean, ed. *Produce and Conserve, Share and Play Square: The Grocer and the Consumer on the Home-Front Battlefield During World War II.* Hanover, NH: University Press of New England, 1994.

Ware, Caroline. *The Consumer Goes to War.* New York: Funk and Wagnalls, 1942.

Yellin, Emily. *Our Mothers' War: American Women at Home and at the Front During World War II.* New York: Free Press, 2004.

CHAPTER 6: LIVELY GOLF BALLS AND TWO-FORD FREEDOM: THE POSTWAR YEARS

BOOKS, ARTICLES, AND REPORTS

The Changing American Market, by the editors of *Fortune.* Garden City, NY: Hanover House, 1955.

Cohen, Lizabeth. *A Consumers' Republic.* New York: Vintage, 2003.

Dichter, Ernest. *Motivating Human Behavior.* New York: McGraw-Hill, 1971.

———. *The Psychology of Everyday Living.* New York: Barnes and Noble, 1947.

———. *The Strategy of Desire.* Garden City, NY: Doubleday, 1960.

For a New Thrift: Confronting the Debt Culture. New York: Institute for American Values, 2008.

Galbraith, John Kenneth. *The Affluent Society*. Boston: Houghton Mifflin, 1958.

Halberstam, David. *The Fifties*. New York: Villard, 1993.

Harvey, Brett, ed. *The Fifties: A Women's Oral History*. New York: HarperCollins, 1993.

Heimann, Jim, ed. *40s: All-American Ads*. Cologne: Taschen, 2001.

Horowitz, Daniel. *The Anxieties of Affluence: Critiques of American Consumer Culture, 1939–1979*. Amherst: University of Massachusetts Press, 2004.

Kaledin, Eugenia. *Daily Life in the United States, 1940–1959: Shifting Worlds*. Westport, CT: Greenwood, 2000.

Katona, George. *The Powerful Consumer: Psychological Studies of the American Economy*. New York: McGraw-Hill, 1960.

———. *Psychological Analysis of Economic Behavior*. New York: McGraw-Hill, 1951.

Katona, George, and Eva Mueller. *Consumer Attitudes and Demand, 1950–1952*. Ann Arbor: Survey Research Center, Institute for Social Research, University of Michigan, 1953.

Manning, Robert. *Credit Card Nation: The Consequences of America's Addiction to Credit*. New York: Basic Books, 2000.

Mazur, Paul. *The Standards We Raise: The Dynamics of Consumption*. New York: Harper, 1953.

Packard, Vance. *The Waste Makers*. New York: D. McKay, 1960.

"2 Providence Banks Drop School Savings Programs." *New York Times*, May 24, 1964.

OTHER SOURCES
Prelinger, Rick. *Ephemeral Films, 1931–1960*. New York: Voyager, 1994.

CHAPTER 7: SPENDTHRIFT NATION

BOOKS, ARTICLES, AND REPORTS
Bucks, Brian, Arthur B. Kennickell, Traci Mach, and Kevin B. Moore. "Changes in U.S. Family Finances from 2004 to 2007: Evidence from the Survey of Consumer Finances." Washington, DC: Federal Reserve Bank, February 2009.

Bucks, Brian, Arthur B. Kennickell, and Kevin B. Moore. "Recent Changes in U.S. Family Finances: Evidence from the 2001 and 2004 Survey of Consumer Finances." Washington, DC: Federal Reserve Bank, 2005.

Cramer, Reid, Rourke O'Brien, and Alejandra Lopez-Fernandini. "The Assets Agenda: Policy Options to Promote Savings and Home Ownership by Low- and Moderate-Income Americans." Washington, DC: New America Foundation, September 2008.

For a New Thrift: Confronting the Debt Culture. New York: Institute for American Values, 2008.

García, José, James Lardner, and Cindy Zeldin. *Up to Our Eyeballs: How Shady Lenders and Failed Economic Policies Are Drowning Americans in Debt.* New York: New Press, 2008.

Gokhale, Jagadeesh, Laurence Kotlikoff, and John Sabelhaus. "Understanding the Postwar Decline in U.S. Saving: A Cohort Analysis." Working Paper 5571. Cambridge, MA: National Bureau of Economic Research, May 1996.

Isaacs, Julia, Isabel Sawhill, and Ron Haskins. "Getting Ahead or Losing Ground: Economic Mobility in America." Washington, DC: Brookings Institution, 2007.

Kennickell, Arthur B., Martha Starr-McCluer, and Brian Surette. "Recent Changes in U.S. Family Finances: Results from the 1998 Survey of Consumer Finances." Washington, DC: Federal Reserve Bank, 2000.

Lansing, Kevin. "Spendthrift Nation." Federal Reserve Bank of San Francisco *Economic Letter.* November 10, 2005.

Lardner, James, and David A. Smith, eds. *Inequality Matters: The Growing Economic Divide in America and Its Poisonous Consequences.* New York: New Press, 2005.

Lusardi, Annamaria, Jonathan Skinner, and Steven Venti. "Saving Puzzles and Saving Policies in the United States." Working Paper 8237. Cambridge, MA: National Bureau of Economic Research, April 2001.

McKibben, Bill. *Deep Economy.* New York: Times Books, 2007.

Mishel, Lawrence, Jared Bernstein, and Heidi Shierholz. *The State of Working America 2008/2009.* Washington, DC: Economic Policy Institute, 2008.

"National Saving: Current Saving Decisions Have Profound Implications for Our Nation's Future Well-Being." Testimony Before the Subcommittee on Long-Term Growth and Debt Reduction, Committee on Finance, United States Senate. Washington, DC: U.S. Government Accountability Office. April 6, 2006.

Shaw, Jonathan. "Debtor Nation: The Rising Risks of the American Dream, on a Borrowed Dime." *Harvard Magazine.* July–August 2007.

Skinner, Jonathan. "Are You Sure You're Saving Enough for Retirement?" *Journal of Economic Perspectives*, vol. 21, no. 3 (Summer 2007), pp. 59–80.

"Trends in College Pricing." Washington, DC: College Board, 2008.

Weller, Christian, and Eli Staub. "Middle Class in Turmoil: Economic Risks Up Sharply for Most Families Since 2001." Washington, DC: Center for American Progress, 2007.

INTERVIEWS
Laurence Kotlikoff, Boston University
Brad Setser, Council on Foreign Relations
Ronald Wilcox, University of Virginia
David Wyss, Standard & Poor's
Stephen Zeldes, Columbia University

OTHER SOURCES
"FAQs about Benefits—Retirement Issues," Employee Benefits Research Institute. http://www.ebri.org/publications/benfaq/index.cfm?fa=retfaq14
Brad Setser's blog on Chinese economic policy: http://blogs.cfr.org/setser/
For credit card statistics: www.cardtrak.com

CHAPTER 8: ECO-CHEAP

BOOKS, ARTICLES, AND REPORTS

Berry, Wendell. *Home Economics.* New York: North Point, 1987.

"The Causes of Global Climate Change." Science Brief 1. Arlington, VA: Pew Center on Global Climate Change, September 2006.

"Greendex 2008: Consumer Choice and the Environment." Survey conducted by National Geographic and GlobeScan, 2008.

Harris, Jonathan. "Overview Essay: Consumption and the Environment," in *The Consumer Society,* ed. by Neva Goodwin, Frank Ackerman, and David Kiron. Washington, DC: Island Press, 1996.

McKibben, Bill. *Deep Economy.* New York: Times Books, 2007.

"Municipal Solid Waste Generation, Recycling, and Disposal in the United States: Facts and Figures for 2007." Washington, DC: Environmental Protection Agency, 2008.

Royte, Elizabeth. *Garbage Land: On the Secret Trail of Trash.* New York: Little, Brown, 2005.

Snyder, Gary *Turtle Island.* New York: New Directions, 1974.

Taylor, Betsy, and Dave Tilford. "Why Consumption Matters," in *The Consumer Society Reader,* edited by Juliet B. Schor and Douglas B. Holt. New York: New Press, 2000.

Worldwatch Institute. *State of the World 2004: The Consumer Society.* New York: W. W. Norton, 2004.

CHAPTER 9: LIVING CHEAP IN THE AGE OF MASS CONSUMPTION

BOOKS AND ARTICLES

Carlsson, Chris. *Nowtopia: How Pirate Programmers, Outlaw Bicyclists, and Vacant-Lot Gardeners Are Inventing the Future Today!* Oakland, CA: AK Press, 2008.

Ferrell, Jeff. *Empire of Scrounge: Inside the Urban Underground of Dumpster-Diving, Trash Picking, and Street Scavenging.* New York: New York University Press, 2005.

Martin, Andrew. "One Country's Table Scraps, Another Country's Meal." *New York Times,* May 18, 2008.

Todd, Richard. *The Thing Itself.* New York: Riverhead Books, 2008.

INTERVIEWS
Adam Dowis
John de Graaf
Christian Gutierrez
Quinn Hechtkopf
Rozie Hughes
Janet Kalish
Shawn Rosenmoss
Helena Shoe
Adam Weissman

OTHER SOURCES
www.freegan.info
www.wastedfood.com
The Gleaners and I. Documentary film by Agnès Varda, 2000.

CHAPTER 10: CHEAPSKATE PSYCHOLOGY

BOOKS AND ARTICLES

Baumeister, Roy, Todd Heatherton, and Dianne Tice. *Losing Control: How and Why People Fail at Self-Regulation.* San Diego: Academic Press, 1994.

Baumeister, Roy. "Yielding to Temptation: Self-Control Failure, Impulsive Purchasing, and Consumer Behavior." *Journal of Consumer Research,* vol. 28, no. 4 (March 2002), pp. 670–76.

Borneman, Ernest. *The Psychoanalysis of Money.* New York: Urizen, 1976.

Camerer, Colin, George Loewenstein, and Drazen Prelec. "Neuroeconomics: How Neuroscience Can Inform Economics." *Journal of Economic Literature,* vol. XLIII (March 2005), pp. 9–64.

Diagnostic and Statistical Manual of Mental Disorders, 4th ed., Arlington, VA: American Psychiatric Association, 1994.

Freud, Sigmund. "Character and Anal Erotism," in *The Standard Edition of the Complete Psychological Works of Sigmund Freud.* Translated from the German under the general editorship of James Strachey, in collaboration with Anna Freud. London: Hogarth Press, 1953–1974.

Freud, Sophie. *Living in the Shadow of the Freud Family.* Westport, CT: Praeger, 2007.

Funder, David. "On the Pros and Cons of Delay of Gratification." *Psychological Inquiry,* vol. 9, no. 3 (1998), pp. 211–12.

Heath, Chip, and Jack B. Soll. "Mental Budgeting and Consumer Decisions." *Journal of Consumer Research,* vol. 23, no. 1 (June 1996), pp. 40–52.

Hoch, Stephen, and George Loewenstein. "Time-Inconsistent Preferences and Consumer Self-Control." *Journal of Consumer Research,* vol. 17, no. 4 (March 1991), pp. 492–507.

Kahneman, Daniel. "A Psychological Perspective on Economics." *American Economic Review,* vol. 93, no. 2 (May 2003), pp. 162–68.

Kahneman, Daniel, and Amos Tversky. "Prospect Theory: An Analysis of Decision Under Risk." *Econometrica,* vol. 47, no. 2 (March 1979), pp. 263–92.

Lastovicka, John L., Lance A. Bettencourt, Renee Shaw Hughner, Ronald J. Kuntze. "Lifestyle of the Tight and Frugal: Theory and Measurement." *Journal of Consumer Research,* vol. 26, no. 1 (June 1999), pp. 85–98.

Loewenstein, George. "Willpower: A Decision-Theorist's Perspective." *Law and Philosophy,* vol. 19, no. 1 (January 2000), pp. 51–76.

Loewenstein, George, and Ted O'Donoghue. "'We Can Do This the Easy Way or the Hard Way': Negative Emotions, Self-Regulation and the Law." *University of Chicago Law Review,* vol. 73 (Winter 2006), pp. 183–206.

Masson, J. Moussaieff. "The Psychology of the Ascetic." *Journal of Asian Studies,* vol. 35, no. 4 (August 1976), pp. 611–25.

Novemsky, Nathan, and Daniel Kahneman. "The Boundaries of Loss Aversion." *Journal of Marketing Research,* vol. XLII (May 2005), pp. 119–28.

Offer, Avner. *The Challenge of Affluence: Self-Control and Well-Being in the United States and Britain since 1950.* New York: Oxford University Press, 2006.

Prelec, Drazen. "Consumer Behavior and the Future of Consumer Payments." Paper presented at the Future of Consumer Payment Conference. Washington, DC: Brookings Institution, September 16, 2008.

Prelec, Drazen, and George Loewenstein. "The Red and the Black: Mental Accounting of Savings and Debt. *Marketing Science,* vol. 17, no. 1 (Winter 1998).

Rachlin, Howard. *The Science of Self-Control.* Cambridge, MA: Harvard University Press, 2000.

Romal, Jane, and Barbara Kaplan. "Difference in Self-Control Among Spenders and Savers." *Psychology: A Journal of Human Behavior,* vol. 32, no. 2 (1995), pp. 8–17.

Rick, Scott. "The Influence of Anticipatory Affect on Consumer Choice." Dissertation. Pittsburgh: Carnegie Mellon University, May 2007.

Rick, Scott, Cynthia Cryder, and George Loewenstein. "Tightwads and Spendthrifts." Working Paper, 2006.

Stearns, Peter. *Battleground of Desire: The Struggle for Self-Control in Modern America.* New York: New York University Press, 1999.

Thaler, Richard. "Anomalies: Saving, Fungibility, and Mental Accounts." *Journal of Economic Perspectives,* vol. 4, no. 1 (Winter 1990), pp. 193–205.

———. "From Homo Economicus to Homo Sapiens." *Journal of Economic Perspectives,* vol. 14, no. 1 (Winter 2000), pp. 133–41.

———. "Mental Accounting Matters." *Journal of Behavioral Decision Making,* vol. 12, no. 3 (Sept. 1999), pp. 183–206.

———. "Psychology and Savings Policies." *American Economic Review,* vol. 84, no. 2 (May 1994), pp. 186–192.

Thaler, Richard, and H. M. Shefrin. "An Economic Theory of Self-Control." *Journal of Political Economy,* vol. 89, no. 2 (April 1981), pp. 392–406.

Tversky, Amos, and Daniel Kahneman. "Loss Aversion in Riskless Choice: A Reference-Dependent Model." *Quarterly Journal of Economics,* vol. 106, no. 4 (November 1991), pp. 1039–61.

VanderEycken, Walter, and Ron Van Deth. *Fasting Saints and Anorexic Girls: The History of Self-Starvation.* London: Athlone Press, 1994.

Warneryd, Karl-Erik. *The Psychology of Saving: A Study on Economic Psychology.* Cheltenham, UK: Edward Elgar Publishing, 1999.

INTERVIEWS
Ken Clark, psychologist and financial planner in private practice
Ron Faber, University of Minnesota
Leon Hoffman, psychoanalyst and director, Pacella Parent Child Center
Erik Kriss, New York State employee
Jim Mitchell, Neuropsychiatric Institute, University of North Dakota
Drazen Prelec, Massachusetts Institute of Technology
Scott Rick, Wharton School, University of Pennsylvania
Jill Slater, food activist
Gail Steketee, Boston University School of Social Work
Rik Treiber, foundation executive
David Weber, author's father

CONCLUSION

Binkley, Christina. "Style Showdown: $1,000 Sweater Faces $100 Rival." *Wall Street Journal,* November 29, 2007.

INDEX